Boswell's *Life of Johnson*

BOSWELL'S
Life of Johnson

New Questions, New Answers

Edited by John A. Vance

THE UNIVERSITY OF GEORGIA PRESS

Athens

© 1985 by the University of Georgia Press
Athens, Georgia 30602
All rights reserved

Designed by Kathi L. Dailey
Set in 10 on 13 Linotron 202 Baskerville
with Caslon 471 Italic display

The paper in this book meets the guidelines for
permanence and durability of the Committee on
Production Guidelines for Book Longevity of the
Council on Library Resources.

Printed in the United States of America

89 88 87 86 85   5 4 3 2 1

Library of Congress Cataloging in Publication Data
Main entry under title:

Boswell's life of Johnson.

Bibliography: p.
Includes index.
1. Boswell, James, 1740–1795.   Life of Samuel
Johnson—Addresses, essays, lectures. 2. Johnson,
Samuel, 1709–1784—Biography—Addresses,
essays, lectures. 3. Biography (as a literary form)—
Addresses, essays, lectures. 4. Authors, English—
18th century—Biography—Addresses, essays,
lectures. I. Vance, John A., 1947–
PR3533.B63B67 1985   828'.609 [B]   84-16351
ISBN 0-8203-0765-3

FOR BERTRAM H. DAVIS

—A Most *Clubable* Man

That I was anxious for the success of a Work which had employed much of my time and labour, I do not wish to conceal: but whatever doubts I at any time entertained, have been entirely removed by the very favourable reception with which it has been honoured.

—JAMES BOSWELL, advertisement to the second edition
of the *Life of Johnson*

Truth like beauty varies its fashion, and is best recommended by different dresses to different minds.

—SAMUEL JOHNSON, *Idler* 85

Contents

Contents

Acknowledgments

*F*irst I wish to thank Paul Zimmer, Karen Orchard, Ellen Harris, Mary Hill, and the staff of the University of Georgia Press for their initial interest in the project and for their expeditious handling of the manuscript from its first journey to an outside reader to its transformation into a published book. The readers engaged by the Press made valuable suggestions for improvement, and the English Department of the University of Georgia provided me with much-needed research time and photocopying.

Perhaps sensing their editor's impatient nature, the contributors were extremely prompt in answering queries and making alterations. My special thanks go to Ralph Rader, Donald Greene, and Frederick Pottle for offering their previously published essays and to Indiana University Press, the *Georgia Review, Modern Language Studies,* and the *Transactions of the Johnson Society* for permission to reprint those pieces. Stan Lindberg gave important counsel when the collection was in its infancy, and John Burke advised wisely on the pitfalls of editing such a volume. For other suggestions and permissions I would like to acknowledge Irma Lustig, Marshall Waingrow, Graham Nicholls, McGraw-Hill Book Company, and the Yale Boswell Office. To Richard Schwartz, John Burke, Thomas Curley, Samuel Woods, and William Siebenschuh—that hearty band of souls who gathered in New York in April 1983 to take part in my seminar "Johnson without Boswell?: Further Perspectives on the Uses of the *Life of Johnson*"—I again extend my appreciation, for their observations at that time were the genesis of this book. An early title of William Siebenschuh's paper was conveniently borrowed and modified to serve as the title of this collection.

From start to finish I have benefited from the encouragement, advice, and assistance of my wife, Susie. My children, Hope and Jimmy, kept things in their proper perspective.

Finally, this volume is dedicated to Bertram H. Davis. Although not formally a festschrift, this book includes essays by those who respect his contributions to eighteenth-century studies, admire his sound scholarship, praise his commitment to dignity and fairness in our profession, and value his friendship. I would be happy to have this volume stand as a small tribute to Bert Davis's career. Perhaps it is more than coincidence that his major professor edited the last collection of essays devoted to the *Life* and that his doctoral student has edited this one.

Boswell's *Life of Johnson*

JOHN A. VANCE

Introduction

*I*n May of 1776, a greatly agitated Samuel Johnson reacted to James Boswell's enthusiastic and inquisitive nature with the remark, "Sir, you have but two topics, yourself and me. I am sick of both."[1] Johnson's words had absolutely no effect in diminishing the Scot's attraction to either of those topics, nor has Johnson's famous retort reflected the attitude of the thousands who over the past two centuries have read Boswell's *Life of Johnson* with considerable delight. As for the scholars and critics, they have found the work an engaging, invaluable, and troublesome study to be sure, but they have never determined it to be a lifeless or tiresome book, the kind one easily gets "sick" of. Indicative of twentieth-century scholarly and critical interest in this accepted masterpiece of world literature was the 1970 publication of James Clifford's collection of essays on the *Life*.[2] Composed of Clifford's excellent introduction and essays by noted Johnsonians and Boswellians,[3] the volume served several important purposes: (1) it reviewed the direction scholarship on the *Life* had taken since Macaulay's memorable characterization of Boswell as a fool who by the freakest of accidents wrote a biographical treasure,[4] (2) it clarified the critical questions twentieth-century commentators had asked about the *Life*, and (3) it offered significant discussion of the major issues and methods of approaching Boswell's book. In addition, Clifford's collection hinted at the future of studies on the *Life*, for the divergence of opinion expressed in the essays, the new critical ground broken, and Donald Greene's full-scale attack on the merits of Boswell's book presaged a lively period of criticism in which some of the issues

1

and problems would be readdressed, the arguments refined, and newer ones advanced. We are now in the midst of such a period.

It is time again to review recent work on the *Life*—specifically, the important studies published since Clifford's collection—so that we can see where we are, how we got there, and where we might go. Although many who wrote significant commentary on the *Life* before 1970 remain in the forefront of the critical debate, newer names have since that time added to the increasingly rich and complex texture of studies on the *Life*. Not only is the following survey of recent criticism a proper prelude to this volume of essays, but it may serve as an initiation for those who know the *Life* only casually and believe it to be generally admired (if not revered) by specialists working in the later eighteenth century. Those harboring such thoughts will be very much surprised (and perhaps pleased) by the critical disagreement and literary warfare characteristic of recent work on Boswell's *Life of Johnson*.

As NOTED, James Clifford's 1970 collection made clear just how far scholarship and commentary on the *Life* had come since the influential assessment of Macaulay.[5] No longer do those familiar with the Age of Johnson conjure an image of Boswell as Johnson's closest associate, constantly in his company with notebook in hand, furiously scribbling down every word spoken by the mighty oracle.[6] But how much effect have the efforts of serious Johnsonians and Boswellians had on the way nonspecialists, students, and the general public view Johnson and Boswell? It is a "truth universally acknowledged" that most conceptions about the two men have been driven into popular imagination by the hammering force of Boswell's narrative art or, to some, his conscious misrepresentation of the truth. References to the Johnson-Boswell relationship and quotations from the *Life* appear frequently in newspaper editorials, magazine articles, popular novels, and even advice columns.[7] Boswell's *Life* has therefore given Johnson *the kind of* popularity—and at times notoriety—his works could not have gained. (And my italics here are material because we should vigorously reject the impression held by some even today that Boswell's book rescued Johnson from the oblivion he would have fallen into by the middle of the nineteenth century.) Students and the general public have formed from a superficial or condensed reading of the *Life* a picture of Johnson so memorable and deeply entrenched that, to borrow from Johnson's *Rasselas,* a "concussion that would shatter" this image would likely "threaten the demolition of the continent."

Students and colleagues in other literary periods are often amazed to learn that the *Life* has both come under fire for its shortcomings as biography and received much scrutiny and praise for its literary, not biographical, merits. Many of those toiling outside the eighteenth century are shocked to know that Johnsonians and Boswellians are often at each other's throats: "Is not, after all, a Johnsonian also a Boswellian?" But serious questions have been raised in recent years about Boswell's depiction of Johnson, his attitude toward Johnson and Johnson's toward him, the various poses Boswell assumes in the *Life,* the weight of the famous conversations in determining Johnson's personality and philosophy, the accuracy of Johnson's conversation as reported by Boswell, Johnson's status as literary hero, the *Life* as a reflection of Boswell's literary artistry, and the reliability of Boswell's depictions of other members of the Johnson Circle. As this volume demonstrates, these issues continue to receive critical attention, and they lead to larger and more fundamental questions: What is the value of the *Life* if it is *not* good biography? How should one approach it, teach it, and use it? How can we still accord it a place among the world's great books while at the same time pointing out its deficiencies? Can we continue to enjoy the *Life* knowing it may distort our perception of the real Samuel Johnson? And is it possible to imagine a Johnson without Boswell?

In the introduction to his collection, Clifford provides a useful summary of how Boswell transferred his notations on events and conversations depicted in the *Life* to the finished product itself.[8] Here, then, we have the first significant area of interest for scholars of the *Life:* Boswell's method as a biographer and the accuracy of his book. The now famous discovery, publication, and subsequent employment of the Boswell journals and manuscript papers have done much to inform us regarding these matters.[9] And Marshall Waingrow's edition of Boswell's correspondence relating to the composition of the *Life* has provided us with an indispensable research tool to augment the journals.[10] The scholarly horizon will widen even further with the publication of the manuscript version of the *Life,* again edited by Marshall

Waingrow. Soon scholars not having access to the Boswell Collection at Yale University will be able to compare this composite of the initial draft and later revisions with the standard Hill-Powell edition of the *Life*. Those concerned with the accuracy of the *Life* will joy in the availability of this important scholarly work.

Boswell's method as biographer has remained a topic of interest for those writing since the Clifford collection (for example, Clarence Tracy in "Boswell: The Cautious Empiricist").[11] Others have found even more stimulating the relationship between the journals (and other manuscript evidence) and the finished *Life*. Irma Lustig has recently shed much light on Boswell's progress from writer of journal entries, letters, and memoranda to the biographer of Johnson.[12] In two other modern studies, Robert Bell and Elizabeth Bruss have discussed this process of transition and the relationship between the *London Journal* and the *Life of Johnson*.[13] (And one might consult A. R. Brooks's Twayne study of Boswell for the basic facts about the composition of the *Life*.)[14] Although scholars now feel relatively comfortable discussing Boswell's talent for recalling details and his skill in turning journal notations into biographical entries,[15] the topic has certainly not been exhausted, as William Siebenschuh's essay in this collection indicates.

The matter of Boswell's accuracy and success as a biographer remains, however, a point of conflict in studies of the *Life*. Donald Greene's "Reflections on a Literary Anniversary," included in the Clifford volume,[16] threw down the gauntlet, and Boswellian champions picked it up immediately: "For, strictly, Boswell's book can hardly be seriously termed a biography at all. It is a series of excerpts from his huge diary, those dealing with the times, during the latter two decades of Johnson's life, when he was in Johnson's company. . . . A biography? Surely not. It is an edited diary."[17] Greene went on to emphasize the inaccuracies, warped perspective, and the gross distortion of Johnson one encounters in the *Life*. In more recent years Greene has, in addition to the essays printed in this collection, reinforced his position in reviews and other pieces that encourage us not only to distrust Boswell but also to consult rival contemporary biographies of Johnson, such as that of John Hawkins,[18] and he has insisted that a modern biography of Johnson's later years is sorely needed.[19]

Richard Schwartz's *Boswell's Johnson: A Preface to the "Life"* (1978)[20] examines Boswell's book from the perspective of then existing theories of biographical art—including Johnson's, as articulated in *Rambler* 60 and *Idler* 84. Boswell's "stress of collection at the expense of systematic organization and shaping," Schwartz argues, "would associate him with the benighted empirics attacked by Bacon, the blind, indiscriminate gatherers. On the other hand, his attempts at compelling authenticity and accuracy mimic the search for mathematical certainty which represents a heterodox facet of Newton's method."[21] In agreement with Greene, Schwartz concludes that far from viewing it as a masterpiece, we should see the *Life* instead "as essentially a book about Boswell, a portion of his autobiography."[22] The *Life*'s "importance necessitates searching criticism. Its uses have often been improper ones. To discourage those uses the book's limitations must be stressed." But softening his blows somewhat, Schwartz adds that a "realization of Boswell's limitations prepares the way for an investigation of his strengths."[23]

Even considering the above qualification and Schwartz's conclusion that "What we need (as always) is a balanced view of Boswell, one which avoids either patronizing him or damning him outright,"[24] Schwartz and Greene have stimulated many into a more skeptical examination of the structure and accuracy of the *Life* as biography. Still others have resented Schwartz's and Greene's conclusions. Frederick Pottle's essay in this volume is one form of challenge to their position; others have answered with even more vigor.[25] Interestingly, any negative criticism of the *Life* as biography tends to brand one an iconoclast (such is the effect of long-standing impressions), and it is often with dauntless conviction on the one hand and nervous timidity on the other that one investigates Boswell's biographical shortcomings. In the introduction to his frequently cited piece "The *Life of Johnson:* An Anti-Theory" (1973), Leopold Damrosch, Jr., carefully weighs his words before entering the fray: "It is far from my wish that the *Life of Johnson* should be less admired; I only mean to argue that it should not be praised for what it is not."[26] Damrosch summarizes the major objections he has to the *Life:* "In the first place, it has real defects of organization and structure; in the second place (and more importantly) it leaves much to be desired as the comprehensive interpretation of a life."[27] And with these words we may turn to the issue over which so much fur has flown and over which the marriage between Johnsonians and Boswellians has been rent asunder: Boswell's presentation of his biographical subject—"Boswell's Johnson."

In his "'Tis a Pretty Book, Mr. Boswell, But—" (1978), reprinted in this collection, Donald Greene writes that one "needs only to chat for a few moments with one's colleagues teaching in other periods of English literature to recognize that, for most, Johnson is still the quaint old 'personality,' the figure of mild fun, that emerges most conspicuously from the *Life*, and very little more."[28] "[I]t is Boswell," Greene asserts elsewhere, "who must bear the chief responsibility for this state of things; Boswell who forged the iron curtain which has fallen between the increasingly complex and sympathetic Johnson discovered by scholarship and the immutable Great Cham of the 'intelligent general reader'; Boswell who must continue to be combated by books like [John] Wain's until the forbidding monolith has begun to be eroded away."[29]

Greene was not the first, of course, to comment on Boswell's portrayal of Johnson in the *Life*. Nineteenth-century commentators, most memorably Macaulay, and critics earlier in this century offered their assessments of the Johnson who emerges from the pages of Boswell's book. A. S. F. Gow wrote in 1931 that "Boswell's Johnson is a great and dominating figure with many admirable and some lovable qualities, yet you do not feel that you would have constantly sought his society or thought it more than worth the price in deference and humiliation at which it was to be attained."[30] Such comments assume, however, that by and large Boswell's Johnson is in fact the historical Johnson. But Greene rejected this assumption and went so far as to question Boswell's motives for making Johnson "a much simpler person than, in his complexity, he really was": "The most serious charge against Boswell, in my opinion, is that his much-touted 'hero-worship' of Johnson is a mask, disguising from himself and others an unconscious wish to cut Johnson down to size and establish, in the end, the superiority of Boswell, the aristocratic, polished man-of-the-world, to this rugged provincial with his uncouth manners and quaint, old-fashioned prejudices." Greene probes even deeper into Boswell's psyche: "The psychology behind this is not hard to comprehend.

Boswell, rejected by his own stern father, seized on Johnson as a substitute father-figure to support his shaky ego. But we all know, or by this time should know, how much suppressed resentment the poor father-figure is subjected to."[31]

Greene would therefore find vexing the basic truth of Marshall Waingrow's observation that no other "hypothesis" of Johnson "has pleased so many, or is likely to please so long, as Boswell's."[32] Both Greene and Richard Schwartz would add, though, that Boswell's portrait has pleased to the detriment of the real Johnson's personality and reputation as a writer. As Schwartz argues, "Boswell's sense of Johnson is too superficial and overlooks (along with much modern scholarship) Johnson's Johnson, the image which emerges in the self-portraits sprinkled throughout Johnson's works."[33] And Schwartz warns students of Johnson not to "forget the type and extent of coloring" Boswell injects into the famous scenes in the *Life:* they "must constantly guard against Boswellian falsification of Johnson."[34]

Both Johnsonians and Boswellians have wrestled with the issue of "Boswell's Johnson." In 1969 Hugh Amory whimsically noted the Johnsonians' quest for the Historical Johnson in the *Life,* compared the relationship of Boswell and Johnson to that of Plato and Socrates, and considered the "resemblance between the *Life of Johnson* and the philosophic lives of antiquity."[35] W. K. Wimsatt's "Images of Samuel Johnson" (1974) set Boswell's portrait in its historical context—in relationship to other contemporary accounts, most notably, Hester Piozzi's: "We are in an especially good position to talk about Boswell's Johnson through the circumstance that Johnson was the cynosure of so many other observers and reporters."[36] And to some a careful examination of the Johnson-Boswell relationship is the best way to understand Boswell's characterization of Johnson.[37] Irma Lustig strenuously objected to those who have utilized that relationship as "one of the sticks used to beat Boswell." She believes that "Boswell's reverence for Johnson as moral and intellectual hero never failed. It is a fixed element of the friendship, and the motive and theme of the *Life*." Her essay seeks to rebut those who contend that the *Life* "is not an act of love and homage, but post-mortem revenge for years of subordination and suppressed resentment."[38]

In 1974 Felicity Nussbaum offered her views on the Johnson who inhabits the world of Boswell's book through an examination of Boswell's revision of his journal entries and the original manuscript version of the *Life*. She observes early in her essay that

> By attributing Johnson's contradictory qualities to the energetic vitality of his mind, Boswell provided an explanation for the great man's idiosyncrasies without idealizing him. Johnson's apparent inconsistency but real consistency is a recurring theme of the *Life*, a conception of Johnson's character which functions as a significant control when Boswell, faced with his memories, the journal records, and the miscellaneous "Papers Apart," sought to impregnate these diverse materials with the Johnsonian ether. Since the Johnson of the *Life* must be larger than the lively and cantankerous traveling companion of the *Tour to the Hebrides* (from which the *Life* sketch was derived), the elaborately expanded *Life* character explained Johnson's apparently rigid piety, gloomy melancholy, and argumentative spirit as characteristics to be duly noted but then subordinated to his extraordinary and admirable virtues.[39]

Nussbaum sees Boswell as protector of Johnson's reputation, interpreter of his eccentricities, and critic and judge of his temperament: "The *Life of Johnson* is not panegyric," she concludes, "not even an idealized picture, but it is Boswell's interpretation of a life well-lived; the contradictions are adjusted within the limits of authenticity, and the 'strange succession' in which these qualities show themselves is shaped without destroying the essential veracity of Boswell's portrait."[40] Hugo M. Reichard, in "Boswell's Johnson, the Hero Made by a Committee" (1980), believes that the Johnson in the *Life* is more than both the historical Samuel Johnson and the Johnson "created" by Boswell; rather, "Boswell's majestic protagonist is largely decided by others, by persons in his shadow."[41] And in this volume, John J. Burke, Jr., assails the very notion of a "Boswell's Johnson."

Whether one blames, defends, or praises Boswell for the way Johnson is depicted, all of us, especially as teachers of Johnson, should appreciate the profound effect the Johnson lifted from the pages of the *Life* has had on the minds of nonspecialists, students, and general readers. As both defenders and detractors of Boswell have observed, Johnson has frequently appeared as a stuffy moralist and inflexible conservative, huffing and puffing out pronouncements on literature and life. Many have seen him as an *old* eccentric, powerful of mind but far less attractive than the exhilarating and shocking Swift and the intoxicating and mystical Blake. So memorable is Boswell's portrait, so powerfully drawn, that readers naturally assume the colossus in the *Life* was the historical Samuel Johnson. Certainly one discovers a literary giant in the *Life,* but from our reading of the book as undergraduates we remember more easily, and therefore place more emphasis on, Johnson's conversations, his seemingly reactionary political views, his hatred of Scotland, his bullying personality, and his belief in his own intellectual infallibility.

From a casual exposure to Boswell's *Life* many have concluded that Johnson "talked" the best literature of his age and that he was always the "Dr." Johnson of his late fifties, sixties, and early seventies. Readers have also recalled with both relish and distaste Johnson's idiosyncrasies: his tics, convulsions, superstitions, habits, and pathetic and often hilarious personal appearance. In his defense, Boswell emphasizes much more in his portrait of Johnson the man and author, and he at times attempts to qualify the impression he leaves. But either despite himself or intentionally so, Boswell injects enough dramatic and comic energy into the major scenes and confrontations between Johnson and his company that they mushroom out of proportion to his stated biographical designs. The student or general reader usually does not come from a reading of the *Life* discussing Johnson's works, the complexity of his personality, or the depth of his humanity. He or she rather remembers with pleasure the colorful anecdotes and retorts and concludes that Johnson was a powerful force to be sure, but more so a cantankerous though often entertaining old man. Johnson of the *Life* is so much fun to talk about and quote, but are we sure he is or is sufficiently close to the real Johnson? Some of those deploring the stereotype of Johnson taken from the *Life* wince even when a colleague or student mentions "Dr." Johnson. To some committed Johnsonians of more recent years, "Dr." has the same connotative value as "Negro" did to younger blacks in the late 1960s and early 1970s.[42]

But the questions remain: Should one blame Boswell or the *Life* for projecting the negative image of Johnson? Or has the *Life* captured the essence of the historical Johnson, even if the portrait is not in all ways accurate? Has the *Life* so affected the reader's view of Johnson that a healthy exposure to Johnson's work and other biographical accounts still would not crack the popular image? Would Johnson have been better off without Boswell? Or is the allure of the *Life* so strong that, like the lotus-eaters, readers will not wish to leave the isle of pleasure that is Boswell's book to return to what is real but to what also may be less exciting and sustaining?

EVEN THOUGH SEVERAL MODERN STUDIES have not been deterred in their quest for the "real" Johnson, much contemporary discussion has been marked by a pronounced shift away from a concentration on the historical Johnson and toward an appreciation of Boswell's literary artistry. In his collection, Clifford commended Boswell's literary talents from the biographer's perspective: "as students of the art of biography we must applaud Boswell's skill in producing a smooth, engrossing narrative."[43] Also in that volume, Paul Alkon examined Boswell's dramatic method and concluded, "It is Boswell's skill as much as Johnson's personality that has created so many partisans and so many detractors."[44] Frederick Pottle's essay in that collection, "The *Life of Johnson:* Art and Authenticity," signalled the direction in which a number of subsequent studies would go—namely, toward seeking a synthesis of the historical and the artistic. Ralph Rader's seminal article (reprinted here) has been the most respected and influential attempt to reconcile the worlds of factual biography and literary artistry, although his remarks on Boswell the creative artist have had the most impact.

Studies on the literary value of the *Life* have considerable range, from the more traditional approach of David L. Passler's *Time, Form, and Style in Boswell's "Life of Johnson"* (1971),[45] which investigates the thematic structure of the book and Boswell's literary proficiency, to the more controversial "deconstructionist" analysis in William C. Dowling's *Language and Logos in Boswell's "Life of Johnson"* (1981),[46] in which he argues, among other points, that historical reality is inoperative in the *Life* because the book is a "self-contained world of motive and speech of action." Ignoring or finding less important questions regarding biographical accuracy, some commentators have followed Sven Eric Molin's lead[47] and have isolated their study to significant sections or scenes in the *Life*. One example would be Donald J. Newman's essay in this collection; another would be Jo Allen Bradham's "Comic Fragments in the *Life of Johnson*" (1980). Boswell,

Bradham writes, "positions Johnson as *alazon,* or the bragging over-speaker, against himself as the quiet, but eventually victorious *eiron,* the foxy fellow who holds his tongue and bides his time. Or, setting Johnson against Sir Joshua Reynolds in the *alazon* role, Boswell draws Johnson as the sly but wise *eiron.* In some situations Boswell throws about the broad strokes and caricature necessary for farce."[48]

Paul Alkon's "Boswellian Time" (1973) sees not only "Boswell's artistry" at issue but also the "still unresolved question" of whether the *Life* "is primarily a static or kinetic experience." "Far from being disjoined," Alkon observes, "the *Life* achieves formal coherence and human significance by means of skillfully created and mutually sustaining narrative counterparts to the dramatic unities of place, time, and action."[49] Recent discussion of Boswell's artistry has also included David E. Schwalm's "The *Life of Johnson:* Boswell's Rhetoric and Reputation" (1976),[50] which questions the generic label affixed to the *Life* and contends that the book is "the end product of an interconnected maze of conscious and unconscious rhetorical devices." Indicative of those studies that seek to bridge the seeming dichotomy between art and authenticity in the *Life,* Schwalm maintains that Boswell "purposely distracted the reader's attention from his artistry in order to enhance the credibility and authenticity of his record."[51]

In his review of Richard Schwartz's *Boswell's Johnson,* William R. Siebenschuh remarked, "However comfortable or uncomfortable one feels about it, it seems impossible to escape the conclusion that the *Life* makes the full impact that it does because Boswell makes Johnson accessible to our imagination in ways we usually associate with fiction."[52] First in his monograph, *Form and Purpose in Boswell's Biographical Works* (1972), later in two essays on the *Life* (1977, 1981), and most recently in his book, *Fictional Techniques and Factual Works* (1983),[53] Siebenschuh scrutinizes the literary techniques Boswell employs in the *Life* and their relationship to the image of Johnson ultimately revealed in that work. Siebenschuh asks, "How is our response to the portrait of Johnson in the *Life* affected by Boswell's use of techniques we usually associate with fiction?" Yet, he argues, "the success of the literary effects depends directly on the credibility of the image of the historical man."[54] This interrelationship of art and authenticity, then, is at the heart of one's response to the *Life.* According to Siebenschuh,

Boswell is an "interpretive biographer" or "artist-biographer"[55] prone to biographical errors, omissions, and occasional misinformation. Even so, the major achievement of the *Life* is not the facts revealed but rather Boswell's "vision of Johnson, the imaginative possession of him that his book allows us to have."[56] Siebenschuh concludes that "Boswell's Johnson is not merely an interpretive portrait of a historical figure; he is a perpetual affirmation of something in us; not, perhaps, of what we always are but of what we are capable of being via the literary dimension of the portrait."[57]

Another recent examination of Boswell's literary artistry in the *Life* (and in his other works) is William Dowling's *The Boswellian Hero*.[58] As does Siebenschuh, Dowling believes that one cannot assume an "essential antagonism between the factual and the imaginative."[59] History and artistry have been placed by many commentators in "false conflict": "to read the *Life of Johnson* as literature is only to begin where all criticism must begin, with an awareness of its self-contained nature as a work of art—something that is in no way inconsistent with its being simultaneously a repository of facts about the 'real' Samuel Johnson."[60] Dowling places Boswell's Johnson within the heroic tradition of literature and determines that he is "the hero in an unheroic world." To Dowling, the "tension between the man and his age" is a "generic tension": "The *Life* is partly the story of Johnson's heroic resistance to these invisible forces of moral anarchy, but its larger theme concerns the cast of such resistance to mind and soul."[61] Dowling asks us to peer below familiar levels of interpretation: "when we think of the world of the *Life of Johnson,* we are really contemplating a world within a world, one transformed by Johnson's presence and symbolically associated with his values." The *Life,* he adds, is "a tragedy taking place inside a comedy."[62] He concludes, "The real problem of imaginative versus factual literature derives, then, from a mistaken tendency to think of a work like the *Life of Johnson* as an object-in-itself existing independent of any universe of discourse whatever." These words look to Dowling's "deconstructionist" reading of the *Life: Language and Logos in Boswell's "Life of Johnson."*

Whereas the two major areas of investigation—the *Life* as accurate biography and the *Life* as great literature—have received the most attention since 1970, scholars and critics have been exploring other avenues of approach. For example, William Siebenschuh has addressed the issue of the *Life*'s accessibility to the modern undergraduate,[63] and scholars, such as Samuel H. Woods, Jr., in this volume, have begun to examine more closely and then question the impression Boswell leaves of other members of Johnson's famous circle. Another topic of growing interest is "Boswell's Boswell";[64] that is, Boswell's presentation of himself in the *Life*. Frank Brady, who has now completed the account of Boswell's later years,[65] discussed in "Boswell's Self-Presentation and His Critics" (1972) the "central paradox about Boswell's reputation: admittedly the world's greatest biographer, Boswell the man has been more consistently sneered at and patronized than any other British writer of the first rank."[66] Did Boswell, as Joseph Reed wrote in 1966, create "a dramatic persona for the sake of his book"?[67] Responding negatively to David Passler's analysis (in *Time, Form, and Style in Boswell's "Life of Johnson"*) of how Boswell's "unstable personality" is inseparable from his achievement as a writer, Brady wonders why we must continue to judge Boswell the man when we evaluate the *Life*. After reviewing Boswell's contemporary reputation, Brady considers how it might have affected the way the Scot portrayed himself in his book. In answer to many modern assumptions about "Boswell's Boswell," Brady ends his essay as follows: "But in one respect, in assuming that his readers could make the elementary distinction between man and writer, Boswell gave his readers far more credit than many have given him."[68]

Part of David Schwalm's "The *Life of Johnson*: Boswell's Rhetoric and Reputation" (1976) is devoted to the question Brady earlier raised: Why would Boswell "display himself so much to his disadvantage"?[69] Schwalm reasons that in "all probability, Boswell's self-portrait was by and large determined by what he chose to include about Johnson. However, Boswell did choose at some point *whether* to appear as a character and adhered to his decision although he was aware that he was not appearing to advantage."[70] Robert Bell describes Boswell's role more simply: "Boswell the character has a variety of guises in the story of Samuel Johnson—gadfly, jester, inquisitor, stage manager, host, *ingénu*, disciple—but all his roles provide a foil for the grandeur of the hero."[71] And more to the discredit of Boswell is Richard Schwartz's position that the *Life* "is a book about Johnson but a book in which crucial attitudes and points of view are those of Johnson's biographer."[72] In any event the matter of "Boswell's Boswell" should command more attention, especially if the trend continues toward evaluating the *Life* more as literature than as biography.[73]

IT WOULD BE WRONG to separate all recent work on the *Life* into two hostile camps: the Johnsonians, who approach the *Life* from a strictly biographical angle and accordingly find it deficient as the major portrait of Johnson and as a repository for information on him; and the Boswellians, who concern themselves far less with the historical Johnson than with Boswell's narrative skill and the artistic merits of his book. In some instances the battle lines are clearly drawn; in others, critics go freely between the two camps, some defending the accuracy and success of Boswell's biography and presentation of Johnson without turning most of their attention to the literary properties of the *Life*. And still others are active in bringing peace to both sides by stressing that the historical Johnson and Boswell's literary artistry can coexist harmoniously in any analysis of the book. But if the nature of the war is occasionally exaggerated, some of the battles have clearly resembled more the ferocity of fighting at Malplaquet than the small-scale skirmishing at Lexington and Concord.

THIS COLLECTION reflects recent debate over the *Life*, reassesses previous assumptions about Boswell's achievement, and offers new perspectives on ways to examine this long-cherished though often misread and misused literary masterpiece. Although three of the essays here are not "brand new" (even though one of them contains new material), they are "new" in the sense of being reflective of the "modern" period of work on the *Life*—post 1970. (And any "new" study of Boswell's *Life* will surely have to contend with the work of Rader, Greene, and Pottle.) The essays in this volume should inform both the specialist and the uninitiated, inspire or incite others to address the issues raised or elaborated on in these pages, and therefore help continue what is now an exciting period in the history of commentary on the *Life of Johnson*.

Since I have discussed in my overview of criticism first the matter of biographical accuracy in the *Life* and second Boswell's literary artistry, as a gesture to fairness I have reversed the order in placing the essays and have given the place of honor to Ralph Rader's seminal study, "Literary Form in Factual Narrative: The Example of Boswell's *Johnson*."[74] And any honor given this piece is well deserved, for the frequent citation of the essay by the contributors to this volume as well as by many who have written recently on the *Life* speaks to its significance. It remains one of the most important studies ever written on Boswell's famous book, and one would not be far from the mark to speak of a "Rader School" of Boswell criticism. Although the essay was initially published in 1968, it belongs in spirit to the post-1970 era of work on the *Life*, for Rader's conclusions have helped stimulate the work of Siebenschuh, Dowling, and others wishing to illuminate the creative and literary force Boswell projects in his book.

In Donald J. Newman's "The Death Scene and the Art of Suspense in Boswell's *Life of Johnson*," the legacy of Ralph Rader is readily apparent, and here Newman directs our attention toward a section of the *Life* that has disappointed many readers. Newman argues that, rather than being out of control, Boswell has a literary principle guiding his selection and arrangement of details surrounding Johnson's last days. "We have trouble seeing the climactic element in the death scene," Newman asserts, "because we do not see its two-part structure." To Newman, the "art of Boswell's suspense is his skill at concealing the story's real ending while amplifying our anxieties concerning the fate of a man we have come to care about a great deal." Newman's essay reminds us that individual scenes or sections of the *Life* offer much to the literary critic as well as to the scholar interested in Johnson, Boswell, and members of their circle. The *Life* as a literary work is filled with tributaries and coves yet to be explored and charted by the critic.

Fredric V. Bogel's "'Did you once see Johnson plain?': Reflections on Boswell's *Life* and the State of Eighteenth-Century Studies" is another example of how critics are forced to consider both the book's "historicism" and its "formalism." Bogel provides a valuable assessment of Johnson's presence in the *Life* but goes on to question the manner in which we have traditionally approached Boswell's book. Reflecting recent developments in literary criticism and the effect they have had—or should have—on eighteenth-century studies, Bogel believes we must "continue the de-historicizing that the formalists began so that, at the very least, we can pose more interesting and fruitful questions about the multiple determination—historical, literary, and so on—of a variety of texts," including the *Life of Johnson*. Bogel gives us a theoretical assessment of the book bound to stimulate serious thinking and debate. This is an essay that, perhaps more than any other in the collection, points in the direction toward which many recent literary theorists will wish studies on the *Life of Johnson* to go.[75]

The reader will see in William R. Siebenschuh's "Boswell's Second Crop of Memory: A New Look at the Role of Memory in the Making of the *Life*" that although much modern criticism has sidestepped—or thrown aside—the issue of historical accuracy in the *Life* the topic continues to engage even those who have written impressively on Boswell's literary gifts. Examining the process by which Boswell recalled the facts and scenes he included in his book, Siebenschuh shows us that one may come to an appreciation of Boswell's achievement without concentrating exclusively on the historical Samuel Johnson or on Boswell's artistry, although his remarks offer important insight on both those topics. The essay helps us discover and value "the principles of selectivity which were peculiar to Boswell." Siebenschuh goes beyond Frederick Pottle's early essay, "The Power of Memory in Boswell and Scott,"[76] and draws on the assistance of contemporary research "in the fields of human memory and perception." This essay suggests that an examination of the *Life* may be informed and enhanced even by nonliterary and nonhistorical fields.

No collection of essays on Boswell's *Life of Johnson* would be complete without something from Donald Greene, who first and foremost pulled down the icon and forced us to consider the defects of an accepted "great book" of world literature. James Clifford's volume included the highly provocative "Reflections on a Literary Anniversary"; this collection reprints the equally famous (or is it notorious?) "'Tis a Pretty Book, Mr. Boswell, But—" (1978), complete with further thoughts and illustrative tables by the author. In shaping their perceptions of the *Life*, students cannot afford to ignore Greene's refutation of Boswell's achievement. Nor would such a volume as this seem complete without something from Frederick Pottle, to whom all students of Boswell and the *Life* owe an incalculable debt. Pottle's

"The Adequacy as Biography of Boswell's *Life of Johnson*" was initially published in the *Transactions of the Johnson Society* (Lichfield) for 1974, but it is in effect an answer to the circulated version of Greene's "'Tis a Pretty Book" piece (1973), to Greene's "Reflections on a Literary Anniversary," and to those, such as Leopold Damrosch, Jr., who have attempted to "degrade the reputation of the *Life of Johnson* for faults of structure and proportion." Pottle sees in Greene's attitude toward the book "a classical case" of "the fear of the usurpative power of biography." In the spirit of the debate that has swirled around the *Life*, Donald Greene provides a short rebuttal to Pottle's objections and to others' emphases on Boswell's literary art, an answer written specifically for this collection. In short, these essays make for a stimulating exchange between the two most prominent scholars of Johnson and Boswell.

The Herculean quality of the issues debated by Greene and Pottle prompts another challenger in John J. Burke, Jr.'s "But Boswell's Johnson Is Not Boswell's Johnson." Burke's piece, which in many ways replies to the conclusions of Greene and Richard Schwartz, confronts one of the most significant questions asked in recent years about Boswell's book: Are we engaged with the historical Samuel Johnson in the pages of the *Life*? Is he more a character created by Boswell's literary imagination or a deliberate distortion perpetrated by a well-meaning and image-shaping or possibly, as Greene argues, a resentful and obtuse Boswell? In his carefully argued study, Burke contends that the Johnson of the *Life* "is not and could not be simply Boswell's Johnson." Although Boswell himself "remained the principal architect," the *Life* was "constructed from the testimony of a large number of Johnson's friends and acquaintances." Burke reminds us, then, that if we confront a "Boswell's" Johnson in the *Life* we also discover a "Hector's" Johnson, an "Adams's" Johnson, a "White's" Johnson, a "Garrick's" Johnson, a "Maxwell's" Johnson, a "Burney's" Johnson, a "Beauclerk's" Johnson, and a "Reynolds's" Johnson. And Burke offers a new perspective on the importance of Bennet Langton to the shaping of the *Life*.

Marshall Waingrow observed in 1969 that "no matter how many new facts are brought to light, Samuel Johnson will always be somebody's hypothesis." Hugh Amory wrote in the same year that Johnsonians have continued in their examination of the *Life* the "Quest for the Historical Johnson" on which commentators embarked in the early nineteenth century.[77] I am one of those, as Amory puts it, "in hot pursuit" of that Johnson, for my essay, "The Laughing Johnson and the Shaping of Boswell's *Life*," not only forwards my "hypothesis" of the historical Johnson in the *Life* but also argues, through an examination of his unique brand of humor, that the contexts of many of the famous scenes and retorts may have all this time been misunderstood. By deliberate deception Johnson distorted himself to others and as a result helped to shape the way in which the *Life* and his own character have come to be judged. We therefore find ourselves engaged less with "Boswell's" Johnson and more with "Johnson's" Johnson. The Johnson who emerges in this essay is one specialists too often forget and one students and general readers do not even know.

Samuel H. Woods, Jr.'s "Boswell's Presentation of Goldsmith: A Reconsideration" treats the problem of accuracy and tone in "Boswell's Goldsmith." As the latest biographer of Goldsmith, Woods brings to the *Life* his special insight on who is perhaps next to Johnson and Boswell themselves the most memorable figure in the book. Woods compares Boswell's presentation of the Irishman in the *Life* with that in the journals and with the reminiscences of Percy, Johnson, and Reynolds to show how Goldsmith came to be perceived as both genius and fool. Woods's essay reflects the continuing interest in Boswell's *Life* as a source of information on and a showcase for members of Johnson's famous circle.

Finally, Richard Schwartz, whose *Boswell's Johnson: A Preface to the "Life"* both articulated the arguments against the biographical accuracy and achievement of the *Life* and crystallized the opposition to his and Greene's arguments, concludes this collection with "The Boswell Problem." Schwartz's piece should be seen as the after-dinner brandy that helps the reader digest the various entrées he or she has either savored here with pleasure or found simply unpalatable. In this epilogue to the volume, Schwartz offers his sense of the major issues scholars and critics have grappled with in recent years and asks and then attempts to answer the question, given the shortcomings of the *Life* as a biography of Johnson, "What then are we to do with Boswell?" Schwartz approaches the answer from a pedagogical as well as a critical perspective. It is important to consider, he reminds us, the way in which the *Life* is taught, because the book should remain "a part of our intellectual and spiritual lives." With its caveats to the student of the *Life,* Schwartz's epilogue looks forward to work yet to be done.

REGARDLESS OF HOW ONE JUDGES the success and importance of any particular essay here, this volume is testimony to the enduring value of Boswell's *Life of Johnson*. The critical emphases have changed considerably since the influential estimations of Macaulay and Carlyle, and one trusts they will continue to change, perhaps dramatically, as we approach and then pass the bicentenary of the book's publication. But one thing has not changed much at all. The *Life* remains a classic, a masterpiece, a memorable reading experience, and a joy even to those inclined to ponder the weighty critical matters about to be discussed in these pages. The true test of a great book, it seems to me, is not so much the longevity of its popularity as its ability to sustain intense critical scrutiny and then, when later picked up by the same hands that annotated it and wrote about its literary value or its shortcomings, provide time and again immense pleasure and satisfaction. The *Life of Johnson* is such a book.

Notes

1. James Boswell, *The Life of Samuel Johnson, LL.D.,* ed. George Birkbeck Hill, rev. L. F. Powell, 6 vols. (Oxford: Clarendon Press, 1934–1964), III:57. This remains the most scholarly edition of the *Life.*

2. James Clifford, *Twentieth Century Interpretations of Boswell's "Life of Johnson"* (Englewood Cliffs: Prentice Hall, 1970).

3. All of the collection's essays and "viewpoints," except for Clifford's introduction and Frederick A. Pottle's "The *Life of Johnson:* Art and Authenticity," had been previously published.

4. Namely, by having Johnson as its subject matter. See Thomas Babington Macaulay's review of John Wilson Croker's edition of Boswell's *Life of Johnson* in *Edinburgh Review* 54 (September 1831): 1–38.

5. Donald Greene, most notably among others, believes that Macaulay's "influence in shaping and perpetuating the Johnson myth of the nineteenth

century and later was enormous—and still remains so." See Donald Greene, ed., [Samuel Johnson's] *Political Writings* (New Haven: Yale University Press, 1977), xxii.

6. For the number of days Boswell was in Johnson's company, see Greene's statistical appendix printed in this volume.

7. The clearinghouse for this information is the *Johnsonian News Letter*.

8. Clifford, *Twentieth Century Interpretations,* 5–21. For further insight into these matters, Clifford follows his introduction with Geoffrey Scott's "The Making of the *Life of Johnson* as Shown in Boswell's First Notes" and Frank Taylor's "The Caldwell Minute." (The latter title is actually Clifford's; the essay is taken from Taylor's "Johnsoniana from the Bagshawe Muniments in the John Rylands Library: Sir James Caldwell, Dr. Hawkesworth, Dr. Johnson, and Boswell's Use of the 'Caldwell Minute' " [1952–1953].)

9. For the history of the Boswell Papers see David Buchanan, *The Treasure of Auchinleck* (New York: McGraw-Hill Book Company, 1974) and Frederick A. Pottle, *Pride and Negligence: The History of the Boswell Papers* (New York: McGraw-Hill Book Company, 1982).

10. Marshall Waingrow, *The Correspondence and Other Papers of James Boswell Relating to the Making of the "Life of Johnson"* (New York: McGraw-Hill Book Company, 1969).

11. In *The Triumph of Culture: Eighteenth-Century Perspectives,* ed. Paul Fritz and David Williams (Toronto: Hakkert, 1972), 225–243.

12. See Irma Lustig, "Boswell at Work: The 'Animadversions' on Mrs. Piozzi," *Modern Language Review* 67 (1972): 11–30, and "Fact into Art: James Boswell's Notes, Journals, and the *Life of Johnson,*" in *Biography in the Eighteenth Century,* ed. John D. Browning (New York: Garland Publishing, 1980), 128–146.

13. Robert Bell, "Boswell's Notes Toward a Supreme Fiction from *London Journal* to *Life of Johnson,*" *Modern Language Quarterly* 38 (1977): 132–148; Elizabeth Bruss, "James Boswell: Genius and Stenography" in Bruss, *Autobiographical Acts: The Changing Situation of a Literary Genre* (Baltimore: Johns Hopkins University Press, 1976), 61–92.

14. A. R. Brooks, *James Boswell* (New York: Twayne Publishers, 1971), 83–127.

15. Of his more recent work, Frederick Pottle's "Art and Authenticity" (in the Clifford collection) offers valuable commentary on Boswell's biographical methods.

16. The essay was initially published in *Queen's Quarterly* 70 (Summer 1963): 198–208.

17. Clifford, *Twentieth Century Interpretations,* 97–98.

18. For a modern abridgment of John Hawkins's *Life of Samuel Johnson, LL.D.* (1787), see Bertram H. Davis's edition (New York: Macmillan Company, 1961). For commentary on Hawkins's *Life,* see Davis, *Johnson before Boswell* (New Haven: Yale University Press, 1960).

19. See Greene, "Do We Need a Biography of Johnson's 'Boswell' Years?," *Modern Language Studies* 9, no. 3 (1979): 128–136. The major biographies of Johnson are James L. Clifford's *Young Sam Johnson* (New York: McGraw-Hill Book Company, 1955) and *Dictionary Johnson* (New York: McGraw-Hill Book Company, 1979); John Wain's *Samuel Johnson* (New York: Viking Press, 1974); and Walter Jackson Bate's *Samuel Johnson* (New York: Harcourt Brace Jovanovich, 1977). Greene is now working on a biography of Johnson's "Boswell" years, 1763–1784.

20. Richard Schwartz, *Boswell's Johnson: A Preface to the "Life"* (Madison: University of Wisconsin Press, 1978).

21. Ibid., 31.

22. Ibid., 102.

23. Ibid., xiii.

24. Ibid., 105.

25. See the reviews of Schwartz's *Boswell's Johnson* by Irma Lustig in *Eighteenth-Century Studies* 13 (1980): 344–348 and by John J. Burke, Jr., in *The Eighteenth Century: A Current Bibliography*, n.s. 4 for 1978 (New York: AMS Press, 1981), 357–359.

26. Leopold Damrosch, Jr., "The *Life of Johnson:* An Anti-Theory," *Eighteenth-Century Studies* 6 (1973): 486–505.

27. Ibid., 493–494.

28. See p. 115 of this volume.

29. Donald Greene, "Johnson without Boswell," *TLS*, 22 November 1974, 1315–1316. For a reaction to Greene's remarks, see David Pole's "Letter to the Editor" in *TLS*, 20 December 1974, 1442.

30. A. S. F. Gow's "The Unknown Johnson," reprinted in Clifford, *Twentieth Century Interpretations*, 88.

31. Greene, "Johnson without Boswell," 1315–1316. See as well "Reflections on a Literary Anniversary," in Clifford, *Twentieth Century Interpretations*, 100–101.

32. Waingrow, "Boswell's Johnson," in Clifford, *Twentieth Century Interpretations*, 50.

33. Schwartz, *Boswell's Johnson*, xii. See as well Donald Greene's "The Uses of Autobiography in the Eighteenth Century," in *Essays in Eighteenth-Century Biography*, ed. Philip B. Daghlian (Bloomington: Indiana University Press, 1968), 43–66. Greene's argument is that the "best biography of Samuel Johnson is not Boswell's" but rather Johnson's autobiographical account.

34. Schwartz, *Boswell's Johnson*, 101.

35. In the "last analysis," Amory concludes, there is "only a mock-resemblance." Hugh Amory, "Boswell in Search of the Intentional Fallacy," *Bulletin of Research in the Humanities* 73 (1969): 24–39.

36. W. K. Wimsatt, "Images of Samuel Johnson," *ELH* 41 (1974): 359–374, esp. 360.

37. In an essay from an earlier period, B. L. Reid argued that Johnson

"required" Boswell "to be a superb companion, and Boswell responded with a superb performance." In "Johnson's Life of Boswell," *Kenyon Review* 18 (1956): 546–575, esp. 575.

38. Irma Lustig, "The Friendship of Johnson and Boswell: Some Biographical Considerations," in *Studies in Eighteenth-Century Culture* 6 (1977): 199–214, esp. 199, 200, and 206.

39. Felicity Nussbaum, "Boswell's Treatment of Johnson's Temper: 'A Warm West-Indian Climate,'" *SEL* 14 (1974): 421–433, esp. 423–424.

40. Ibid., 433.

41. Hugo M. Reichard, "Boswell's Johnson, the Hero Made by a Committee," *PMLA* 95 (1980): 225–233.

42. Donald Greene writes, "Johnson was no more in the habit of speaking or thinking of himself as 'Doctor Johnson' than any other sensible holder of an honorary doctorate. But thanks to Boswell, the average reader is probably convinced that he did; and so he seems stupidly pompous." Donald Greene, "Reflections on a Literary Anniversary," in Clifford, *Twentieth Century Interpretations*, 101. For further discussion of these matters, see John J. Burke, Jr., "The Unknown Samuel Johnson," in Burke and Donald Kay, eds., *The Unknown Samuel Johnson* (Madison: University of Wisconsin Press, 1983), 3–16.

43. Clifford, *Twentieth Century Interpretations*, 21.

44. Paul Alkon, "Boswell's Control of Aesthetic Distance," first published in *University of Toronto Quarterly* 38 (1969): 174–191. See Clifford, *Twentieth Century Interpretations*, 58.

45. David L. Passler, *Time, Form, and Style in Boswell's "Life of Johnson"* (New Haven: Yale University Press, 1971).

46. William C. Dowling, *Language and Logos in Boswell's "Life of Johnson"* (Princeton: Princeton University Press, 1981). At least one commentator, William H. Epstein, is unwilling to consider Dowling's book as a deconstructionist interpretation of the *Life:* "it borrows some of the terminology of the Derridean project to pursue an approach which is, ideologically and methodologically, contrary to and even subversive of the so-called deconstructionist enterprise." Epstein, *"Bios* and *Logos:* Boswell's *Life of Johnson* and Recent Literary Theory," *SAQ* 82 (1983): 246–255.

47. Sven Eric Molin, "Boswell's Account of the Johnson-Wilkes Meeting," *SEL* 3 (1963): 307–322. Molin writes of Boswell's "comic-novelistic presentation," which "anticipates Dickens." Boswell, Molin argues, was a "conscious artist."

48. Jo Allen Bradham, "Comic Fragments in the *Life of Johnson*," *Biography* 3 (1980): 95–104, esp. 95. Consult as well Bradham's "Boswell's Narrative of Oliver Edwards," *Journal of Narrative Technique* 8 (1978): 176–184.

49. Paul Alkon, "Boswellian Time," *Studies in Burke and His Time* 14 (1973): 239–256, esp. 239, 256.

50. David E. Schwalm, "The *Life of Johnson:* Boswell's Rhetoric and Reputation," *Texas Studies in Literature and Language* 18 (1976): 240–289.

51. Ibid., 286.

52. *Modern Philology* 78 (1980): 93.

53. William R. Siebenschuh, *Form and Purpose in Boswell's Biographical Works* (Berkeley: University of California Press, 1972); "The Relationship between Factual Accuracy and Literary Art in the *Life of Johnson,*" *Modern Philology* 74 (1977): 273–288; "Who Is Boswell's Johnson?," *Studies in Eighteenth-Century Culture* 10 (1981): 347–360; and *Fictional Techniques and Factual Works* (Athens: University of Georgia Press, 1983).

54. Siebenschuh, *Fictional Techniques,* 55, 73.

55. Ibid., 76, 96.

56. Ibid., 80.

57. Ibid., 98.

58. William C. Dowling, *The Boswellian Hero* (Athens: University of Georgia Press, 1979). See as well Dowling's "The Boswellian Hero," *Studies in Scottish Literature* 10 (1972): 79–93; "Boswell and the Problem of Biography," in *Studies in Biography,* ed. Daniel Aaron (Harvard English Studies 8 [1978]), 73–93; and "Biographer, Hero, and Audience in Boswell's *Life of Johnson,*" *SEL* 20 (1980): 475–491.

59. Dowling, *Boswellian Hero,* xi–xii.

60. Ibid., xv.

61. Ibid., 2, 16.

62. Ibid., 122, 127.

63. William R. Siebenschuh, "Modern Undergraduates and the Accessibility of *The Life of Johnson,*" *Eighteenth-Century Life* 5, no. 3 (1979): 54–59.

64. Bertrand H. Bronson wrote earlier on this topic. See Bronson, "Boswell's Boswell," in *Johnson Agonistes and Other Essays* (Berkeley: University of California Press, 1965), 53–99. (The essay first appeared, however, in 1944.)

65. To finish the biographical project begun with Frederick A. Pottle's *James Boswell: The Earlier Years, 1740–1769* (New York: McGraw-Hill Book Company, 1966). See Frank Brady, *James Boswell: The Later Years, 1769–1795* (New York: McGraw-Hill Book Company, 1984).

66. Frank Brady, "Boswell's Self-Presentation and His Critics," *SEL* 12 (1972): 545–555.

67. Joseph Reed, *English Biography in the Early Nineteenth Century* (New Haven: Yale University Press, 1966), 134.

68. Brady, "Boswell's Self-Presentation," 555.

69. Schwalm, "The *Life of Johnson,*" 273.

70. Ibid., 285.

71. Robert Bell, "Boswell's Notes toward a Supreme Fiction," 144.

72. Schwartz, *Boswell's Johnson,* 69–70.

JOHN A. VANCE

73. Other more recent studies not discussed in this overview would include Peter Steese, "Boswell Walking upon Ashes," in *English Symposium Papers,* Vol. 1, ed. Douglas Shepherd (Fredonia: SUNY College at Fredonia, 1970), 46–69; Donald Greene, "The Making of Boswell's *Life of Johnson,*" *Studies in Burke and His Time* 12 (1970–1971): 1812–1820; Frank Brady, "The Strategies of Biography and Some Eighteenth-Century Examples," in *Literary Theory and Structure,* ed. Brady, John Palmer, and Martin Price (New Haven: Yale University Press, 1973), 245–265; and Allan Ingram, *Boswell's Creative Gloom: A Study of Imagery and Melancholy in the Writings of James Boswell* (New York: Barnes and Noble, 1982).

74. First published in Daghlian, *Essays in Eighteenth-Century Biography,* 3–42.

75. See Dowling's *Language and Logos in Boswell's "Life of Johnson."* William Epstein believes the *Life* has not received the kind of critical attention it deserves and needs in large part because of our long-standing infatuation and preoccupation with the Boswell papers: "As literary redemption, scholarly myth, and academic enterprise, the Papers have described—and to some extent circumscribed—study of Boswell's canon, in which the status of the *Life of Johnson,* for so long that canon's salient text, has been diminished or perhaps shared during the past fifty years by a mythic hoard of revelatory manuscripts" ("*Bios* and *Logos,*" 251).

76. Frederick Pottle, "The Power of Memory in Boswell and Scott," in *Essays on the Eighteenth Century Presented to David Nichol Smith* (Oxford: Clarendon Press, 1945), 168–189. See as well Pottle's "Art and Authenticity" in Clifford, *Twentieth Century Interpretations,* 66–73.

77. Waingrow, "Boswell's Johnson," in Clifford, *Twentieth Century Interpretations,* 50; Amory, "Boswell in Search of the Intentional Fallacy," 28.

RALPH W. RADER

Literary Form
in Factual Narrative:
The Example of Boswell's
Johnson

*A*lthough factual narrative, that is to say, history and biography, is certainly an art, only a few biographies and histories are unequivocally literature. This paradox deserves explanation and will in fact provide the whole subject of my remarks in this essay. While much biography and history has a clear if relatively low place in literature, only Boswell and Gibbon in English have constructed factual narratives which stand unquestioned as literary masterpieces of the very first rank. On the other hand, much excellent biography and history has no place in literature at all. The explanation for these facts lies in the fundamental contrast between the fictional and the factual narrative modes. Literature in general is, in Coleridge's phrase, that species of composition which proposes pleasure rather than truth as its immediate object. The purely literary artist is free to invent, dispose, weight, and vivify his or her materials as a means to the greatest intensity of effect, whereas the immediate object of the biographer or historian cannot be effect but fidelity to truth.

Some works of history and biography nevertheless produce a distinct and powerful effect closely akin to those which characterize works of the imagination, and these of course are, as they should be from Coleridge's definition, the very works which rank as literature.

But though we speak of Gibbon's epical sweep and force and Macaulay's dramatic powers, we ought not to succumb to the temptations of analogy and talk as if the *Decline and Fall* were in fact an epic, or the *History of England* a drama, or even as if the most celebrated contemporary work of factual narrative is what its author calls it, a nonfiction novel. To do so would be to evade the terms of the question we want to answer, which is not how literary works are literary, but how works whose primary commitment is distinctly nonliterary nevertheless become literature.

The answer which I am going to propose is that such works become literature by transcending while fulfilling the usual purpose of history and biography, to provide true knowledge of the human past. I am going to suggest that factual narratives in order to compass a literary effect must raise their subjects constructively out of the past and represent them to the imagination as concrete, self-intelligible causes of emotion. My claim will be that these works of history thereby become, paradoxically, "a more philosophical and a higher thing than history." They become universal, in Aristotle's sense, because they are displayed to the imagination not as contingent but as concretely probable and valuable in terms of that general human nature which as human beings we all share and intuitively know. I choose as my text Boswell's *Life of Johnson* but shall return intermittently and at the close to a view of the overall subject.

It has not been obvious to the authors of the two most extensive and scholarly modern treatments of biography that the greatest work of factual narrative in our language has a structure which is the cause of its greatness, and that effective structure, as all writers should know, is never an accident. Donald Stauffer, though he gives high praise to Boswell's artistry, says flatly that "the structure of the *Life* is open to serious question." It lacks narrative connection and temporal development, it fails to scale itself to the proportions of Johnson's life, and (astoundingly) it fails to create Johnson, affording rather "materials from which Johnson may be created by an imaginative act."[1] John Garraty repeats the charges and adds a few of his own: the book is "all out of proportion"; it is merely "one man's recollections of another"; it lacks "not so much unity as cumulative effect and a comprehensive estimate of its subject and his importance."[2] As we shall see, it would make as much sense to blame Shakespeare for not providing a comprehensive estimate of Hamlet. Most of these criticisms point to real facts about the substance and structure of the *Life*, but they do not point to faults. Only the inadequate theoretical conception which underlies the criticism could make these facts seem faults, for no reader intuitively reacts to them as such. The problem lies in conceiving Boswell's work as if it were an ordinary explanatory narrative, like Krutch's biography of Johnson. If it were such a biography, then it would be a manifestly defective one, and we should have to pronounce it inferior to Krutch's. This would be absurd, for fine as it is, Krutch's biography is not great literature and Boswell's is. That is the whole point. It is literature. It is not an explanatory narrative but an emotive narrative of the type I have indicated, one whose whole principle is not to give instrumental information and explanation but rather to reconstruct and present as concrete and universal an aspect of human fact so as to render it inherently the cause of a distinct effect. What aspect of fact does Boswell reconstruct, and what is its effect? The answer lies in the last sentence of his book: "Such was Samuel Johnson, a man whose talents, acquirements, and virtues, were so extraordinary, that the more his character is considered, the more he will be regarded by the present age, and by posterity, with admiration and reverence." The subject of Boswell's book is not the life of Johnson but the *character* of Johnson as revealed in the facts of his life; and his purpose is to make us feel that admiration and reverence which is the natural emotive consequences of full empathetic perception of the character.

Unlike Scott's life, Johnson's career as a connected sequence of actions could not have been presented as the cause of a powerful effect. It is his character alone—the extraordinary strength, subtlety, and depth of his mental powers, joined with the nobility and magnanimity of his moral nature and his astonishing powers of expression—that contains the potentiality of such an effect. This Boswell knew. That concluding sentence is no accident, nor is the brilliant character sketch which precedes it and pulls together into a single retrospective view the subject which the myriad pieces of his book have together evoked.

Character must be manifested in the concrete, and Johnson's character is known primarily from its concrete manifestation in the *Life*. Just because the concrete is or seems to be a given reality, however, Boswell has gained small credit for showing it to us. So discerning a critic as Joseph Wood Krutch can see Boswell's technique as wholly naturalistic: "What he [needs is] not imagination or insight, or even, primarily, the judgment to select. It is documentation and more documentation."[3] The well-known, often answered, but still recurring charge that Boswell was nothing but a tape recorder is a ghost that ought to be permanently laid, but it will continue to haunt us until we perceive with more clarity and certainty than we yet have that Boswell's book is, in the part and in the whole, not a recording of fact but always and everywhere an implicitly affecting artistic selection and construction of an aspect of fact. George Mallory pointed out long ago that the effect of the *Life* does not depend on its factuality but upon Boswell's power of "picking out [from the facts] all that was characteristic and important, of ruthlessly discarding unnecessary details and presenting only the salient points." "He gives not the whole of Johnson's words but the essence of them," preserving only "the spirit [and, we may add, the effect] of Johnson's talk and the atmosphere of the moment as the listeners felt it." The talk is "too deliberate, too close, too well-winnowed, as it were" to be a transcript of the actual. The effect of Boswell's operation on the facts, Mallory nevertheless concludes, was to make the whole more real, "a better representation of Johnson."[4]

All this implies the creative secret of Boswell's art: he had within his mind not a series of disjunctive photographic impressions but a single dynamic image of Johnson which, though it derived from innumerable manifestations of Johnson's character, was nevertheless quite independent of any particular manifestation and even independent of their sum. He knew Johnson's image mimetically, and he knew it in its essence. We remember that he could impersonate Johnson more vividly and exactly than Garrick, giving something that approached a full psychosomatic impression. We remember that he could make fresh Johnsoniana with the ring of the true coin: "Dine with Jack Wilkes, Sir! I'd as soon dine with Jack Ketch!" But just because he possessed Johnson's image so completely within himself, he knew its value immediately and fully through the involuntary psychic comparison with himself which the act of mimetic participation implied. In Johnson's presence Boswell always felt an intense exhilaration as he imaginatively participated in Johnson's powers. It is easy to understand how in retrospect that exhilaration became an unshakable reverence and admiration.

In creating the *Life*, then, Boswell was in a real sense creating an objective correlative of a grand emotive idea. His idea was not so much an aid to him in his task as it was the very principle of that astonishing reconstruction. No other assumption can account for the fact, indicated by Mallory and others, that the Johnson of the *Life* is more Johnsonian than Johnson himself could invariably be. To breathe life into the concentrated dust of the notes and to shape from them the form of the living Johnson can in no sense be conceived as a mechanical act directed toward a string of discrete memories but only as a fully organic act of the creative imagination.[5] Boswell had not to record dead memories but to construct a reenactment of Johnson that would be concretely adequate in itself to reproduce and release in the reader the emotion which the living man had once produced in him. And the fullest proof of the truly imaginative nature of his act is that he found the correlative of his idea not only in the facts which he himself had witnessed but in all the other facts which his industry had brought to light. His book, he says, is made up of "innumerable detached particulars," but it is not therefore a mélange; the particulars are not a heterogeneous collection of facts but a homogeneous presentation of character. Each of the particulars is displayed by Boswell, to the degree that each inherently permits, as an epiphany of an infinitely varied but always single character. Boswell's image of Johnson is the selective, constructive and controlling principle of the *Life*, the omnipresent element that vivifies and is made vivid in the whole. The image is the unity—the real and living unity—of the *Life*.

It is obvious therefore why the book lacks narrative connection and temporal development. The uniqueness of Johnson's character manifested itself in moments of time and not over a temporal sequence.

There is no external connection of parts in the *Life* because the subject can be expressed only as the essence of its individual manifestations; there is no development because the character *in its uniqueness* was static. It is obvious also why the book is not scaled to the proportions of the actual life: more facts expressive of character were available from the late than from the early life.

The creative and unifying role which Boswell's internalized idea of Johnson plays in the *Life* can be forcefully demonstrated from his treatment of those portions of the life in which he himself had played no part. Critics have not sufficiently noticed the very many occasions when Boswell shows his dramatic talent quite independent of his memory. One recalls, for example, the vivid and pleasing scene where Langton and Beauclerk rouse a comically formidable Johnson in the middle of the night and take him on a midnight frisk. It is alive before us, yet Boswell was a boy in Edinburgh when it occurred. How many such scenes in the *Life* Boswell never saw but makes the reader see because he saw them not in reality but where the true artist always sees—in the mind's eye. But of the parts in which Boswell's memory played no part, the most instructive for our present purpose are those which may be compared with parallel parts from the works of Boswell's rivals, Hawkins and Mrs. Piozzi. Neither of those writers, of course, was moved by any detached sense of Johnson's magnificent mystery to discover every possible sign of it; they were content with what lay at hand. The very immensity of Boswell's *Life* is itself evidence, in comparison with their works, of the way in which he was possessed by the essence of his subject and motivated to give it body. They were prompted to write about a particular man whom they had known, from private emotion; Boswell was driven to write about a man who was intrinsically of interest to all men, by disinterested universal emotion. Both Hawkins and Mrs. Piozzi held and expressed the same general estimate of Johnson that Boswell does (that he was an astonishingly great and good man), but neither is consistently able to show us the materials of their works as the cause of their estimate. Too often they allow merely personal feeling to interfere with their presentation of the universal Johnson. Consider the following anecdote told by both Boswell and Mrs. Piozzi. Boswell first: "In the playhouse at Lichfield, as Mr. Garrick informed me, Johnson having for a moment quitted a chair which was placed for him between the side-scenes, a gentleman took possession of it, and when Johnson on his return civilly demanded his seat, rudely refused to give it up; upon which Johnson laid hold of it, and tossed him and the chair into the pit."[6] Mrs. Piozzi's version is as follows: Garrick "said that in their young days, when some strolling players came to Lichfield, our friend had fixed his place upon the stage, and got himself a chair accordingly; which leaving a few minutes, he found a man in it at his return, who refused to give it back at the first intreaty: Mr. Johnson, however, who did not think it worth his while to make a second, took chair and man and all together and threw them all at once into the pit."[7] There is a good deal of difference in precision and elegance of narration here, of course; Boswell's is much the shorter, with no irrelevant detail, the whole laid out in the clean curve of a single sentence. And Boswell's works together with a series of short epiphanies he is giving at the moment to illustrate his nicely discriminated immediate thesis that Johnson was afraid of nothing but death, not even what might occasion death. But the most basic difference is that Boswell's version in itself supports his claim that Johnson was a great and good man. Mrs. Piozzi's does not support her claim and thereby fails to display that which she has pointed to as the natural interest of her subject. The choice which she made in evaluating Garrick's story was as a personal moral choice just as justifiable as Boswell's, but as an artistic choice it was not defensible at all, since it diminished the inherent potential of the subject. If Johnson had been as she shows him here, we would feel no interest and take no pleasure in reading about him. Mrs. Piozzi's mistake was repeated, on a much larger scale, by a much greater biographer—Froude, in his *Life of Carlyle*.

There is an example of parallel tendency in Hawkins, who writes thus of a famous incident at Oxford: Johnson had "scarce any change of raiment, and, in a short time after Corbet left him, but one pair of shoes, and those so old, that his feet were seen through them: a gentleman of his college, the father of an eminent clergyman now living, directed a servitor one morning to place a new pair at the door of Johnson's chamber, who, seeing them upon his first going out, so far forgot himself and the spirit that must have actuated his unknown benefactor, that, with all the indignation of an insulted man, he threw them away."[8] The essential facts are as Boswell is to present them: the

shoes were given and Johnson was indignant. The problem is in evaluation: it was a fault in Johnson to be indignant. It may be true, yet in
judging Johnson on a narrow moral base Hawkins diminishes him.
Johnson is seen to fall away from a universal standard of virtue and to
become by that much less the man because of whose greatness
Hawkins is writing. Boswell, without at all changing the facts, reads
and relates them in a much different way: "Mr. Bateman's lectures
were so excellent, that Johnson used to come and get them at second-
hand from Taylor, till his poverty being so extreme, that his shoes
were worn out, and his feet appeared through them, he saw that this
humiliating circumstance was perceived by the Christ-Church men,
and he came no more. He was too proud to accept of money, and
somebody having set a pair of new shoes at his door, he threw them
away with indignation. How must we feel when we read such an anecdote of Samuel Johnson!"[9] Hawkins's inert details and judgments
drop out as Boswell makes us feel Johnson's poverty and the reality of
his consequent humiliation. Boswell construed his pride convincingly
as a sign of his majestic independence, and, suppressing the irrelevant
clergyman, evaluates the incident not in relation to him but to Johnson's essential character and the fact of his permanent greatness,
something to which Bateman's excellent lectures and Johnson's desire
for them are not of course irrelevant. Critics often seem to assume
that the Boswellian record is superior to the Hawkins and Piozzi records largely in its greater material fullness: there is more documentation. If this were true, then it would have been no literary crime for
Croker to have conflated as he did all three works together; facts are
facts. But it *was* a crime because the records are different not in extent
but, as Professor Clifford has seen, in their fundamental nature.[10]
Boswell's facts are created according to the model of a living universal
idea of a great man, the minor biographers' as impressions of the
contingent acts of a contingent man who sometimes displayed his
greatness.

(The passage quoted from Hawkins, incidentally, witnesses to an
interesting point. In attempting to impose universal moral judgment
on Johnson's imperfect action, Hawkins is imitating Johnson's own
biographical practice, just as he attempted to imitate Johnson's style.
Johnson succeeds in his biographies because he genuinely does im-

pose his judgment on the facts. His biographies are literature because they achieve universality of judgment, not because they display the inherent universality of their subject. The pleasure of Johnson's *Lives* is Johnson, not Pope or Addison. This shows how untrue is the usual statement that Boswell followed Johnson's biographical example. He followed it in its emphasis on character and on characterizing particularity, but he departed totally from the basic Johnsonian mode of presentation. Johnson's practice, of course, was ideally suited to his gifts, for the same reasons that made him the ideal subject for Boswell's kind of biography.)

Once the nature of Boswell's image of Johnson has been pointed out, its presence and constructive function are everywhere apparent. Many facts in the *Life*, however, would not in themselves contribute directly to our vivid sense of the character, and it is not immediately clear why they should have been included if the subject of the work is as I describe it. Briefly we may say that Boswell treats the full range of facts in the life on the assumption, amply born out by modern scholars, that anything connected with such a man will contribute a little bit more to our attempt to fill out and confirm the inherently fascinating reality of his image. In factual literature, we do want to know how many children had Lady Macbeth. But Boswell, as may easily be illustrated, always proportions his treatment of a fact to the relevance it has for the image of essential character, so that he dismisses quickly much that has great importance in the progress of Johnson's life and devotes pages to what does not affect its progress at all. He explains the substantive biographical facts adequately as facts but always in such a way as to shape and control their significance as emblems of the admirable character. Take, for instance, Boswell's account of Johnson's pension.[11] We see at once that it is not an account of a fact in itself but a transformation of a potentially hostile fact into the terms of the image. He begins by placing the grant in the glowing context of George III's liberal and disinterested patronage and only then contemptuously characterizes the charges of venality which had been made against Johnson. He then refutes the charges by a detailed citation of witnesses, painstakingly and concretely recreating the motivation on both sides, and emerges with the dramatically won conclusion that the pension had been granted on "liberal and honourable terms." The passage closes with Johnson's nobly dignified letter to Bute, which concretely confirms and amplifies the judgment Boswell has offered, so that the reader is left secure in truth and admiration, the image not only intact but fortified. Examples of such essay-parts, as we may call them, clearly shaped to the large end of the book, could be multiplied.

But the fact that the shaping role of Boswell's grand image of Johnson is especially obvious in particular passages should not prevent our perceiving its active presence in every part of the *Life*. We hear it vibrate in the fanfare of the very first sentence: "To write the Life of him who excelled all mankind in writing the lives of others, and who, whether we consider his extraordinary endowments, or his various works, has been equalled by few in any age, is an arduous, and may be reckoned in me a presumptuous task." A grand and confident claim has been made upon our attention. We necessarily infer that the claim has a cause in reality external to the narrator, and we respond as to a perceived fact with a corresponding mental and emotional assumption of our own. The narrative posture thereafter continuously asserts the real existence of the image thus evoked and continues to demand its counterpart in us. Thus, even when the facts immediately produced do not actively validate the image, the reader never doubts its reality because the narrator does not evaluate such facts as validation but only as necessarily interesting and relevant in relation to the curiosity which the continuing image naturally generates.

More than narrative assertion is required, of course, to call Johnson's spirit from the vasty deep, particularly in the opening pages where so little of the concrete is available, and the discerning critic can only admire the many subtle means Boswell employs to bring the permanent Johnson quickly before us. In the facts of the youth he discovers the greatness of the man, and with the voice of the man he makes the youth vivid. He selects, compresses, dramatizes, vivifies to such a degree that when at last the figure of Johnson walks through Davies's doorway, he is an old and beloved acquaintance.

More largely, throughout the *Life*, many subtle features, quite distinct from its factual substance, conspire to renew and intensify our sense of the grandeur of the subject. Recurring epithets like "my illustrious friend" give us a tug of pleasure and reanimate our established estimate as we think subconsciously, "he *was* illustrious." Even such apparently irrelevant aspects of the book as its praise of great men, or its literary allusions, or Boswell's digression on the qualities of a noble estate contribute in the aggregate to the massive special effect of the whole. (Only consider how much grander and more spacious is the world of the *Life* than the world of Boswell's *London Journal*.)

In a moment I shall pay detailed attention to the means by which the image is given redundant concrete specification, but I should not leave the subject of the peripheral means Boswell employs in connection with it without noticing two directly related matters: his citation of the testimony of others and his use of Johnson's letters. Both these dimensions of his work serve as necessary guarantees that we are encountering not a personal but a universal view of the subject. The testimony of others validates and extends the view Boswell himself takes, and the letters, each of which, as Professor Daghlian has recently noted, powerfully images Johnson's noble character,[12] offer the strongest possible objective corroboration of the image: the Johnson we meet in the letters is indubitably the same as the Johnson Boswell elsewhere shows us. From all this we understand how the image becomes a covert but omnipresent reality in the *Life*, even in those facts which in themselves would not evoke it. The explanation offered here as confirmed by the actual experience of a continuous reading of the *Life* allows us to understand how such seemingly inert facts are drawn into relevance by the unseen lines of magnetic force which the large image and emotional flow of the whole exert and how each functions as one of the myriad particles which together make the lines real and distinct. The image constructs the facts, and the facts in turn construct the image; the process, circular and progressive, constitutes the linear coherence and material unity of the *Life*.

But unity and coherence do not by themselves make literature. To understand why the *Life* is a supremely literary work, we must explain its power, unmatched among factual narratives, of producing literary pleasure. The explanation lies in the unusual degree to which the *Life* is able, within the limits of truth, to meet Coleridge's supplementary requirement that literary works ought to be so designed as to give in each of their parts as much pleasure as is consonant with the greatest pleasure in the whole. Lockhart's *Life of Scott*, for instance, has a plotlike structure, a single line of developing tragic perception, that produces a powerful single effect, but the constituent parts are relatively inert. As a whole, consequently, it is much less a work of literature than Boswell's. The *Life of Johnson* gives maximum pleasure just because it is so preponderantly made up of images of Johnson's acts, each of which has its own particular pleasure which, when most fully realized, most contributes to the peculiar pleasure of the whole. To understand this, we must remember what Aristotle teaches: that literary pleasure results from the vivid representation to our consciousness of striking human acts, morally determinate, which move us through our perception of the internal probability and ethical consonance of their inception, continuance, and completion. Now, as I shall more fully illustrate, all the acts in the *Life* are represented according to this formula. Boswell renders them vivid and striking, makes us see them as internally probable in terms of motive and circumstance, and adjusts our view so that we always see them as ethically consonant both in themselves and with the morally determinate image of an admirable Johnson. Each of the representational parts, then, has its own local pleasure, but the parts are of such a nature that in sum they also form the basis of the larger literary pleasure of the entire book—the single continuing, growing, and self-reinforcing pleasure of encountering in new and striking but always probable manifestations the astonishing character of Samuel Johnson. That we know these new manifestations as probable and encounter them with anticipatory pleasure demonstrates the fact that the image, though it has no single material expression, nonetheless exists as an active essence in the reader's mind which, as I have already said, effectively renders even the inert parts concrete. (That we possess the liberated image of Johnson even after the fact of reading the *Life* is demonstrated by the effect upon us of the words "Sir" or "Why, No Sir" spoken out of context but with appropriate inflection. The utterance immediately brings to mind that amusing but admirable conjunction of sincere deference and rational aggression which together reflect the essence of Johnson's character. A similar phenomenon obtains for no other historical figure.)

It may help to clarify the large structural principle of the *Life* if we recall that we have already seen it in action in the episodes compared with their counterparts in Hawkins and Mrs. Piozzi. When Boswell's Johnson throws the interloper off the stage, we are made to see his action as ethically consonant with, though conventionally disproportionate to, the provocation he has received and his own dignity, so that the scene becomes comically pleasing; at the same time, Johnson's overall moral stature is pleasurably confirmed and reinforced. Mrs. Piozzi's Johnson, by contrast, is neither amusing nor admirable. When Boswell's Johnson throws away the shoes at Oxford, we are moved by a momentary pulse of admiring compassion, because we understand the grounds of his act fully and evaluate it as justified; at the same time, we see a permanently grand aspect of his nature. Hawkins's Johnson is shown to neither purpose.

But Coleridge's principle about the relation of parts to the whole has in view not only such material parts as episodes in a representation but also purely qualitative parts. The pleasure of any literary work will increase in proportion as all its elements, including those of language itself (syntax, diction, and pure sound), are arranged so as actively to support the effect. For example, other things being equal, a representation in verse is more intensely pleasing than one in prose. Here, then, is another cause of the supreme literary quality of the *Life*. Johnson's speech—edited and pointed by Boswell to preserve and heighten its Johnsonian essence—makes him the only character in factual literature whose speech is equal or superior to that of fictional characters. The graceful elasticity and full vital expressiveness of Boswell's own purposefully unobtrusive style work toward the same end to make the *Life* unique as a factual work which to the large pleasure of concrete character and the smaller pleasure of concrete act can add the fully perfecting concrete pleasures of language itself (At least once in the *Life* we get the pleasure of speech as a pure increment to the already forceful sense: "He seemed to take pleasure in speaking in his own style," says Boswell, "for when he had carelessly missed it, he would repeat the thought translated into it. Talking of the Comedy of 'The Rehearsal,' he said, 'It has not wit enough to keep it sweet.' This was easy; he therefore caught himself, and pronounced a more rounded sentence; 'It has not vitality enough to preserve it from putrefaction.'"[13] Pure style, pure pleasure—but as always in Johnson, the style is the man.)

But the vital corpuscles of the *Life*'s body are the acts. Let us take them first at their simplest and then at their most complex. The simplest kind of complete act represented in the *Life* is an aphorism or generalization by Johnson without context. Now any general truth even independent of a speaker has a representational character and force: the mind perceives it as a self-caused, inherently purposeful, surprising but probable act of cognition, carrying with it therefore its own distinct pleasure. The pleasure of a generalization will be greater in proportion to the degree in which it is both true and unobvious, to the inherent human relevance of its substance, and to the concision and force of its expression. To describe the conditions of pleasure in generalizations is to suggest the qualities of Johnson's. As much as La Rochefoucauld's and Pascal's, Johnson's sayings have literary value in and of themselves, with the additional pleasure of their spontaneity. It is not too much to say that the recorded impromptus of all other men together do not equal the total of his in pleasure and value. Yet all of his remarks in the *Life* give additional pleasure, on the large grounds sketched out above, in that they satisfy as fresh but unforeseeable signs of the power of the character and at the same time add an increment to the total pleasurable image. Let us take one of the myriad examples, the statement "All censure of a man's self is oblique praise. It is in order to show how much he can spare. It has all the invidiousness of self-praise, and all the reproach of falsehood."[14] The initial sentence, paradoxical and surprising, is quickly and pleasingly rendered inherently probable (that is, true) by the explanatory second sentence. The compelling analytic judgment of the third sentence converts what might have been a cynicism of La Rochefoucauld's into an implicit positive base of moral operations. It is not directed scornfully at *other* men but put instructively for the use of *all* men, including the speaker. The statement surprises, pleases, and teaches, and it leaves the mind with a renewed and augmented sense of the simultaneously good, wise, and articulate man who made it. But even when Johnson's statements are perfectly particular they are pleasurable merely as fresh revelations of the established admirable character. "Sir, I would walk to the extent of the diameter of the earth to save Beauclerk." Or "Sir, you have not travelled over *my* mind, I promise you."[15] Notice that the hyperbolical first statement would not please if our conviction of Johnson's majestic rectitude and the depth of his feeling did not give it substance, and that the second, if said by Goldsmith to Johnson, rather than the other way around, would be merely an egotistical impertinence.

But the most massively pleasing parts of the *Life* are its scenes. The art of the major scenes is so plain that they have often drawn praise upon Boswell for the vividness of their pointing and their parenthetical stage directions ["Johnson (puffing and blowing): . . ."]. But these praises are often analytically empty because the critics who give them have no conception of the form and effect to which the devices are subordinate. After "vivid" and "dramatic" there is nothing left. Space does not permit me to work in full detail through the most famous scene in the *Life*, the Wilkes episode,[16] but a partial analysis can sufficiently demonstrate how much its effect depends upon Boswell's handling. Its essential structure may be described by expanding the basic formula already set down: it is a full Aristotelian action which follows the predicament of a central character from a beginning which defines the terms of that predicament, through a middle which develops and complicates it and our reactions to the full, to an end which resolves the complications and brings our emotional participation to satisfactory discharge and close. More particularly, it is a comic action. Now in a comic action the hero is of mixed character: essentially and predominantly good, so that we wish him finally well, but at the same time flawed or restricted in a way that involves him in embarrassments which are the substance of the complications of the plot. We view these embarrassments with delight both because they are of the hero's own making and because the conduct of the story assures us throughout that he will in some way that our perplexity cannot foresee ultimately achieve the due which his fundamentally good character deserves and that meanwhile nothing really harmful or painful will befall him.[17] Boswell shows us the Wilkes episode according to just this formula.

At the outset, Johnson is already secure in our admiration, but Boswell must make us actively desire to see a kind of trick played on him. He does this initially by making us feel that the meeting will be a delightful experiment in human nature which will end much to the Doctor's credit and by heightening our sense of that awful personal power in Johnson which by itself guarantees the preservation of his dignity while it enhances our comic sense of Boswell's resourceful daring ("How to manage it, was a nice and difficult matter"). Boswell sets the terms of the story by defining Johnson and Wilkes as "celebrated men" who, though as different as they could possibly be, are yet both friends of Boswell. The meeting is thus neatly characterized as potentially productive either of an explosion or a conciliation. We are made to feel that the last will and ought to be the result but are left to wonder how, considering Johnson's strong moral and political prejudices, the first will be avoided. The terms are quickly sharpened with the apparently gratuitous paragraph about Sir John Pringle who, like Wilkes, was also linked to Johnson through the middle term of Boswell's friendship but who, though an excellent man, was "not sufficiently flexible" to meet agreeably with him. The paragraph has a very precise function: it underlines the potential explosiveness of the desired meeting and Boswell's own underlying assurance that the explosion will somehow not occur, while at the same time it defines any inflexibility which might stand in its way as a regrettable human limitation. From this point on, therefore, the reader must actively hope that Johnson will be able to meet Wilkes on affable terms, while he is all the more aware of the piquant difficulties.

The paragraph on arrangements with Dilly increases with every detail our sense of the necessity that Johnson for his own sake meet the standards of social sophistication, while Dilly's represented alarm reinforces our sense of the internal barrier to his doing so. The next scene shows Boswell with consummate meekness and guile inducing Johnson to accept the invitation through a subtle challenge to his vanity as a social man. The paragraph could sustain a page of analysis, but I will only say that its brilliance consists in Boswell's heightening our comic sense of Johnson's majestically cantankerous nature at the same time that he makes us sympathetic to Johnson's full if inadvertent commitment of his pride to the fact that he is not ultimately limited by his prickliness. "And if Jack Wilkes *should* be there, what is that to *me*, Sir?" Johnson must make good this commitment, but all the more we wonder, how is he to do it?

The obstacle presented by Mrs. Williams is used fully by Boswell to heighten by opposing the wishes we have formed to see the meeting take place, as well as for other purposes, and when the obstacle is overcome we exult with Boswell as his prize is carried off. Snug and silent, we watch with delight the impact upon Johnson of Mr. Arthur Lee and then Mr. Wilkes. Boswell defines Lee's comic function with brilliant economy by juxtaposing a description of him in the idiom of Johnson's prejudice—he was both a "patriot" and an "American"— with a comment that underlines his membership in the civilized world of which we desire Johnson to be fully a member—Lee was, Boswell says, later American ambassador to the Court of Madrid. In other words, we see Lee at once as Johnson in his comic limitation sees him and also as he really is and as Johnson must therefore finally accept him if he is to maintain and increase our regard. But just at this moment we are most aware of the resources it will require in Johnson to overcome the strength of his prejudice as Boswell vividly communicates his comic distress—"too, too, too." The distress is visible, but if the effect is to be maintained, we need as well some assurance that the hoped for if as yet unspecifiable triumph will eventually come and that it will come not accidentally but as a result of Johnson's deliberate attempt to master himself and the situation. No sign is available, and so Boswell boldly goes into Johnson's mind to get it for us: "His feelings, *I dare say*, were awkward enough. But he *no doubt* recollected his having rated me for supposing that he could be at all disconcerted by any company, and he, *therefore*, resolutely set himself to behave quite as an easy man of the world, who could adapt himself at once to the disposition and manners of those whom he might chance to meet." The sympathetic vanity and our hopes for its triumph are strong in our minds.

Despite his resolution, Johnson's "surly virtue" is shown to yield only gradually as the conciliatory gestures of the suave but sincere Wilkes make us wish all the more for Johnson's triumph of sophistication. All the matter now heightens and foreshadows the climax, in ways we cannot pause to notice, until we get the climactic interchange: "*Johnson.* (to Mr. Wilkes) 'You must know, Sir, I lately took my friend Boswell and shewed him genuine civilised life in an English provincial town. I turned him loose at Lichfield, my native city, that he might see for once real civility: for you know he lives among savages in Scotland, and among rakes in London.' *Wilkes.* 'Except when he is with grave,

41

sober, decent people like you and me.' *Johnson.* (smiling) 'And we ashamed of him.'" The speeches please not just in themselves but because they resolve with such unexpected and delightful fullness the underlying tensions which have been so clearly and vividly represented from the outset. Johnson's first speech—"and among rakes in London"—covertly and politely acknowledges and thus neutralizes the antagonism which he has felt toward Wilkes and which has been the source of our comic concern. Wilkes, just as politely, denies any antagonism by defining himself with Johnson as among the "grave, sober, decent people"—the three adjectives are a giveaway—as opposed to the rakes. Johnson's smiling "And we ashamed of him" accepts the denial, cancels the animosity, joins himself to Wilkes, and, in a complete reversal of the original terms of the incident, leaves the Boswell who had challenged Johnson's civility comically out in the social cold, a barbarous Scot. The single adjective, "smiling," applied to Johnson is, of course, not just a piece of random vividness but is crucially important to our full sense of the active benevolence with which Johnson reconciles himself to Wilkes; it is not the limited triumph of self-control over ineradicable and debilitating prejudice, but the full-hearted triumph of a capaciously human soul whose prejudice is only a temporary defect of its large virtues. It should be clear even from this brief analysis that the pleasurable effect not only of the climax but of the whole depends on the facts *only* as they are selected, revealed, and evaluated by Boswell's art.

The interchange does not end the episode, but we cannot pause to follow Boswell's means of bringing it to full aesthetic completeness. Enough has been said to show how the episode, like the other parts we have examined, makes its fullest contribution to the overall purpose of the *Life* when its own appropriate pleasure is most realized. The inherent particular effect of the Wilkes episode is comic pleasure, and that pleasure has been seen to increase in proportion to Johnson's triumph. The greater, the more surprising, and yet characteristically probable the triumph, the greater the comic pleasure. But obviously then the greater the comic pleasure, the greater our residual admiration for Johnson. We should notice, too, that the episode necessarily depends on the preceding part of the *Life,* for an active idea of Johnson's character is a requisite of its comic effect. No one who reads the episode without experience of the *Life* will think it very funny.

A great part of the pleasure of the scenes taken as a whole is their wide range of effect from somberness to the gayest lightness, while all express the same Johnson and all are indebted to Boswell's art. Consider, for instance, the grand scene where Boswell introduces "the subject of death, and [endeavors] to maintain that the fear of it might be got over."[18] The conversation must have lasted some time but Boswell gives only its heart. Johnson's defense of his own fear of death as against the alleged lack of fear in Hume and Foote justifies him immediately in our estimation because he finds evidence for his own feelings that we cannot deny: "Hold a pistol to Foote's breast, or to Hume's breast, and threaten to kill them, and you'll see how they behave." Still, we would not be really prepared to absorb the gigantic outburst that follows Boswell's "But may we not fortify our minds for the approach of death?" if Boswell had not been able, without breaking the rhythm of the scene, to specify and ennoble Johnson's inner state:

> I am sensible I was in the wrong, to bring before his view what he ever looked upon with horrour; for although when in a celestial frame, in his "Vanity of human wishes," he has supposed death to be "kind Nature's signal for retreat," from this state of being to "a happier seat," his thoughts upon this aweful change were in general full of dismal apprehensions. His mind resembled the vast amphitheatre, the Coliseum at Rome. In the centre stood his judgement, which, like a mighty gladiator, combated those apprehensions that, like the wild beasts of the *Arena*, were all around in cells, ready to be let out upon him. After a conflict, he drove them back into their dens; but not killing them, they were still assailing him. To my question, whether we might not fortify our minds for the approach of death, he answered, in a passion, "No, Sir, let it alone. It matters not how a man dies, but how he lives. The act of dying is not of importance, it lasts so short a time." He added, (with an earnest look) "A man knows it must be so, and submits. It will do him no good to whine."

Boswell's grand simile, though necessary, is dangerous. Were it not for its manifest accuracy and truth and its immediate validation by the grandeur of Johnson's reply, so artificial a comparison could easily

43

have been a disaster. But it succeeds by forcing us to understand that Johnson's unusual fear of death does not diminish him, since it makes us feel how constant and tremendous the pressures upon him were, how great was the effort needed to hold them in equilibrium, and how near to breaking without ever really breaking his majestic nature was. The agitated but noble reply confirms all this and releases Johnson from the blame of personal defect because, though it functions fully as the sign to us of his particular emotion, it is perfectly general and fully applicable to all other human beings, so that we see him not as a particular fearful man but as an exemplar of the most basic kind of human heroism. Our sense of the splendid agony of his bravery carries over to his full credit as Boswell goes on to tell of his "Give us no more of this" and of his expressing himself "in a way that alarmed and distressed me." When the peremptory "Don't let us meet to-morrow" comes, we feel not that Johnson has been blamably irritable but only that we have seen a nature, like ours but much grander, unintentionally provoked beyond endurance. Boswell, of course, had at the moment been himself made "extremely uneasy." "All the harsh observations which I had ever heard made upon his character, crowded into my mind." But in retrospect the causes of this uneasiness had faded away, irrelevant to the grand epiphany to which he had been witness, and we ourselves actively perceive only the universality and not the contingency of the occasion.

But Boswell can preserve not merely the grand essential moments but also the very small ones. It is sometimes said that he does not show us the light, trifling Johnson we know from Burney and Thrale, but consider the following vignette:

> Johnson was prevailed with to come sometimes into these [blue-stocking] circles, and did not think himself too grave even for the lively Miss Monckton (now Countess of Corke), who used to have the finest *bit of blue* at the house of her mother, Lady Galway. Her vivacity enchanted the Sage, and they used to talk together with all imaginable ease. A singular instance happened one evening, when she insisted that some of Sterne's writings were very pathetick. Johnson bluntly denied it. "I am sure (said she) they have affected *me*."—"Why (said Johnson, smiling, and rolling himself about,) that is, because, dearest, you're a dunce." When she some time afterwards mentioned this to him, he said with equal truth and

politeness; "Madam, if I had thought so, I certainly should not have said it."[19]

Boswell's quick definition of the established mutual regard of the two, the brief glimpse we get of Johnson's usually ominous tendency to roughness ("bluntly denied") joined to the surprising adroitness and sophistication of his immediate and ultimate responses to Miss Monckton's momentary and fetching vulnerability conspire to make the little scene extremely pleasing. Even so, however, the immediate response would not have given much pleasure if Boswell had not marked Johnson's inner spirit so accurately by his description of the Doctor's physical posture. The language ("dearest") and the movements together wonderfully communicate the delighted premeditation and benign condescension with which the ponderous Johnson makes his affectionate thrust. And so Boswell reveals another aspect, surprising but entirely consonant, of Johnson's astonishing being.

Despite his intention of evoking consistent admiration and reverence for Johnson, Boswell as we have already seen does not suppress our sense of his faults. Boswell set out to write "not his panegyric, which must be all praise, but his Life; which, great and good as he was, must not be supposed to be entirely perfect."[20] Boswell did not suppress faults but deliberately included them and thereby induced Fanny Burney's fear, already noticed, that the portrait of Johnson with all his blemishes would lessen him forever in the eyes of posterity. But Boswell knew that without the blemishes the portrait would not be true and concretely convincing. Unless the reader were to see an image which in its basic structure corresponded to his own imperfect nature, he would not recognize either the paradigmatic likeness or the particular otherness that are the essence of biographical portraiture; he would not admire because he would not believe.[21] Besides, to be as Johnson was, with all his defects, constituted, as Boswell says, "panegyric enough to any man in this state of nature." But Boswell had an artistic motive even higher than verisimilitude for his honesty. He can make Johnson even more admirable by showing that he was so in spite of his faults and uglinesses. As in all art, the greater the ugliness overcome, the greater the ultimate beauty and pleasure.

As Hume showed long ago,[22] any emotion arising from the contemplation of a painful object is, in the presence of a predominant sentiment of beauty, converted into the higher feeling. Any emotive reaction to faults or ugliness is overcome consistently in Boswell by the emotion attaching to our immediate or residual impression of Johnson's essential greatness and goodness.[23] When Mrs. Piozzi tells us that Johnson was a "gross feeder," the brief image is ugly and painful, while a much more particular and materially ugly description of Johnson's eating by Boswell is not.[24] Mrs. Piozzi's description images her own disgust, Boswell's a more complex but affirmative reaction that assimilates our perception of the intense passion with which Johnson eats to our sense of the gigantic will which drives his being and which does not, except in indifferent matters, break through his moral control. Consistently in the *Life,* as in most of the episodes we have examined, faults are pleasurably rendered as temporary foibles or necessary defects of the great virtues, while the fully represented physical grotesqueness, the eccentricity and ugliness, ultimately serve only to make Johnson's achievement the more concretely real, particular, and astonishing.

But even when Johnson's defects cannot be converted to immediately sympathetic pleasure, Boswell faces them directly in order to show, we may say, how much Johnson can spare. He makes little defense, for instance, of *Taxation No Tyranny.* Johnson should not have written it, and Boswell quotes with approval two animadversions on the pamphlet. Both of these, however, share with Boswell the assumption that the work is an uncharacteristic and unworthy product of the great mind which produced it, and when Boswell goes on to indicate as fully and concretely as he can that Johnson probably shared this view, the effect is complete. Finally, in extreme cases, where Johnson has been excessively rude or violent, Boswell will report an outburst in general terms sufficient to make us understand its character and effect, but not vividly enough to make it actively disagreeable. The most notable example precisely because it is so seldom noted is the occasion when Johnson attacks Boswell himself so fiercely that Boswell is angry for days and almost goes away to Scotland without seeing the Doctor again.[25] The shock was obviously nearly traumatic to Boswell, and affected him personally more deeply perhaps than all but a few of the scenes in the *Life*. His handling of it is characteristic: he *tells* us accurately the substance and effect of Johnson's rudeness, but he does not *show* it to us; in the sequel, however, he dramatizes the reconciliation with great particularity and happy effect. Despite his personal investment, he proportions the weight he gives the scene strictly to its relative value as a sign of his subject—Johnson's character as it is of interest to all men, not Johnson's character as it might appear momentarily to and affect one man. Boswell sees not for himself but for all of us; his book is by no means "one man's recollections of another."

This brings us to our final topic in the *Life*: the general matter of its truth. Most students have emphasized that the strictest truth is essential to biography, but they have meant by truth, ordinarily, authenticity; that is, fidelity to ascertainable empirical fact. The authenticity of Boswell's account has often been investigated and checked against his own records and the records of others. The verdict is nearly unanimous: the *Life* is as authentic as human effort could have made it. Yet we have seen fully characteristic instances when Boswell goes quite beyond the limits of literal truth, as when he dramatizes scenes he has not witnessed, or directly enters Johnson's mind. Even the speeches, we have noticed, must be understood as true more in effect than in substance. If, as Johnson himself and many since have insisted, the inherent value of biography depends directly upon its literal truth, how can we justify Boswell's editing, shaping, and evaluation? More generally, how can we explain the fact that we experience the full value of Boswell's book while reading it in complete innocence of all the existing external corroboration of its accuracy? The answer is implicit and to a degree explicit in all that I have been saying. Certified truth in Boswell's book is a requisite as in all factual narrative, but its truth is ultimately relevant not to the external facts of Johnson's life but to the essence of his character, for the book is not about an eighteenth-century man of letters, not about an external life and career, but about a man, significant independent of history, who manifested himself in the events of a life and career. All of Boswell's authenticating assiduity, all the innumerable certified details, are valuable finally not as they give us true external facts but as evidence of the conjunction of that magnificent image with reality; like Defoe's circumstantiality, Boswell's constantly implies that the fact is not fiction but real, but unlike Defoe's, Boswell's circumstantiality is not a lie. An inherent part of the pleasure of the character is that it *was* real, and without Boswell's endless certification of what might seem the aesthetically indifferent reality around it, our pleasure in the image could not be as certain and full. Our emotion is toward a timeless image but it is nonetheless an image of fact with location in time and place. Nevertheless the only inherently essential fact of the work is the character, and the truth of the character itself, as we understand by now, is something internal to the *Life* itself. We know intuitively that the character is what it appears to be because it is so complex, so various and astonishing in its endless manifestations and yet so obviously consistent and coherent as a whole that its image could have proceeded from no cause except itself. It is not, as some have sneeringly said, that we know that Boswell could not have invented Johnson; rather we know with the fullest intuitive certainty that no one—not Defoe, not even Shakespeare—could have invented him. No fictional personality approaches the capacities and complexities of Johnson's. Insofar as the reality of the character is concerned, the book is more compelling than any other evidence of any kind could possibly be. The truth about Johnson's life will change and grow, but the essential truth of his character will never be different from what we feel it to be in Boswell; our residual impression of Johnson must always be such as to produce admiration and reverence. And so we end where we began. Boswell's book is literature because it lifts an aspect of human reality from the contingency of history and displays it as a concrete universal—self-validating, self-intelligible, inherently moving, permanently valuable. For what we experience finally in the book—and this is the most fundamental source of its literary greatness—is not the sum of Johnson's particular actions but the essence of his character, an essence deeply relevant not to the contingency of history but to the permanence of human nature and therefore immediately to ourselves.

Every man desires to be both bound and free. He desires to be free to express his own deepest passions, and he desires to be bound by the ties of morality and convention that link him to other men in love and respect. It follows from this that he desires at the same time to bind his deepest passions and to break through the internalized restraints of society. His pride requires that he be potent; his dignity requires that he be moral. The powers of most men are unequal to the paradox: dignity suffers when the passionate self breaks down, or corrupts, the moral commitment, or pride is diminished as the self in meeting the commitment succumbs to the seductions of the protean forms of hypocrisy. Literature in general may be understood as, at bottom, a series of symbolic solutions to this paradox, with success dependent upon the degree to which both its dimensions are satisfied. And Johnson's image is the functional core of a great work of literature because his extraordinarily passionate and powerful being, while fully committed to the restraints of convention, morality, and reason, was yet neither corrupted nor rendered impotent. Perpetually he broke powerfully through the ordinary restraints of convention to express his most primal impulses in vindication of his commitment to convention, morality, and reason. He thereby created his dignity and justified his pride on the most general human grounds, so that his image could become for all of us a token of the simultaneous freedom and commitment which is possible to human beings. Symbolically in our imaginative sympathy and actually as an example, that image frees us from the burdens of conventional impotence and falsity— from the rehearsed response, the coward's stance, the liar's quinsy— and restores our dignity and our pride in ourselves and in the human nature which we share with him. That is why the pleasure of the book is so real and so deep.

Johnson's image is therefore one of the most valuable of our cultural possessions, but without Boswell it would never have been freed from the bondage of time. His book is, as Carlyle said, "a revocation of the edict of Destiny; so that Time shall not utterly, not so soon by several centuries, have dominion over us."[26] Not over Johnson, notice, but over us, who have our stake in Johnson. Boswell's construction of his book was a supremely important artistic act. Because it was so fully artistic, however, it *is* fully real and therefore has seemed to many to manifest no art at all. But it should be clear from what we have said that the *Life of Samuel Johnson* is a great book not because the subject was great or because the biographer was great but because both were great; it was a magnificent literary symbiosis. Johnson was all activity, Boswell all potentiality. He—a truly reverent man, as Carlyle says—filled himself with Johnson's greatness and displayed it to posterity shorn of accident and unblemished by any stain of his own private feeling or immense personal ego. That ego indeed had been deeply wounded in the midst of his task when he learned what Johnson had said of him in his letters to Mrs. Thrale, but this did not at all deflect him from his high purpose.

Johnson, if he had known, would have been more grateful to Boswell than posterity has often been. "Sir, it was generous and noble beyond expectation." But even in his life he was not indifferent to Boswell's devotion. We remember the unusual gesture he made in going with Boswell down to Harwich to see him off to Holland. One of the finest moments in the *Life* is our view of him tarrying on the Harwich pier as the receding Boswell perceives him in the distance, "rolling his majestic frame."[27] The moment is strangely moving, because it triggers in proportion to its slightness such a flood of sentiment. Boswell's two epithets render the for once inarticulate figure a sudden and forceful evocation of all the benevolent affection that our experience as shaped by Boswell has attached to his image. Boswell repaid the Doctor for his kindness. His majestic rolling frame is fixed there forever in its particular and universal humanity.

Notes

Many of the concepts articulated here were first developed in a graduate seminar which I gave in the spring of 1964 at the University of California, Berkeley. I wish to acknowledge my debt to the students in that seminar, particularly Gerry Brookes, William Chace, Peter Collier, Robert Hirst, John Hunter, and James Johnson. Since the lecture was written, it has benefited from the criticisms of Paul Alkon, Bertrand H. Bronson, James L. Clifford, Philip B. Daghlian, and Frederick A. Pottle, to all of whom I am grateful. This essay is reprinted from a longer version in Philip B. Daghlian, ed., *Essays in Eighteenth-Century Biography* (Bloomington: Indiana University Press, 1968), 3–42.

1. Donald A. Stauffer, *The Art of Biography in Eighteenth-Century England* (Princeton, 1941), 445–446.
2. John A. Garraty, *The Nature of Biography* (New York, 1964), 26, 95.
3. Joseph Wood Krutch, *Samuel Johnson* (New York, 1941), 386.

4. George Mallory, *Boswell the Biographer* (London, 1912), 293, 278, 271, 281.

5. Professor Pottle has put the case for Boswell's imaginative creativity more explicitly (and accurately, I believe) than any other critic. See Frederick A. Pottle, *James Boswell: The Earlier Years, 1740–1769* (New York, 1966), 87–90, and an earlier article, "The Life of Boswell," *Yale Review* 25 (Spring 1946): 445–460.

6. *Life*, II, 299.

7. Hester Lynch Piozzi, *Anecdotes of the Late Samuel Johnson, LL.D.*, ed. G. B. Hill, in *Johnsonian Miscellanies* (Oxford, 1897), 1:224.

8. Sir John Hawkins, *The Life of Dr. Samuel Johnson*, in *The Works of Samuel Johnson* (London, 1787), 1:11.

9. *Life*, II, 76–77.

10. James L. Clifford, *Hester Lynch Piozzi (Mrs. Thrale)* (Oxford, 1941), 357: "Boswell's superiority over his rival biographers . . . lies not only in the completeness of his picture of Johnson, but also in the significant definition, the delicate shading, and the general coherence of his portrait. He justifies himself as a creative artist."

11. *Life*, I, 372–377.

12. Philip B. Daghlian, "Samuel Johnson," in *The Familiar Letter in the Eighteenth Century*, ed. Howard Anderson et al. (Lawrence, Kans., 1966), 109, 128.

13. *Life*, IV, 320.

14. Ibid., III, 323–324.

15. Ibid., IV, 10, 183.

16. Ibid., III, 64–79.

17. The conception of a comic action offered here is obviously indebted to R. S. Crane's "The Concept of Plot and the Plot of *Tom Jones*," reprinted in *Critics and Criticism*, abridged ed. (Chicago, 1957), 82–83.

18. *Life*, II, 106–107.

19. Ibid., IV, 108–109.

20. Ibid., I, 30.

21. Hallam Tennyson's attempt to sustain an attitude of reverence in his *Memoir* of his father is largely unsuccessful because Tennyson's character is consistently presented as without defect and because Hallam's represented reverential attitude has no adequate correlative in the facts as presented.

22. In "Of Tragedy."

23. I am well aware that all readers of Boswell do not admire Johnson consistently throughout the book and that some do not admire him at all. This does not alter the fact that, formally speaking, Johnson is always presented so as to sustain the effect of admiration. That Boswell should fail of his intended effect in some passages or with some readers is no more evidence of a lack of consistent artistry than that Wordsworth, for example, should often fail of his effect in similar ways. The strong wine that Boswell offers can some-

times be fully savored only if the reader has the capacity to take the same disinterested delight in the powers of human nature that Boswell does. But that Boswell in fact achieves his effect with most readers the unique position of his book in literary history testifies.

24. *Life*, I, 468.

25. Ibid., III, 337.

26. Thomas Carlyle, "Boswell's Life of Johnson," *Critical and Miscellaneous Essays* (London, 1899), 3:80.

27. *Life*, I, 472.

DONALD J. NEWMAN

The Death Scene
and the Art of Suspense
in Boswell's *Life of Johnson*

*W*ould the death scene in Boswell's *Life of Johnson* really be much better if Boswell had been in London instead of Scotland when Johnson died? A number of scholars, noting what they see as disappointing biographical and artistic deficiencies in the second-hand account Boswell provides, certainly think so.[1] The difficulties they perceive in the ending arise out of Boswell's emphasis on Johnson's religious conflicts and their effect on his fear of death, knowledge that creates in readers a strong expectation of drama in an account of Johnson's last days. But, because he was absent from London, Boswell was unable to gather those intimate, revealing details that would have enabled him to attend to the biographical and dramatic needs the last act of his story demands—and that his audience expects. Thus, handicapped by the lack of "minute particulars" and first-hand observations, Boswell is unable to exploit the drama in Johnson's death, so he is forced to fall back on conventional religious themes as a means of organizing the death scene.[2] "So strong was the attraction of the proper moral end for a Christian Hero," O M Brack observes, "that even Boswell failed to escape it."[3]

Our disappointment, no doubt, is sharpened by imagining what Boswell could have, should have, and would have done if he had had the raw material of drama that permeates the portrait of Johnson Sir John Hawkins presents, a portrait we expected to find in a biography that promises to show Johnson "as he really was" (I, 30). Boswell's rival shows us

> a man worn out with literary labour and disease, contemplating his dis-solution, and exerting all his powers to resist that constitutional malady which now, more than ever, oppressed him. To divert himself from a train of thinking which often involved him in a labyrinth of doubts and difficulties touching a future state of existence, he solicited the frequent visits of his friends and acquaintance, the most discerning of whom could not but see, that the fabric of his mind was tottering; and, to allay those scruples and terrors which haunted him in his vacant hours, he betook himself to the reading of books of practical divinity.[4]

If we compare this portrait to Boswell's it is understandable how we might feel that Boswell welshed on his promise to let us "'live o'er each scene' with him, as he actually advanced through the several stages of his life" (I, 30), and it is equally understandable how we might conclude that, as fine as the rest of the book is, Boswell's lapse into convention dulls the finishing touches on what is otherwise an inspired portrait in one of the finest biographies in English.[5]

There is no denying the presence of orthodox Christian themes in "a deathbed scene so orchestrated as to seem almost a ritual,"[6] but it is a mistake to assume that these themes are included at the expense of Boswell's biographical integrity or his art. To automatically assume that the presence of these conventions is the mark of biographical or artistic failure prevents us from seeing what a truly fine ending the death scene is, for we then do not bother to examine how Boswell enlists these conventions in the service of biography to achieve, in the words of William Siebenschuh, "a very special literary effect in the service of a higher kind of truth."[7]

One of the reasons we have difficulty seeing beyond the conven-tions is that we ignore what Boswell tells us about his literary intent regarding the conclusion of his book. Although he does not tell us specifically what it is, he does tell us what it is not, for he deliberately abandons the biographical method that has been his constant boast: "It is not my intention," he declares, "to give a very minute detail of Johnson's remaining days" (IV, 398–399). Although he is shifting liter-ary gears, Boswell is not dropping into neutral and letting the scene roll forward under its own momentum: "I am conscious that this is the most difficult and dangerous part of my biographical work, and I cannot but be very anxious concerning it. I trust that I have got through it, preserving at once my regard to truth,—to my friend,—and to the interests of virtue and religion" (IV, 398).

In light of this obviously intense concern, it is not reasonable to assume that he is suddenly abandoning that biographical vision that has been his guiding principle all along, which the absence of graphic details suggests to some he has done. Suppose, however, that Boswell's literary objective, to show Johnson "as he really was" (I, 30), remains unchanged. Then, the absence of the details we expected to have could very well signify a change, not in Boswell's biographical goal, but in the biographer's artistic approach to his biographical problem.

William Dowling suggests the nature of this shift in an observation he makes about the dramatic qualities of the death scene: "The drama of Johnson's death as a Christian hero remains dramatic precisely because the *Life* insists on the existential dimension of his religious struggle until the last possible moment, throwing into sharp relief themes that have run submerged throughout the earlier story."[8] Dowling is referring to Boswell's art of suspense, the ingredient in his narrative that enables him to write a death scene that soars above the ruts of religious triviality. Boswell infuses his religious themes with suspense, which he then exploits to bring the *Life* to a subtle yet dramatic climax laden with biographical significance. To exploit this suspense, Boswell had to change his approach to the death scene.

We have trouble seeing the climactic elements in the death scene because we do not see its two-part structure. The long series of vignettes in the *Life* conditions us to look at every scene in the book as an anecdote, so we tend to see the death scene as just another anecdote, the last in the sequence, and we evaluate it accordingly. The problem, though, is that we then apply an inappropriate set of standards to the death scene. The differences we note between this scene and the earlier anecdotes (that is, the lack of unity and focus, details selected without apparent regard for biographical value or artistic effect, the repetition) automatically become shortcomings. But if we evaluate the death scene's structure as it is rather than as we think it should be, these supposed flaws vanish.

Rather than looking at the death scene as the artistically unified narrative we expect to find in one of Boswell's anecdotes, we should see it as a narrative in two parts that appear interchangeable but are not. The first part is drama: Boswell's artistic rendering of the death of Samuel Johnson. The second is exposition: various accounts pieced together by Boswell the editor from the pens of others and intended to serve, apparently, as his ever-present collection of "proofs" (I, 50; IV, 149) that his account is indeed "authentick" (I, 40) and his understanding correct. No doubt Boswell also intends that the second part serve as a repository for those particulars that he wants to include, but which, for aesthetic and artistic reasons, he is obliged to leave out of the first part.

The first part of the death scene, and that which is both the more artistically and biographically significant, begins with Boswell's announcement that "It was now evident, that the crisis was fast approaching, when he must *die like men, and fall like one of the Princes*'" (IV, 399), and it ends with Mr. Strahan's "agreeable assurances, that, after being in much agitation, Johnson became quite composed, and continued so till his death" (IV, 416). The second part begins immediately after with Dr. Brocklesby's trustworthy remarks and continues until "His schoolfellow, Dr. Taylor, performed the mournful office of reading the burial service" (IV, 419–420). Although the second part of the death scene contains more concrete details than the first, it is the first part that is the focus of Boswell's artistry and the climax of the *Life*.

The biography's closing scenes contain what Dowling considers "the end of an existential drama," which he accurately describes as "the long and complex story of Johnson's struggle throughout the *Life* . . . to work out his spiritual destiny within the confines of Christian orthodoxy."[9] Boswell tells us early in the book that an important article in the biography will be "The history of [Johnson's] mind as to religion" (I, 67), a subject he treats in such extensive detail that Dowling rightly isolates it as "Boswell's major theme." This theme of religious conflict is developed after a pattern Ralph Rader describes as the "basic formula" underlying Boswell's more dramatic anecdotes.[10] Boswell is following Aristotle's lead; we are given a beginning that places a central character in a predicament whose outcome we cannot foresee, a middle that develops the situation and molds our responses to it and the character, and an end in which the predicament is resolved and our emotional tensions released.

Johnson's predicament, and the source of suspense in the story, is the conflict created by Johnson's belief that he must lead a life of "obedience and repentance" (III, 295) to earn the "hope that a good life might end at last in a contented death" (I, 365), and the disturbing contradiction he held most of his life that "the better a man is, the more afraid is he of death" (III, 154). At the root of this conflict is Johnson's "supposed orthodoxy" (II, 104). He believes that God's mercy flows from His sense of justice, not from His infinite goodness, and since "No man can be sure that his obedience and repentance will obtain salvation" (III, 295), the only rational response is fear.[11] The desirability of a peaceful death is a theme that appears early in the *Life* and is developed in such a way that it is both a symbol of the validity of Christianity and, for Johnson, who never looked upon death but "with horrour" (II, 106), of fear conquered.

Boswell captures the drama of Johnson's religious conflicts in dramatic irony, and the tension it creates vibrates throughout an account relating "a thousand instances of his benevolent exertions in almost every way that can be conceived" (IV, 344). We watch Johnson earnestly practice a brand of Christianity that is creating the anxiety religion is intended to relieve. The irony is honed every time Johnson expounds on, or defends, Christian revelation. But readers never see Johnson grappling with the fear itself. All we see is evidence of the struggle manifested in Johnson's ever-present fear of death, a theme reinforced and emphasized continually by dozens of oblique references to Johnson's anxieties about death, judgment, and immortality. Even the most casual reader senses the continual struggle for religious peace, and few are surprised when Boswell's apparently tactless prodding on the subjects of death and immortality provokes an irritated or violent response from Johnson.[12]

Our response to this conflict is shaped to a great extent by Boswell's portrayal of Johnson as a "sincere and zealous Christian" (IV, 426). And here Rader's analysis of a hero deepens our insight into Boswell's methodical molding of our responses to Johnson's religious paradox. Rader describes a hero thusly:

> The hero is of mixed character—essentially and predominantly good, so that we wish him finally well; at the same time flawed or restricted in a way that involves him in embarrassments which are the substance of the

complications of the plot. We view these embarrassments with delight both because they are of the hero's own making and because the conduct of the story assures us throughout that he will in some way that our perplexity cannot foresee ultimately achieve the due which his fundamentally good character deserves.[13]

Does this not describe Boswell's portrayal of a troubled Johnson's "religious progress" (I, 67)? Although Johnson's character is far from perfect, his essential goodness is never in question, and it is emphasized by Boswell's development of Johnson's other admirable qualities: his genius, his personal courage, his charity, his determination, his sincerity. As a Christian, however, he is flawed; his religion should be effortless for a man of such virtue and piety, yet his religious life is unnecessarily complicated by "his notion of the ethicks of the gospel" (IV, 397). It is impossible for us not to wish that a man with a "most humane and benevolent heart" (IV, 426) like Johnson's will discover a way to escape his religious torment and find peace. Our desire to see him relieved is intensified by our early awareness that his religious difficulties are the product of yet another brutal irony: the powerful genius that made him "the brightest ornament of the eighteenth century" (I, 9) is also the "obstinate rationality" (IV, 289) that is preventing him from resolving his religious dilemma. The irony is the more painful for us because Boswell makes it clear that Johnson's orthodoxy, the cause of his anxiety, is a "chain which early imagination and long habit made him think massy and strong, but which, had he ventured to try, he could have snapt asunder" (II, 104).

Rader's analysis concerns itself with the development of Boswell's comic anecdotes, which remain comic because we are assured all will end well. But there is no such assurance of a happy ending for Johnson in Boswell's treatment of Johnson's religious fears. In fact, Boswell litters his narrative with subtle hints that things could get worse for Johnson, a strategy that makes us anxious that Johnson just might not die the peaceful death he obviously deserves and that we want him to have. This anxiety in the reader is the stuff out of which Boswell fashions a subtle yet dramatic climax.

"The Death," as Boswell calls it, works as a climax because he successfully uses suspense to focus our hopes and fears for Johnson on a single moment, that instant when Johnson realizes he has at last come face to face with death, for it is this moment and this moment only when we learn for sure which prevails in the struggle for control of Johnson's mind: his fear or his faith?[14] Will Johnson's personal and religious courage crumble under the reality of his own death? Or will his religious faith sustain him through his last great trial? We do not know, until the last moment, how Johnson will behave, so we can be surprised, and our surprise illuminates the profound significance of an event in Johnson's "religious progress" that, in lesser hands, might have passed unnoticed. We can be surprised because Boswell's art of suspense keeps the outcome of Johnson's confrontation with death in doubt.

The art of Boswell's suspense is his skill at concealing the story's real ending while amplifying our anxieties concerning the fate of a man we have come to care about a great deal. In short, we can be both surprised and relieved. Boswell diverts our attention from the book's most probable ending, that Johnson will die peacefully, by encouraging us to imagine the worst. We are threatened with the possibility that if Johnson does not resolve his religious paradox we will witness a most distressing scene: the courageous and pious Samuel Johnson cowering hysterically before the Grim Reaper. We really do not want to see Johnson's stature diminished from that of a "majestick teacher of moral and religious wisdom" (I, 201) to that of an "ordinary mortal" (IV, 374). Boswell's recording of Johnson's physical decline makes us feel that the resolution of his religious conflict is a matter of utmost urgency, a sensation that Boswell intensifies by his management of dramatic time.[15] By the time we arrive at the climax, we are, figuratively speaking, on the edge of our seats.

Boswell is able to promote the possibility that Johnson will die a death embarrassing to a Christian because he envelops Johnson's physical decline in an atmosphere of uncertainty and foreboding. There are strong hints that Johnson's Christian fortitude may be weakening as well, and we are never provided with the kinds of details that will enable us to divine the story's future. We do not know, any more than does Johnson himself, when or how he is going to die. Obviously, Boswell knows, but he withholds the information until he can get the greatest dramatic impact out of it. Because we do not know the dramatic future, we are reacting to the Johnson that is rather than the Johnson that will be, and the Johnson that is, is a man "much oppressed by the fear of death" (IV, 299). By concealing John-son's ultimate religious temperament Boswell prevents his more dra-matic scenes from becoming mere exploitation of the public's pru-rient interest in watching a great man trembling in his unbuckled shoes, and he avoids the predictability of the Ars Moriendi tradition.

The effectiveness of Boswell's approach to his handling of the drama in Johnson's fear of death is evident in the scene in which Boswell wonders aloud whether David Hume and Samuel Foote might really have been afraid of death despite their insistence to the contrary. Boswell brings up the issue to support his contention that a man might indeed fortify his mind against death. The discussion provokes an impassioned response from Johnson:

> "No, Sir, let it alone. It matters not how a man dies, but how he lives. The act of dying is not of importance, it lasts so short a time." He added, (with an earnest look,) "A man knows it must be so, and submits. It will do him no good to whine."
>
> I attempted to continue the conversation. He was so provoked, that he said, "Give us no more of this;" and was thrown into such a state of agitation, that he expressed himself in a way that alarmed and distressed me; shewed an impatience that I should leave him, and when I was going away, called to me sternly, "Don't let us meet to-morrow." (II, 106–107)

Readers will not respond emotionally to this scene and to Boswell's distress if they know that Johnson's fear is unwarranted; his passion-ate response and Boswell's naive anxiety and persistence would then be reduced to melodrama.

Boswell leads us to the death scene with his reporting on Johnson's failing health, but Boswell chronicles the decline without providing any clues as to what the future holds for Johnson. Most of the specifics we are given about Johnson's health problems come from Johnson himself, and Boswell seldom comments directly about the nature of Johnson's problems. But Boswell does interpret them for us, and what he tells us is sufficiently vague that he increases our anxiety about Johnson without telling us anything concrete, thus cultivating our perception that Johnson's religious conflicts are becoming a critical issue.

An especially good example of Boswell's technique of heightening our sense of the urgency of Johnson's situation while cultivating our feelings of uncertainty is his account of the concert the pair attended in 1777. Boswell becomes "conscious of a generous attachment to Dr. Johnson, as my preceptor and friend, mixed with affectionate regret that he was an old man, whom I should probably lose in a short time" (III, 198). There is no solid information here that enables us to guess what the future holds, and a guess by its very nature reduces uncertainty. Nor do we even know what specifically led to Boswell's realization. He describes Johnson as old, but, strength-wise, how old? If there is some clue as to how fast Johnson's strength is ebbing, we can guess what Boswell means by a short time. But then our attention is diverted from Boswell's coming surprise to an evaluation of our own ability to interpret clues, and the shock value of the climax is lessened. In addition, the fact that we cannot guess what a "short time" is heightens our sense that Johnson could die at any moment, with or without his religious difficulties resolved.

Boswell makes sure two facts are evident to the most casual reader: Johnson is in a predicament that must come to a "crisis" (IV, 399), and the crisis will occur during that "approaching trial" (IV, 395). Since 1782 we have been watching Johnson's health deteriorate rapidly; he is "battered by one disorder after another" (IV, 153) until even he is forced to admit he is failing. "I am loth to think I grow worse; and cannot fairly prove even to my own partiality, that I grow much better" (IV, 354), he confesses with apprehension. Our anxiety for him is sharpened by our suspicion that the "manly fortitude" (II, 190) that for so long has held his powerful emotions in check is no longer strong enough to restrain his dread of the end. His strength seems drained. When Dr. Adams and Boswell bring up the subject of death, Johnson, who once would have retaliated with a flash of anger, seems beaten: " 'Let me alone, let me alone: I am overpowered,' and then he put his hands before his face, and reclined some time upon the table" (IV, 294).

Only once does Boswell reveal prematurely anything about the ending. Again, Boswell and Dr. Adams are discussing death, and Boswell comments:

> If what has now been stated should be urged by the enemies of Christianity, as if its influence on the mind were not benignant, let it be remembered, that Johnson's temperament was melancholy, of which dire-

ful apprehensions of futurity are often a common effect. We shall
presently see that when he approached nearer to his aweful change, his
mind became tranquil, and he exhibited as much fortitude as becomes a
thinking man in that situation. (IV, 300)

Although Boswell reveals, without emphasizing it, that Johnson became tranquil, Boswell's comment that Johnson exhibited "as much
fortitude as" leaves open the possibility that the initial confrontation
with death might have been a very emotional one.

Right to the last our feelings of uncertainty and anxiety are being
cultivated. Even when Boswell tells us at the start of his chapter covering 1784 that he is now "arrived at the last year of the life of Samuel
Johnson" (IV, 257), we still do not know when, or how, his dissolution
will take place. His near breakdown in front of Boswell and Dr.
Adams makes any appearance of calmness and fortitude suspect.
Johnson was once "much pleased" with General Paoli's observation
that those dying easy "are not thinking of death, but of applause, or
something else, which keeps death out of their sight" (III, 154). How
can we avoid applying this observation to Johnson too? Our confidence in the strength of his faith must be somewhat diminished by a
comment obviously describing his own emotional state as he prepares
to face death: "what must be the condition of him whose heart will not
suffer him to rank himself among the best, or among the good? Such
must be his dread of the approaching trial, as will leave him little
attention to the opinion of those whom he is leaving for ever; and the
serenity that is not felt, it can be no virtue to feign."[16] By showing
behavior that implies fear and by quoting Johnson on his own inner
turmoil, Boswell suggests that Johnson still fears that "No rational
man can die without uneasy apprehension" (III, 294).

Boswell deepens our sense of foreboding by throwing a sinister pall
over what remains of Johnson's uncertain future, which the artist ac-
complishes with a pattern of foreshadowing that continually hints at
unpleasant events to come. He emphasizes his "anxious apprehensions" (IV, 227) with remarks like his observation in 1783 that Johnson's health "was in a more precarious state than at anytime when I
had parted from him" (IV, 225), or like the comment he makes upon
his departure, when he confides to us: "I walked away from his door
to-day, with fearful apprehension of what might happen before I

returned" (IV, 226). The last time Boswell says goodbye to Johnson, it is "with a foreboding of our long, long separation" (IV, 339). This sense of foreboding about an event in the vague future, frequently emphasized, gradually settles over us too.

Since we are uncertain as to when the end will come, Boswell is able to intensify our apprehension with the press of dramatic time that shortens, but we never know by how much, the time until even Johnson can no longer turn his gaze from death. Boswell dramatizes the critical passage of time in three distinct ways. The most obvious is by his reporting of Johnson's health problems, which visibly sap the strength from his vigorous constitution. Until 1782 Johnson's health problems are reported unobtrusively, usually through brief comments made by Johnson in his letters, so that his bad health seems a part of the background. But in 1782 Johnson's health problems loom in the foreground: suddenly, dramatically, graphically, time has taken what seems to be a quantum leap, leaving in its wake an old, ailing man whose days are obviously numbered.[17]

Second, we watch with Johnson as his lifelong friends drop into the grave one by one, and every time he hears the news of the death of a friend we are reminded, as he is, that his turn is coming. The urgency of his situation is emphasized by his stroke. It is a warning with a significance that neither Johnson nor the reader misses. "Let us, my dear, pray for one another," he writes to Lucy Porter a little more than a year before his death, "and consider our sufferings as notices mercifully given us to prepare ourselves for another state. . . . The world passes away, and we are passing with it" (IV, 233).

And, lastly, Boswell provides us with a sort of countdown. We see Johnson for the "last time" (IV, 326) in the company of the Literary Club. We "behold Johnson for the last time . . . in his native city" (IV, 372). Boswell sends him two letters, "the last of which came too late to be read by him, for his illness encreased more rapidly upon him than I had apprehended" (IV, 380). When we arrive at "the Death" we bring to it a full appreciation of Johnson's dread of this last great trial and our own anxious apprehensions about its outcome.

Even at this late point Boswell keeps us on edge by being vague about time. We do not even know exactly how long a period the death scene covers, except that it is "about eight or ten days" (IV, 400). Nothing in the death scene hints at any lessening of the "terrour and anx-iety" (III, 99) that plague Johnson. He lances his leg deeply, a mark of that "extraordinary eagerness to retard his dissolution" (IV, 400), and he warns a woman attending a bedside service to "Live well, I conjure you; and you will not feel the compunction at the last which I now feel" (IV, 410)—and that we feel for him.

Boswell encourages us to wonder if Johnson's periods of calmness are simply the result of his "power of turning his . . . sight away" (III, 154) from death. When discussing the possibility of publishing an edi-tion of his works, Johnson seems to accept his fate: "I may possibly live . . . or rather breathe, three days, or perhaps three weeks; but find myself daily and gradually weaker" (IV, 409), he tells John Nic-hols. But, then again, he later expresses an interest in a project he once rejected because it would have been too much work: "I have been thinking again, Sir, of *Thuanus*: it would not be the laborious task which you have supposed it. I should have no trouble but that of dictation, which would be performed as speedily as an amanuensis could write" (IV, 410).

Our anxieties are sharpened by Boswell's acceleration of time. We see the last of events we suppose to occur at relatively short intervals. We have heard the last service read in the presence of Nichols, a long-time friend attending Johnson during his final illness, and we witness the last meeting of Johnson and Burke. By this point, all our emo-tional responses to Johnson, shaped by a long and sympathetic nar-rative, have been evoked; all are in agitated motion. Because we do not know what to expect, nor when, Boswell is able to surprise and shock us. Johnson is discussing Christianity with Dr. Brocklesby when the subject is abruptly changed by a question that strikes like a bolt of lightning from a clear sky: "Johnson, with that native fortitude, which, amidst all his bodily distress and mental sufferings, never forsook him, asked Dr. Brocklesby, as a man in whom he had confidence, to tell him plainly whether he could recover" (IV, 415).

Perhaps Johnson, at last tired of patronizing uncertainties that "make me hope" (IV, 259), could stand the suspense no longer himself. For just a moment we can feel the shock and chagrin that Dr. Brocklesby must have felt at the question. Does he catch himself the way we do, and hesitate while he quickly tries to assess what impact the truth will have on his dear friend and patient? Does Brocklesby hesitate long enough to estimate the consequences of violating a dictum similar to one Johnson recently pronounced while at Dr. Taylor's?:

> I deny the lawfulness of telling a lie to a sick man for fear of alarming him. You have no business with consequences; you are to tell the truth. Besides, you are not sure what effect your telling him that he is in danger may have. It may bring his distemper to a crisis, and that may cure him. Of all lying, I have the greatest abhorrence of this, because I believe it has been frequently practised on myself. (IV, 306)

Brocklesby's hesitation would explain the earnest entreaty that follows: "And give me (said he,) a direct answer."[18]

Will Dr. Brocklesby, knowing the violence of Johnson's fear of death as we do, tell him the truth? And if he does, how will Johnson take the news? Will the truth "bring his distemper to a crisis"? Our emotions, animated by images of a Johnson terrified by death, cause us to hold our breaths as we wait for Brocklesby's answer; but Boswell keeps us dangling. Brocklesby asks if Johnson "could bear the whole truth, which way soever it might lead?" (IV, 415), and that question is in our minds too. Johnson replies that he can, and suddenly he is face to face with that which has always been to him an "object of terrour" (IV, 394). "Then, (said Johnson,) I will take no more physic, not even my opiates; for I have prayed that I may render up my soul to God unclouded."[19] That this single line is able to carry so much biographical weight with ease argues convincingly against the notion that Boswell just slapped the ending together out of whatever materials he could scrounge up.[20]

Our surprise is a relief, and the shock makes us realize a significant fact: this Johnson, composed and resigned to death, is not exactly the same Johnson who insists nearly all through the *Life* that a rational man cannot die peacefully. Something has changed; it is clear that Johnson's death is not of a piece with his life, for until he was near death "he never had a moment in which death was not terrible to him" (III, 153). Boswell then brings the scene to an immediate close while the audience is still stunned by the sudden turn of events. All we are told at this point, since we get the details in a moment, is that the change is sincere because Johnson remains calm until he dies.

The rest is denouement. In the second part of the death scene Boswell explains why Johnson is able to die peacefully: he has come to trust "in the merits and *propitiation* of Jesus Christ," which means that, imperfect as his life might have been, he found hope and comfort in his religion.[21] Thus, by his example, Johnson undermines the arguments of the infidels by demonstrating that a rational man can find solace in faith.[22] Perhaps the attentive reader will recall an observation Boswell made early in the book about the validity of Christianity: "If there be any thoughtless enough to suppose such exercise the weakness of a great understanding, let them look up to Johnson, and be convinced that what he so earnestly practised must have a rational foundation" (I, 305).

Actually, the change had become obvious earlier than it does in Boswell's story, but Boswell does not disclose this fact until well after the event, until after he reveals the change dramatically, and only then do we get an insight into what has happened to Johnson: "Johnson having thus in his mind the *true* Christian scheme, at once rational and consolatory, uniting justice and mercy in the DIVINITY, with the improvement of human nature" (IV, 416, my italics). The significance of the change is obvious: Johnson's understanding of the nature of God has changed. Mercy can be extended to the sincere individual, not necessarily out of God's sense of justice, but out of His goodness, an attribute Johnson seldom ascribed to God when it came to the Divinity's relations with individuals.[23] As Johnson's biographer, Boswell also reveals a profound truth: his subject has, at last, realized "his approaches to religious perfection" (IV, 410).

It can be argued that the last two or three chapters of the *Life* are littered with extraneous material that does not contribute directly to the artist's attempts to create suspense, and that this extra material often works against Boswell's efforts to increase narrative tension. Especially conspicuous in this regard is Boswell's belated fulfillment of a promise to insert somewhere in his narrative specimens from the pens of Johnson's imitators. He includes them just before the start of the death scene, and there is no question he could not have found a worse place for them had he tried. On the whole much of Boswell's material does not directly contribute to the suspense in the ending, but that does not diminish the accomplishment of making the most of the material he has. We must remember that Boswell does not claim the liberty of the novelist, so he is obliged to use materials that in a novel would be considered extraneous.[24]

However, the validity of the criticism of Boswell's decision to insert the imitations of Johnson's style where he did is undeniable. Boswell put them in a position where they work against the flow of his narrative. As an artistic choice his decision is inexplicable, but one can speculate as to how these specimens wound up where they did. Could not the choice for their location be a manifestation of Boswell's unconscious resistance to reliving the pain of his loss seven years earlier? We know he took Johnson's death hard. He noted in his journal for 17 December 1784:

> This must be ever remembered as a melancholy day; for it brought me the dismal news of my great and good Friend, Dr. Samuel Johnson. His Physician Dr. Brocklesby favoured me with a very full letter dated on Monday the 13 the night of his death. I was stunned, and in a kind of amaze. . . . I did not shed tears. I was not tenderly affected. My feeling was just one large expanse of Stupor. I knew that I should afterwards have sorer sensations.[25]

Boswell's reference to the death scene as "the Death" suggests an attempt emotionally to cut himself off from it, to put distance between himself and Johnson's death. Certainly, trying to recreate the event on paper must have rekindled unpleasant memories. This emotional resistance would explain the absence of more obvious devices for building suspense, but it does not explain why he let a bad decision stand in every subsequent edition. However, this flaw is not severe enough to reduce our appreciation for Boswell's literary gifts and his biographical achievement. Given the genre, the question is not whether the ending of the *Life* could really have been much better, but how much better could it really have been?

Notes

1. For instance, see Maurice Quinlan, *Samuel Johnson: A Layman's Religion* (Madison: University of Wisconsin Press, 1973), 183; O M Brack, Jr., "The Death of Samuel Johnson and the Ars Moriendi Tradition," *Cithara: Essays in*

the Judaeo-Christian Tradition 19 (1980): 3; and Bertram Davis, *Johnson before Boswell* (New Haven: Yale University Press, 1960), 110. The comments about the death scene made by these scholars suggest they share at least some of the disappointment of D. B. Wyndham Lewis, who observes: "To admit Boswell's *Life of Johnson,* so packed with riches, lacks its natural and artistic conclusion is grievous but inevitable. The work has no climax. The disciple was not at the master's death-bed. . . . Without a doubt Boswell's absence in Scotland robs the *Life* of what should have been its great final scene." D. B. Wyndham Lewis, *James Boswell, a Short Life,* 2d ed. (England, 1952; reprint, Westport, Conn.: Greenwood Press, 1980), 168. For a discussion of how eighteenth-century biographers typically treated the deaths of their heroes, see Donald Stauffer, *The Art of Biography in Eighteenth Century England* (Princeton: Princeton University Press, 1941), 515–517.

2. James Boswell, *The Life of Johnson,* ed. George Birkbeck Hill and L. F. Powell, 6 vols. (Oxford: Clarendon, 1934–1964), III, 191. An excellent description of the conventional religious themes in the *Life* can be found in William Dowling, *The Boswellian Hero* (Athens: University of Georgia Press, 1979), 167–181. See especially p. 172, where Dowling observes, "The dramatic context of Johnson's death as a Christian hero . . . is the total context of his inward struggle through the *Life* as a whole. The story of that struggle is what prepares us for Boswell's elaborate and detailed account of Johnson's final days and hours, an account that at last presents us with the conventional image of the Christian hero who has passed through a torment of self-doubt and repentance to the tranquility that lies beyond."

3. Brack, "The Death of Samuel Johnson," 9.

4. Sir John Hawkins, *The Life of Samuel Johnson, LL.D.,* ed. Bertram Davis (New York: Macmillan Company, 1961), 242.

5. There are those, however, who will not allow this assessment to stand unchallenged. The most vocal of this group is Donald Greene, whose antipathy to Boswell is legendary. For a comprehensive summary of Greene's complaints against Boswell, see Donald Greene, " 'Tis a Pretty Book, Mr. Boswell, But—," *Georgia Review* 32, no. 1 (1978): 17–43. See also his "Reflections on a Literary Anniversary," *Queen's Quarterly* 70 (1963): 198–208. Another indictment of Boswell worth reading is Richard Schwartz, *Boswell's Johnson* (Madison: University of Wisconsin Press, 1978).

6. Dowling, *The Boswellian Hero,* 172.

7. William Siebenschuh, "The Relationship between Factual Accuracy and Literary Art in the *Life of Johnson,*" *Modern Philology* 74, no. 3 (1977): 285. This essay has been included in Siebenschuh's latest book, *Fictional Techniques and Factual Works* (Athens: University of Georgia Press, 1983). I am especially indebted to Siebenschuh for the insights he has provided into Boswell's art of the anecdote. Particularly illuminating in this regard is his *Form and Purpose in Boswell's Biographical Works* (Berkeley: University of California Press, 1972), 51–75.

8. Dowling, *The Boswellian Hero,* 171. Dowling also perceives Boswell to be using conventional themes for unconventional purposes. See Dowling's remarks on p. 168, where he writes: "For though Boswell's account of his hero's confrontation with death draws on the conventions of earlier narrative, the final meaning of Johnson's passing is anything but conventional in the more ordinary sense. In this final portion of the *Life* we are dealing in a heightened and ultimate sense with the major theme of Boswellian narrative, the theme of the genuine hero existing in an unheroic age. The death of Johnson is not merely the death of a great and good man but the final disappearance of heroic potentiality from a world alien to heroism."

9. Ibid., 168–169.

10. Ralph Rader, "Literary Form in Factual Narrative," in *Essays in Eighteenth Century Biography,* ed. Philip B. Daghlian (Bloomington: Indiana University Press, 1968), 22. My debt to Professor Rader will be apparent throughout this essay.

11. For an excellent discussion of the rationalism in Johnson's fear of death, see Arieh Sachs, "Reason and Unreason in Johnson's Religion," *Modern Language Review* 59 (1964): 519–526. See also Quinlan, *Samuel Johnson,* 125–149. Any study of Johnson's religion would be grossly incomplete if one neglected Chester Chapin, *The Religious Thought of Samuel Johnson* (Ann Arbor: University of Michigan Press, 1968).

12. Although Quinlan does not disagree that Johnson did indeed fear death, he observes: "The view that Johnson had an obsession about dying was created largely by James Boswell." Quinlan, *Samuel Johnson,* 127. The death scene, then, derives its artistic power from Boswell's emphasis on Johnson's fear of death.

13. Rader, "Literary Form," 22–23.

14. Marshall Waingrow, ed., *The Correspondence and Other Papers Relating to the Making of the "Life of Johnson,"* vol. 2, *Yale Edition of the Private Papers of James Boswell,* ed. Frederick Pottle et al. (New York: McGraw-Hill Book Company, 1969), 384. Boswell writes in a letter dated 10 February 1791 to Edmond Malone: "I have now before me p. 488 in print, the 923 page of the Copy only is exhausted, and there remain 80, besides the Death, as to which I shall be concise though solemn. . . ."

15. Paul Alkon provides some illuminating insights into Boswell's control of dramatic time in his "Boswellian Time," *Studies in Burke and his Time* 14 (1973): 239–256. Alkon meticulously describes Boswell's methods for controlling our "inner clock," the mechanism by which we perceive the passage of dramatic time. By slowing us down Boswell focuses our attention on the life-like repetition of events, which causes us to feel, says Alkon, that we "are living over with Johnson a series of episodes that seem to approximate the duration of their counterparts in the clock time of real life" (p. 250). Alkon continues to observe that "Since readers already know the main outcome—Johnson wrote excellent books, became famous, and received a pension on

which to live ever after—there is no suspense to quicken the pace by throwing attention forward. Nor does Boswell much resort to the devices which, for such a story, *might* have stepped up the tempo." I would argue that Boswell does indeed throw our attention forward, thereby creating suspense, with his development of Johnson's religious conflicts, for we are wondering right to the last what the outcome will be.

16. *Life*, IV, 395. Boswell is quoting from "Mrs. Thrale's Collection, March 10, 1784. Vol. II, p. 350." Although Boswell places this quotation just before the start of the death scene, it actually was written nine months before Johnson died. His use of it implies that the sentiment expressed is what Johnson was feeling just shortly before he died.

17. I have discovered that most of the references to Johnson's health up to the period beginning in 1782 are ones that would be unlikely to have much effect individually on the reader's response to Johnson's health problems, and therefore their effect on the reader is cumulative. The references in the narrative previous to 1782 tend to cluster around the introduction of a new year, although references are sprinkled in especially long sections. The effect is to provide a subtle background of poor health. After 1782, the narrative is dominated by references to Johnson's health.

18. See Waingrow, *The Correspondence and Other Papers*, 31–35. Boswell has rearranged Brocklesby's account a little and polished up the dialogue. This is how Brocklesby related the conversation in a letter to Boswell dated 27 December 1784: "3 days before his death he asked me as an honest professional Man in whom he confided most, whether he could recover. 'Give a direct answer.'" The polishing of the language of Johnson's request heightens the suspense hanging on the answer by emphasizing the possibility that Brocklesby might evade the question.

19. Ibid., 33. Brocklesby says Johnson's reply was this: " 'Then' says he 'Ill take no more Physick, not even my opiates any more for I have earnestly prayed to render up my Soul to God just as it may be unclouded and simple, for' said he 'Opiates though they ever lulled my bodily pains yet they usually filld my imagination with horrors and visions that disturbed for several hours my clear judgem[en]t and I should be loth to dy in that state with any overcast to cloud it.'" The potential damage to Johnson's virtuous image aside, much of the impact of Johnson's reply would have been lost had this entire quotation been used. As Boswell presents it, the revelation of change is effective.

20. Thus it is questionable whether his presence in London would have made much of a difference in his artistic choices. He does not lack details, for he uses less than he has. Not only does he have Hawkins's account to draw on, but he has yet another detailed chronicle kept by John Hoole, eyewitness accounts, and, as Waingrow notes, some that went unrecorded: "For much of Boswell's research there is of course no record. The *Life* was composed in London, where countless investigations must have been made in person—

only a few of which are mentioned in the journals" (p. xxv). And even if Boswell had been handicapped by his absence, it is unlikely that the deficiency would have showed up in his craftsmanship, for he has demonstrated a superb ability to use secondhand materials. There are many instances in the *Life* where it is difficult, if not impossible, to tell which anecdotes come from his journals and which are extracted from his correspondence. Waingrow comments on this aspect of the *Life:* "the estimate of the actual extent of this first-hand element in the *Life* [the conversations] is usually exaggerated. Chapman, for example, succumbed to the common impression, stating that the record of the journal constitutes 'by far the greater part of the *Life*.' In fact, it constitutes less than half" (p. xxiii). It is not likely this mistake would be so common if there was a great disparity between the quality of Boswell's handling of his first-person accounts and the anecdotes he was passing along. See also p. xxv, where Waingrow adds, "Only the sleuthing reader would have guessed how dependent the writing of the *Life* was upon the writing of letters."

21. Boswell has kept a promise. In *The Journal of the Tour to the Hebrides*, Boswell records some of Johnson's remarks on the role of Jesus Christ's sacrifice as an example provided by God to show men how to lead a Christian life and as an example of God's abhorrence of sin. In a footnote Boswell observes, "What Dr. Johnson now delivered, was but a temporary opinion; for he afterwards was fully convinced of the *propitiatory sacrifice*, as I shall *shew* at large in my future work, *The Life of Samuel Johnson, LL.D.*" (*Shew* is my italics; see *Life*, V, 88). Quinlan agrees that a change did take place in Johnson's view of the Atonement, but Quinlan sees the alteration as more of a shift in emphasis rather than a profound and sudden change (p. 50). Chapin discusses the development of Johnson's view of the Atonement in "Samuel Johnson's Religious Development," *Studies in English Literature* 4 (1964): 457–474. That Boswell never uses this information or his knowledge that Johnson died peacefully to mitigate the effect on us of Johnson's terror of death and judgment is evidence that Boswell withheld the information for dramatic effect.

22. Although Dowling's analysis of the death scene is both perceptive and extensive, he introduces some confusion as to what he perceives the ultimate function of the scene to be. Dowling is correct in his assessment of the structure on p. 175: "Throughout the final portion of the *Life*, as a counterpoint to the Christian hero motif, Boswell balances two important themes, the personal and the culturally symbolic, until at the end they converge in the actuality of Johnson's passing. The first of these themes concerns the underlying meaning of the final period as the last spiritual crisis of Johnson's existence, of his ultimate response to the inevitability of death, the event that has horrified him for so many years. The second dwells on the permanent meaning of Johnson's death to his society and age; ultimately, to posterity and the world." Clearly, Johnson's death is meant to have public significance, but Dowling

seems to contradict himself as to what the significance is. Earlier he noted that the death scene represents the "final disappearance of heroic potentiality from a world alien to heroism" (p. 168). I would argue that just the opposite is the case, that Johnson's death is a symbolic example showing it is still possible for an individual to find in Christian orthodoxy a faith that coexists with reason, an opinion that Dowling seems to support as well on p. 171: "In an age of spiritual dissolution, the strongest evidence for the truth of Christianity is neither theological nor metaphysical; it is the presence among lesser souls of a great man whose inward struggle ends within the boundaries of Christian orthodoxy." By following Johnson's example and coming to the same realization he does, every man can become, though perhaps to a lesser degree, a Christian hero. If the death scene is indeed the symbolic passing of heroic potentiality from the world, then it seems the scene is merely catering to the public's curiosity about whether the philosopher-hero does indeed, as Dowling points out, "confront death in a manner different from that of ordinary men" (p. 176). Dowling does not seem to think, however, that Boswell is merely catering to a prurient public; nor do I. The point at which Johnson's personal experience becomes symbolic, the convergence of the two themes mentioned by Dowling, is the point at which the shift in Johnson's religious views is revealed, and this shift is represented by Johnson's response to Brocklesby's acknowledgment that Johnson is dying. Dowling ignores the matter of this shift in Johnson's religious views.

23. *Life*, IV, 299. The "true Christian scheme" described by Boswell as the one accepted by Johnson just before his death is very like the one Boswell wanted to believe in. "I ventured to ask him whether, although the words of some texts of Scripture seemed strong in support of the dreadful doctrine of an eternity of punishment, we might not hope that the denunciation was figurative, and would not literally be executed" (*Life*, III, 200). Not only did Boswell frequently wrestle with the teachings of Christianity as a doctrine, but he could never be certain as to God's benevolence. His journals contain many references to his fear of the Old Testament God of his Calvinistic upbringing. Aside from what is in the biographies of Boswell, there has not been much study of his religious beliefs. However, one might look at the following: Mary Margaret Stewart, "Boswell's Denominational Dilemma," *PMLA* 76 (1961): 503–511, and "Boswell and the Infidels," *Studies in English Literature* 4 (1964): 475–483. See also A. Russell Brooks, "Pleasure and Spiritual Turmoil in Boswell," *College Language Association Journal* 3 (1959): 12–19.

24. This issue was indeed raised by Donald Greene when an abbreviated form of this essay was delivered to the Western Society for Eighteenth-Century Studies at its annual conference in 1983.

25. Waingrow, *The Correspondence and Other Papers*, 29.

FREDRIC V. BOGEL

"Did you once see Johnson plain?": Reflections on Boswell's *Life* and the State of Eighteenth-Century Studies

lthough critical discussion of Boswell's *Life of Samuel John-son* has grown modestly in the last two decades, the terms of that discussion—the rules of the game—have remained re-markably constant since the early years of this century. And while time has removed certain individuals from the roster and replaced them with others, the teams, too, are recognizably the same, as are their slogans: Truth and Art. To the Truth team, the *Life* is great because Johnson was great, while Boswell was very good because he got it all right. "The *Johnsoniad* of Boswell turns on subjects that in very deed existed," gasps Carlyle; "it is all *true*."[1] To the Art team, the *Life* is a great book because Boswell is a great writer, and though Johnson was as-suredly an extraordinary man, his greatness in Boswell's biography is largely Boswell's achievement. "There is no more difficult art," asserts one scholar, "than to give the impression that nothing intervenes be-tween the reader and what is being described."[2]

The central dispute is clear: it concerns the sources of greatness of Boswell's *Life*. But that dispute can be enlisted in a range of larger critical debates and made to serve a variety of symbolic functions. In the 1950s and 1960s, the debate over the *Life of Johnson* carried a particular symbolic weight. To claim that the *Life* owed its greatness chiefly to documentary accuracy and to the singularity of the real Samuel Johnson was to align oneself with the Old School of historical scholarship. To insist on the art of the *Life* and on Boswell's imaginative realization of the character of Johnson was to align oneself with the New Criticism. This debate, of course, reenacted an ancient controversy between history and poetry. William Nelson summarizes the form which that controversy took in the Renaissance:

> The aspiring poet is . . . faced with a dilemma. In order to inherit the laurel of the great writers of antiquity, he must invent stories; by so doing, he opens himself to the charge of frivolity. . . . Alternatively, the story-teller may reject fictional invention, minimizing or even denying the difference between his tales and historical verity, and so assert his title to the respect that the tellers of true things generally enjoy. But adoption of this last course constitutes surrender to the historians, for those who record true events are denied the name of poet.[3]

In the mid twentieth century, the tension between history and poetry became a debate between alternative ways of conceiving a text, especially a problematic text like Boswell's *Life of Johnson*, and alternative ways of accounting for its power and meaning.

What does that debate signify at present, when the conflict between scholarship and criticism has been largely superseded by other kinds of critical controversy, and when formalist criticism—the old New Criticism—is almost universally, if over-hastily, regarded as a historical stage that we have decisively passed beyond?

The present case for the historical Johnson does not, I think, express prejudice against Boswell himself (except in some quarters, where it is often a disguised disappointment at his refusal to be a hero rather than simply portray one) or against the claims of biographers to be genuinely imaginative or "literary" writers, though such prejudices do at times appear. To see what the hidden agenda of the current debate is, we must ask exactly what is being claimed by the insistence on Johnson's historical reality. Not that one Samuel Johnson, sharing many traits with the hero of Boswell's biography, actually inhabited England in the years 1709 to 1784 rather than being merely a Boswellian invention.

No one has ever denied this, or accused Boswell of being an eigh-teenth-century Borges. What those who affirm Johnson's reality are actually claiming, however wishfully or mistily, is that the power of the Johnsonian presence that speaks to us from the text of Boswell's *Life* derives not from that text but from the historical Johnson himself. This is to claim not only that Boswell's text transmits to us the power and the reality of the actual Johnson, but that Johnson's reality manages some-how to reach us quite apart from the textual mediation of the *Life*— that Johnson is a real toad in an imaginary garden, or, rather, a real, breathing king in a painting of a throne room. To insist on Johnson's historical reality as against Boswell's biographical artistry is thus to insist that the historical order can remain distinct from the textual order and yet be transmitted by it, and that what Boswell's biography somehow delivers to us is the historical Johnson, the *real* Johnson, unenmeshed in the web of textuality: "Johnson plain."

This is an extraordinary claim, and one that involves its advocates in a variety of difficulties. Most obviously, it relies on an unexamined notion of what a historical fact is. Comparing the accounts that Hawkins and Boswell offer of Johnson's rejecting the shoes left outside his Oxford chambers, Ralph W. Rader summarizes thus: "The essen-tial facts are as Boswell is to present them: the shoes were given and Johnson was indignant. The problem is in evaluation."[4] But those are not the "essential facts," the irreducible historical granules around which Hawkins and Boswell secrete different evaluative pearls. For "facts" are themselves products of interpretive schemata, of frames of reference, and such frames are, in part, evaluative constructions. In-stead of "was indignant," after all, Rader might have said that Johnson "was petulantly ungrateful," or "was justly outraged," or even that he "chose not to accept them." What Rader terms the essential facts are actually least common denominators of the two accounts, areas of overlap between Hawkins's and Boswell's texts, common features of two (necessarily) derived conceptions of "the facts." Since nothing about the facts is more basic or essential than the "evaluation," the principal effect of an assumption like Rader's is to enshrine as primi-tively historical givens the products of what are inescapably in-terpretive procedures.

Rader's discussion of literary form in factual narrative is one of the subtlest and most valuable treatments of the problematic character of Boswell's *Life*. What, then, accounts for its confusion, and thus for the striking nonuniformity of its intellectual sophistication? This is a question that could be addressed to a number of writers on Boswell. Nearly every critic who addresses seriously the question of truth and art in the *Life* at some point makes a claim—usually a claim for the historical Johnson—that the rest of his or her argument ought to have ruled out, either because it represents a significant lapse in methodological rigor, or because it is inconsistent with the argument as a whole, or both. Why is it that readers relatively untroubled by the problem of the factual and the literary in Augustine's *Confessions* or Wordsworth's *Prelude* or even Boswell's *London Journal* are led into oddities of assertion and argument when treating the *Life of Johnson*? For two reasons, I think, one having to do with the particular character of the *Life* itself, the other with the present state of eighteenth-century studies.

One reason that the *Life* invites the kind of confusion I have been sketching is that Boswell was extraordinarily successful in portraying Johnson as a certain kind of hero, a hero of presence: a figure whose full power must be experienced to be known, and experienced at first hand. "The *Life* reminds us again and again that Johnson's greatness is something that can be fully comprehended only by those who move in his presence."[5] A remark offered late in the *Life* underscores this special kind of greatness that consists not so much in the possession of powers denied to other men as in the ability to make those powers evident and apprehensible to others:

> His superiority over other learned men consisted chiefly in . . . a certain continual power of seizing the useful substance of all that he knew, and *exhibiting* it in a *clear* and *forcible* manner; so that knowledge, which we often see to be no better than lumber in men of dull understanding, was, in him, true, *evident,* and *actual* wisdom.[6]

In portraying Johnson as this kind of hero, Boswell focuses not on traditionally heroic or transcendent confirmations of worth or self-hood but on what Lionel Trilling terms "the idea of authentic personal being": the individual's experience of himself as strong, coherent, substantial, indubitably present.[7] Johnson's conversations, above all, emphasize this side of his heroism, for in them he confirms, and makes powerfully evident to others, the authenticity and presence of his personal being; he exhibits, to adapt another remark of Trilling's, "such energy as contrives that the centre shall hold, that the circumference of the self keep unbroken, that the person be an integer, impenetrable, perdurable, and autonomous in being if not in action."[8]

This emphasis on Johnsonian presence is a principal source of the critical fantasy that Johnson's greatness touches us directly when we read Boswell's *Life*. For it speaks to our desire to keep alive the possibility of unmediated presence in the relam of character—of character as a "transcendental signified," in the current jargon. This desire has to do with our relation to Johnson, but also with our relation to what Johnson is thus taken to symbolize: the very possibility of experiencing an individual existence—another's, but also perhaps one's own—as fully present. For what is remarkable about Boswell's Johnson is that—despite all the forces that keep other figures in the *Life* muffled, over-mediated, and incompletely realized, including the structurally essential low-mimetic figure of Boswell himself—he breaks through again and again into what seems to be unmediated existence. This is his heroic singularity:

> He has made a chasm, which not only nothing can fill up, but which nothing has a tendency to fill up.—Johnson is dead.—Let us go to the next best:—there is nobody;—no man can be said to put you in mind of Johnson. (IV, 420–421)

An insistence that the historical Johnson reaches us by somehow breaking through the textual mediacy of Boswell's *Life* is thus not really a critical assertion about the character of the historical order. It is rather an investment of faith in the ability to break through the mediacy of one's own life, an ability that Johnson, in his moments of heroic presence, seems to demonstrate. Carlyle's own insistence on the truth of the *Life* is intimately connected with his investment in Johnson as just such a figure. For him, Johnson was one of the chosen "whose existence was no idle Dream, but a Reality which he transacted *awake*."[9] Like Carlyle, we want to liberate Johnson from the text that delivers him to us so that, even if we ourselves only rarely, if at all, escape the unrealizedness that enshrouds us in daily life, we need not wholly surrender the possibility of doing so. The fancied bursting forth of the "real" Samuel Johnson from the pages of Boswell's biography is an image of our own potential liberation from the complex web of mediacy within which we are installed and which, worse still, largely constitutes us.

Given such an investment in the figure of Samuel Johnson, it is *necessary* that we elevate Johnson over Boswell and that we deny, explicitly or implicitly, that the Johnson in whom we are thus invested is in any sense Boswell's creation. This denial can even, by the same logic, amount to a denial of the possibility of biography, or of its worth. For to believe in the unmediated Johnson, especially to do so uncritically, requires that we counter or deny assertions of his mediacy, whether these take the form of insistences that anyone's life, Johnson's included, must be caught up in signifying systems, or that the illusion of Johnson's presence derives from the artistry of Boswell's biographical method. We need not, then, invoke either annoyance at Boswell's unheroic character or distrust of biography's claims to be genuinely literary in order to account for the strand in criticism of the *Life* that I have been trying to unravel. For to invest oneself in Johnson not just as a figure of presence but as an object of uncritical belief is to be required to demote both the *Life* itself as a work of biography and Boswell as its author. As Frank Kermode says of a strikingly comparable instance, the effort to read the Gospels critically, "It remains exceedingly difficult to treat them as stories, as texts totally lacking transparency on event," for we are "habituated to the myth of transparency." That habituation is especially powerful when our investment in the historical figure at the center of those texts—Jesus, Johnson—represents a possibility of liberation and realization that we refuse to surrender or to acknowledge as textually (or otherwise) derived.[10]

Interestingly, the literature of the Age of Sensibility tells a more complex story of such longing for presence. Here is Cowper in a mood at once nostalgic and skeptical:

> Would I had fall'n upon those happier days
> That poets celebrate; those golden times,
> And those Arcadian scenes, that Maro sings,
> And Sidney, warbler of poetic prose.
> . . . .
> Vain wish! Those days were never: airy dreams
> Sat for the picture; and the poet's hand,

Imparting substance to an empty shade,
Imposed a gay delirium for the truth.
Grant it:—I still must envy them an age
That favour'd such a dream.[11]

In an analogous fashion, Boswell's biography itself both insists on and denies the accessibility of the very immediacy that Johnson represents. For one thing, the *Life* appeared in 1791, over six years after Johnson's death had forever sealed the possibility of his being actually present to anyone again. Thus the historical pastness of Johnson becomes an emblem of the intransigent *thereness* (not hereness) that always keeps us from encountering the presentness of which we nevertheless cannot cease to dream. For another, as one of Boswell's shrewdest modern critics puts it, "the true subject of the *Life* . . . is the impossibility of the biographical enterprise, not presence but the illusion of presence ultimately revealed as an illusion, the dilemma of narrative trying and failing to reach through to a world beyond itself."[12]

The modern investment in the "real" Samuel Johnson thus recapitulates a fundamental gesture of the later eighteenth century: the search for repositories of presence, locations of the immediate, reservoirs of real existence. But in the Age of Sensibility, whether in Boswell or Gray or Cowper or even Ossian, this gesture is accompanied by various forms of skepticism, demystification, self-awareness, and knowledge of the impossibility of its success—even if, as in Cowper, the skepticism does not annihilate the dream. In this sense, the texts of the Age of Sensibility might be usefully brought to bear on modern criticism of the period, might teach us that to discover the sources or the textual embeddedness of our dreams is not necessarily to cease dreaming but only to know that we are doing so. Even Browning did not claim to see Shelley plain; he only saw someone else who had. It's always someone else who has.

THE CONFUSIONS OF THE HISTORICAL and the literary that the *Life* has endured are clearly invited by features of Boswell's biography, yet modern criticism has been unusually forward in accepting the invitation. It has been so, in part, because criticism of eighteenth-century English literature has proven more resistant than criticism of other periods to the incursions of recent critical theory. A reading of journals devoted to the eighteenth century shows quite clearly that contemporary theory is not, for most eighteenth-century specialists, a prominent part of the Knowledge Most Worth Having.[13] Such knowledge, of course, will not necessarily improve one's ability to interpret particular texts, but neither will an aggressively atheoretical posture. Murray Cohen has complained that "formalist critical assumptions still reign in eighteenth-century studies,"[14] but the truth, I think, is more disheartening still. For in too many instances recent discontent with formalist criticism has been invoked to license not a more advanced critical practice but an untroubled return to preformalist assumptions. One well-known critic of eighteenth-century literature recently remarked that we are about to advance beyond what he termed the "myth criticism" of Maynard Mack, Reuben Brower, and others and to recognize that Pope was a historical person involved in the political realities of his age. I do not see that this will be an advance, and I worry about the state of a field of specialization in which it can be regarded as one.

If anything, we need to continue the dehistoricizing that the formalists began so that, at the very least, we can pose more interesting and fruitful questions about the multiple determination—historical, literary, and so on—of a variety of texts. What we do not need is more annotation-as-criticism: the effort to interpret a text or passage by detailing the historical circumstances that may have surrounded or given rise to it, and to assume that those circumstances constitute its meaning. Such activity is precisely analogous to the claim that Boswell's text somehow delivers to us the historical Samuel Johnson, and it is as effective as that claim has been in stifling fresh interpretive activity.

The development of criticism of satire, from the late 1950s to the present, provides an interesting parallel to the critical fortunes of Boswell's *Life* (and of biography generally) because it illustrates the way in which an incomplete formalist critique of the historical has impoverished both formalism and historicism. The development falls into three stages. The first is the preformalist investigation of satire, devoted to unearthing historical targets: "Sporus" is really Lord Hervey; the Emperor of Lilliput is George I, though as Louis Landa wonderfully adds, "the descriptive details are not accurate";[15] and Timon is, well, someone historical, even if we don't quite know who.

The publication of such works as Mack's "The Muse of Satire," Northrop Frye's *Anatomy of Criticism*, and Alvin Kernan's *The Cankered Muse* inaugurated the second stage.[16] Now, whatever the historical circumstances that may have given rise to such satiric portraits as those of Sporus, Atossa, and others, those circumstances were not to be confused with the meaning and functioning of the portraits "in the poems." The opposition between satirist and victim was not a matter of personal spite, at least not within a framework of *critical* explanation. Rather, the attack, like the satirist's temperamental touchiness or the disordered scene he depicts, was to be understood as a generic requirement, like marriage at the end of a romantic comedy or suffering in a tragedy. Whatever the enmity between Pope and Hervey may have signified in historical reality, "Pope" versus Sporus was a particular instance of an eternal, symbolic conflict, what Pope elsewhere called "the strong Antipathy of Good to Bad."

Itself a historical phenomenon, of course, formalist criticism arose in part to defend the work of art against a style of reading that threatened to erase the distinction between a work and its historical context—the style of reading that I have called annotation-as-criticism. Without denying the existence of the historical sphere, formalism encouraged the abstraction of the literary work from that sphere in the interests of a criticism aimed at ascribing "universal" (that is, largely ahistorical) significance to formal patterns of all kinds. It was at this point that readers became able to conceive of the *Life of Johnson* as a coherent work of verbal art and not just a more or less accurate portrayal of Samuel Johnson.

The formalist approach, however, left something to be desired. The conflict between "Pope" and Sporus may be symbolic and universal, and it may take place purely within the confines of the *Epistle to Dr. Arbuthnot*, but that's not quite how it sounds when you read it. And a passage like the following seems still less a well-wrought Augustan urn, or a satiric Klein bottle turned back on itself:

> Come harmless *Characters* that no one hit,
> Come *Henley's* Oratory, *Osborn's* Wit!
> The Honey dropping from *Favonio's* Tongue,
> The Flow'rs of *Bubo*, and the Flow of Y——*ng!*
> The gracious Dew of Pulpit Eloquence;

And all the well-whipt Cream of Courtly Sense,
That first was *H——vy's, F——'s* next, and then
The *S——te's,* and then *H——vy's* once again.[17]

Like the countless references to names, places, and events that fill the pages of Boswell's *Life,* such a passage seems to require a return to annotation and thus to history, and this, more or less completely, is what took place in the development of satire criticism. A few years after the formalist arguments of Mack, Frye, and Kernan appeared, a counter-movement arose, or resurfaced, contending that satire is precisely that literary form that requires us to proceed from text to context. The following is one of the clearest statements of this position:

> All satire is not only an attack; it is an attack upon *discernible, historically authentic particulars.* The "dupes" or victims of punitive satire are not mere fictions. They, or the objects which they represent, must be, or have been, plainly existent in the world of reality; they must, that is, possess genuine historic identity. The reader must be capable of pointing to the world of reality, past or present, and identifying the individual or group, institution, custom, belief, or idea which is under attack by the satirist.[18]

At that moment in the history of criticism of satire, the historical road was partly resumed and the formalist road somewhat less confidently traveled. As a result, criticism of satire is precisely where it was twenty years ago: poised guiltily between a formalist analysis that seems incomplete and a historical analysis that seems retrograde and antiliterary. The typical activity of satire criticism in this, its third phase, is thus a form of fence-sitting: Sporus functions in such and such a way, but of course he represents Lord Hervey; or, Pope is attacking Lord Hervey in the Sporus portrait, but of course the portrait itself functions in such and such a way. (Ambivalence like this will be familiar to students of the *Life of Johnson,* since it pervades critical treatments of biography as well as satire.) This twenty-year fixation on a single critical gesture seems to have troubled few critics, even though it resembles nothing so much as a disastrous, compulsive repetition of an initially compromised effort of liberation.

What went wrong, and what might further progress down the formalist road have looked like? One thing is certain: it would have had to confront the challenges posed by a passage like the one quoted above from Pope's *Epilogue to the Satires,* a passage densely allusive, bristling with historical particularities, and seeming to require, by the ellipses in its name-calling, that we fill its gaps with history. An intenser formalism would have confronted such challenges, however, not by still more aggressive annotation but by distinguishing between reference (a relation between this text and that object) and referentiality (a textual gesture outward, whether to a historical object or not), and by formulating what might be called a rhetoric of the centrifugal, subclass satiric, capable of describing and interpreting—of lending meaning to—the repertoire of namings, pointings, allusions, and presuppositions that constitute one of the central conventions of satire: the assumption that there exists a historical world, "out there," elements of which are both solidly specifiable and distinct from the order of discourse in which they are specified. This convention, in fact, is one that satire shares with biography and, indeed, with virtually every literary form that we typically label "factual."

A useful place to begin might have been with the linguistic category of deixis, which allows us to distinguish centrifugal from centripetal gestures ("here" versus "there") without also requiring us to contend that every "here" or "there" presupposes a historical referent. From this point of view, the assertion that satire is "an attack upon *discernible, historically authentic particulars*" is not a description of satire's relation to historical reality but a claim that is an important convention of satire itself—indeed, one of satire's principal claims. To look for the particulars attacked is like searching for the real gods invoked by an epic poet instead of investigating the structure of invocation. This is not to say that we need know nothing of Walpole or George II to read Pope's satires, or of Goldsmith and Burke in order to read the *Life of Johnson*. Only that a critical account of those satires, or of the *Life*, will require us to interpret the function of those figures in the structure of the work and to interpret, as well, the very energy of referentiality that directs us to the extratextual world. In satire, referentiality and factuality are essential conventions, products of certain rhetorical strategies, and the kind of historical analysis to which we have mostly been treated blinds us to the nature and significance of those strategies.

Why, moreover, does the satirist engage in so much attack anyway? The usual answer, presupposing a historical world that gives rise to the poet's disapproval ("Mad Ireland hurt you into poetry," or "Fools rush into my Head, and so I write"), offers two possibilities: either the

world is unpleasant and so the satirist attacks it, or the satirist is unpleasant and so he attacks the world. In either case we start with historical reality, satirist's world or satirist's personality (whether high- or
low-minded). Again, what such an approach keeps us from investigating is a form of rhetorical activity: not gestures of referentiality, in this
case, but acts of exclusion, efforts of boundary-policing, and introduc-
tions of difference and distinction that create—rather than grow out
of—an opposition between the satirist and the satiric scene or world.
Such an approach could help to free criticism of satire from what has
been one of its most traditional and debilitating tasks: accounting for
features of a literary mode by turning one's attention away from
literature.

It could also go far to end the charade of moralistic apology in
which critics of satire have been encouraged to engage: justifying a
writer's satiric attacks by arguing that such attacks serve moral ends
and that the satirist may thus escape charges of negativism or superiority or attraction to the debased and repellent. (When this claim has
proven too difficult to sustain, critics have encouraged us to accept the
allegedly bracing fact that a satirist—usually Swift—may indeed be
motivated by prurient attraction to his subject matter. What remains
constant in both versions of this argument is the moral standard,
which the satirist's conduct affirms whether he honors or violates that
standard.)

Such defenses are based on the belief that gestures of exclusion,
and the passing of negative judgments generally, can be excused only
by positing a prior offense still more heinous. If we were to examine
the textual function of such acts of casting-out and exclusion, however, as we examine the function of acts of identification like invocation,
apostrophe, and free indirect discourse, we might begin to recognize
their necessity and indeed inescapability in whatever affirmations the
text puts forth. We would also see that the moral argument is intimately tied to a belief in satire as a response to preexisting reality, and
that these stand or fall together. I think they have stood for altogether
too long. It is a symptom of critical uneasiness with satire that Mary
Claire Randolph's argument of 1942—that formal verse satires attack
X and praise not-X—was taken as a major insight promising significant critical investigation.[19] Only an anxiety about the very idea of
attack or exclusion could have led critics to embrace so warmly an

argument that scarcely needed to be made, since the impulses of advocacy and exclusion are different aspects of a single, two-sided gesture.

Investigations like these, pushing the formalist inquiry beyond the major gains of the 1940s and 1950s, might have given us what we do not yet have: a general account of the strategies of referentiality, a rhetoric of biography comprehensive enough to make visible Boswell's remarkable transformations and thematizing of conventional elements in the *Life of Johnson,* and a rhetoric of satire adequate to the power, the subtlety, and the range of eighteenth-century satiric poetry and prose. And they might have given us something else as well: a powerfully worked-out formalist account of satiric textuality that any new historicism would have to match in order to compete with it. As it is, a half-hearted and guilty formalism has helped dig its own grave and has unintentionally ensured the slackness of a historicism that is too rarely distinguishable from the annotation industry of old or from the pious social insistences of a Leavis or the early Marxist critics. By losing faith in itself, that is, formalism made it too easy for its successors to succeed. Considering the incompletely worked-out idea of rhetoric and textuality offered by the formalist critics of satire and of biography, was a really powerful theory of the historical dimension of a text necessary? What gloomier evidence of the weakness of the case mounted by formalism could there be than this recent displacement of the impulse to mutilate library books?

> Would it not be better to break up [the *Life*] into the component parts which Boswell so loosely and perfunctorily strung together—to extract the parts deriving from the journal and publish them separately as *Boswell's Conversations with Johnson,* following the example of Eckermann? Does not whatever artistry Boswell contributed to the *Life* consist in them alone, and would not that artistry be enhanced by such a procedure?[20]

Given such a suggestion, it is difficult to deny that the formalists failed to teach many readers even the elements of what a text, critically conceived, might look like.

THE QUESTION OF BOSWELL'S "ARTISTRY" returns us to questions of value. It was not just against the reduction of literary texts to their historical origins that the formalists struggled (or, as we might now say, against the refusal to admit the possibility of conceiving a text ahistorically) but also against the displacement of questions of meaning by questions of value. The concern with history and the concern with value, moreover, are deeply related, and the more simply they are conceived the more they tend to converge. A powerful association between a literary text and historical reality, especially if that reality can somehow be conceived as residing within the text (never mind how), almost ensures two responses: the text will be valued more highly because of the historical association, and the act of evaluation will displace efforts of interpretation. In what remains, in many ways, the subtlest and most forthright discussion of literature and history in Boswell, "The Fact Imagined: James Boswell," W. K. Wimsatt enacts both of these responses, even though he did more than any other person to establish the theoretical basis for formalist analysis.[21] Of Boswell's account of the trial of John Reid, Wimsatt says: "This true drama refuses to be measured completely by the norms of the fictional" (p. 168); of Boswell's journal generally he remarks: "Boswell writes a true story—beyond question—and this . . . is one undoubted source of its peculiar power" (p. 182). And he offers this fuller statement of his position:

> Let the literary critic be ready to concede that for diaries and journals the conviction of the individual historic verity does count heavily. Given a certain degree of fictive, of symbolic, of universal interest in a writing, if then the fact be known also to be present, a great enhancement does occur. A measure even of dead weight in the design, of mere fact, will be tolerated and will work in its own way to fortify the imaginative substance.[22]

The operative terms in these passages belong to the vocabulary of value: "measured completely," "peculiar power," "count heavily," "a great enhancement," "fortify the imaginative substance." Wimsatt's essay has much to say, in an interpretive mode, about Boswell's journals, but when the central question of fact and imagination arises, his language becomes resolutely evaluative, and much the same can be said of the history of criticism of the *Life of Johnson*.

This is not to say that a more rigorous formalist analysis is what the factual requires. Since (as I would argue) "the factual" is not a feature of certain texts but the name for a relation between certain texts and extratextual reality, Wimsatt is correct to avoid submitting "the individual historic verity" to critical analysis. What he does not question, however, is whether the historical can be an intrinsic feature of a text. His language is heavily weighted toward a view of historical fact as precisely something that is *in* texts. He speaks of "the fact" as something that can "be *present*" in a writing, and of "a measure even of dead weight *in the design*, of mere fact," fact both present and operative, "working to fortify the imaginative substance." Both the fictive and the factual, in this language of distinct yet comparable and interactive substances, are things we may find in the textual complex, like the brown and the white in a marble cake.

The direction that formalist analysis might have taken but did not (in part because of its anxiety to secure "literariness" as a feature of certain texts so as to distinguish them from other kinds of linguistic construct: the languages of science and of everyday verbal intercourse, for example) would have involved a repudiation of the idea of the intrinsic: intrinsic value, intrinsic meaning, intrinsic literariness, intrinsic historicality or factuality. The consequences would have been multiple. First, questions about factuality or literariness would have been seen as questions about the perspective from which we view a text, or the framework within which we constitute it, or the demands we wish to make on it. Certainly, some texts might lend themselves more readily to a literary construction, and others to, say, a historical construction. But it would not always be obvious which texts these would be, and it would be clear that the same text could function in a variety of different and even heterogeneous ways. The effect for formalist analysis, moreover, would be the liberation of even more textual data. That is, every element in the text that had been regarded as part of its factual or historical "substance," and therefore impervious to a formalist analysis concerned only with the "literary" elements of the text, would now become properly the object of formalist critical analysis. At the same time, all those textual features regarded as intrinsically literary would be susceptible of historical analysis once the text was viewed from a historical rather than a literary-critical perspective.

The alliance of a concern with factuality and a concern with value, then, insofar as it has functioned as a debilitating, anti-interpretive force, rests on an untenable faith in the intrinsic, and it was the formalists' inability to criticize this faith—even to see it *as* a faith—that constituted the greatest single impediment to the realization of their project and to the subsequent criticism of that project by what might have been a rigorous, informed, and subtle historicism. As it is, the challenge to formalism (though it is rarely posed as such) has come from deconstruction, and some of the most promising recent efforts in eighteenth-century studies have attempted to stage a confrontation, at times a benign confrontation, between these two forces that, strictly speaking, have never encountered each other. Such a staging requires the production (in the geometric sense) of lines from a formalism encumbered by notions of the intrinsic to a deconstruction at times similarly compromised but more often unaware of the degree to which it depends on the closural and logocentric impulses that dominated the New Criticism, and unaware of the fact that *differance,* which is the name of a relation that both requires and denies the possibility of priority, is in one sense the hermeneutic circle—or even "organic unity"—seen from the other side.

Whether familiarity with recent critical theory is in itself a good thing, or whether it can significantly improve critical practice, are general questions that I do not wish to take up here. Such familiarity, however, holds a particular promise for eighteenth-century studies. By leading critics to investigate afresh the concept of the intrinsic and thus to see the degree to which this concept grounds a whole range of assumptions about "the literary" and "the historical" in eighteenth-century texts and modes (not just the satiric and the biographical), theoretical considerations might render more fruitful the dreary and often sterile debates that have marked eighteenth-century studies in the past few decades. One of the principal strengths of William C. Dowling's recent *Language and Logos in Boswell's "Life of Johnson,"* for example, is that it treats the topics of Johnson's presence, and of the mixture of what might have been called literary and historical elements of the text, in terms available to critical investigation. It does not, that is, reject the formalist contribution, but neither does it unquestioningly accept formalist notions of textual closure and unity and of the homogeneous discourse of a "literary text," or antiformalist notions of the *Life* as composed of mixed kinds of discourse—literary

and historical—that render parts of it critically unrecuperable. Instead of returning us to preformalist days, that is, or proceeding as
though formalism raised no issue that could possibly bear on contemporary criticism, this study attempts to go beyond formalism by taking
formalism beyond itself. As a result, it begins to heal what has looked
for some time now like the equivalent, in intellectual history, of trau-
ma resulting from an elided stage of development.

I do not know what the present state of eighteenth-century studies
would look like if the formalist analysis had proceeded further along
its initial lines instead of losing its nerve. I am fairly certain, though,
that it would have posed a far more difficult—and therefore far more
productive—challenge to the historicism that has in many quarters
taken its place. Such a challenge, and an adequate response to it,
would make clear that an informed historicism cannot do without the
significative power of formal patterns any more than deconstruction
can claim to dispense with "logocentric" categories of boundedness,
entity, meaning, and hierarchy. In the case of Boswell's *Life of Johnson*,
what has to be accounted for, whatever one's critical approach, is both
the power of the Johnsonian presence (or historical actuality) that the
work provides and the textual (or rhetorical or "literary") structures
that generate this illusion of presence.

The question of approach, moreover, may be less important than
the way in which an approach is understood and employed. Any text,
that is, is a multiply determined—or multiply construable—structure.
It can serve a variety of heterogeneous needs and accommodate a
variety of heterogeneous characterizations (heterogeneous to the
point of stark incompatibility). Recognizing this can, first, free us from
idle arguments about what a text "really" is ("Is Boswell's *Life*
biography or art?") and perhaps enable us to ask more searching
questions about a given text as it is viewed from one or another perspective. At the same time, the recognition of a text's multiple or over-
determined character can bring to the fore the necessarily partial
nature of the interpretive strategy on which we are engaged at any
given moment. This does not mean that every act of interpretation
should be conducted half-heartedly since it is only "an" interpretation. On the contrary, having decided to investigate, say, *Robinson
Crusoe* as a document in economic history, we should do so thor-

oughly, trying to discover how much of the text (projected as such a document) can be thus interpreted: not just its treatment of money, property, exchange, and so on, but anything else that is conceivably open to an economic interpretation. The idea that certain parts of a text naturally "belong to" strategies of reading—discussions of property to the Marxists, of dreams and sexuality to the psychoanalytic critics, of absence and marginality to the deconstructionists, for example—simply perpetuates the notion of the intrinsic that a recognition of the plural character of a text was designed, in part, to combat. As a given interpretation draws to a close, however, if not long before, the critic will become aware that certain features of the text yield relatively little to his present approach, though they promise to respond more fully to another, that certain features yield a great deal even as they promise to yield as much or more to a different approach, and that neither the multiplicity of the text's modes of signification nor our inability (much of the time) to support "the claim to unequivocal domination of one mode of signifying over another" constitutes an argument against interpretation in general or against a particular mode of interpretation.[23]

This is why the readiness to deny distinctions, or the import of distinctions, that is a fairly common feature of the contemporary critical scene seems to me both worrisome and traceable, in part, to what I have called the elided stage in the development of formalism. To restore that step, even privately and imaginatively, is to set against the various nonformalist interpretive procedures of our moment a worthy antagonist and one that, in its relative definability *as* an antagonist, can serve as an emblem of the inescapable role of difference and distinction—even though these must be criticized—in any enterprise that countenances multiplicity. As Murray Cohen writes of "fictions of connectedness, objectivity, and continuous identity" in Hume: "These functional illusions acquire a crucial status throughout Hume's writings, for they are both necessary *and* artificial."[24] To deny the necessity of such distinctions is to bring all thought to a grinding halt. To deny their artificiality is to prolong pointless debates about the true or essential character of Pope's political satires (politics or poetry?) or of Boswell's *Life of Johnson* (truth or art?). Debates like this at times rise to prominence in eighteenth-century studies, but far more often they exert an implicit and thought-retarding force on the investigation of major and minor texts that are still, in many ways, in serious need of patient, energetic, and inventive interpretation. By virtue of its scale, its greatness, its undeniable importance to critics of the eighteenth century, and its uncanny power to cloud the minds of otherwise sage and serious scholars, the *Life of Johnson* is one of the neediest of such texts.

Notes

1. Thomas Carlyle, "Boswell's Life of Johnson," in *Critical and Miscellaneous Essays*, 6 vols. (London: Chapman and Hall, 1869), 4:43. Compare F. A. Pottle's argument that the *Life* is rich in particulars because Boswell wished to demonstrate that Johnson was "a fact and not a fiction" ("The Adequacy as Biography of Boswell's *Life of Johnson*," *Transactions of the Johnson Society* [Lichfield, 1974], 9).

2. Frank Brady, introduction to James Boswell, *The Life of Samuel Johnson*, ed. and abridged by Frank Brady (New York: Signet, 1968), 16. Marshall Waingrow tries to bridge the gap between these two positions by showing that the accuracy of Boswell's presentation of Johnson's conversations is not "overall or complete" but a matter of "local verbal precision . . . key words and phrases" (Marshall Waingrow, ed., *The Correspondence and Other Papers of James Boswell Relating to the Making of the "Life of Johnson"* [New York: McGraw-Hill, 1968], xxxiv, n. 1). Such an argument, of course, moves between two very different ideas of "accuracy," and this movement recapitulates the debate it attempts to transcend. Something similar occurs in Elizabeth W. Bruss's stimulating account of the different Boswells that appear in the *Life* and in the *London Journal*. See her *Autobiographical Acts: The Changing Situation of a Literary Genre* (Baltimore: Johns Hopkins University Press, 1976), 71.

3. William Nelson, *Fact or Fiction: The Dilemma of the Renaissance Storyteller* (Cambridge, Mass.: Harvard University Press, 1973), 54–55.

4. Ralph W. Rader, "Literary Form in Factual Narrative: The Example of Boswell's *Johnson*," in Philip B. Daghlian, ed., *Essays in Eighteenth-Century Biography* (Bloomington: Indiana University Press, 1968), 12. Elsewhere in his essay, Rader offers a far more searching account of the factual, and this intermittent sophistication makes assertions like the one quoted in my text still more remarkable.

5. William C. Dowling, *The Boswellian Hero* (Athens: University of Georgia Press, 1979), 141. I have tried to investigate the question of Johnson's presence in chapter 5 of *Literature and Insubstantiality in Later Eighteenth-Century England* (Princeton: Princeton University Press, 1984).

6. G. B. Hill, ed., *Boswell's Life of Johnson*, rev. and enlarged by L. F. Powell, 6 vols. (Oxford: Clarendon Press, 1934–1964), IV, 427–428, my italics.

7. Lionel Trilling, *Sincerity and Authenticity* (Cambridge, Mass.: Harvard University Press, 1972), 93.

8. Ibid., 99.

9. Carlyle, "Boswell's Life of Johnson," 56.

10. Frank Kermode, *The Genesis of Secrecy: On the Interpretation of Narrative* (Cambridge, Mass.: Harvard University Press, 1979), 121, 118.

11. William Cowper, *The Task*, 4:513–530, my italics.

12. William C. Dowling, *Language and Logos in Boswell's "Life of Johnson"* (Princeton: Princeton University Press, 1981), 97.

13. See Murray Cohen's occasionally mechanical though often pertinent complaints in "Eighteenth-Century English Literature and Modern Critical Methodologies," in *The Eighteenth Century: Theory and Interpretation* 20 (1979): 5–23.

14. Ibid., 5.

15. Louis Landa, ed., *"Gulliver's Travels" and Other Writings by Jonathan Swift* (Boston: Houghton Mifflin, 1960), 503. Though this edition appeared in 1960, it is still, for the most part, governed by preformalist assumptions.

16. Maynard Mack, "The Muse of Satire," *Yale Review* 41 (1951): 80–92; Northrop Frye, *Anatomy of Criticism: Four Essays* (Princeton: Princeton University Press, 1957); Alvin B. Kernan, *The Cankered Muse* (New Haven: Yale University Press, 1959).

17. Alexander Pope, *Epilogue to the Satires*, "Dialogue I," lines 65–72.

18. Edward E. Rosenheim, *Swift and the Satirist's Art* (Chicago: University of Chicago Press, 1963), 23.

19. Mary Claire Randolph, "The Structural Design of Formal Verse Satire," *PQ* 21 (1942): 368–384. Randolph's work on satire, in this and other essays, is often acute and useful. My point here has to do with the inflation, by critics, of one of her points.

20. Donald J. Greene, "'Tis a Pretty Book, Mr. Boswell, But—," unpublished paper, p. 7, quoted in Richard B. Schwartz, *Boswell's Johnson: A Preface to the "Life"* (Madison: University of Wisconsin Press, 1978), 95.

21. W. K. Wimsatt, "The Fact Imagined: James Boswell," in *Hateful Contraries: Studies in Literature and Criticism* (Lexington: University of Kentucky Press, 1965), 165–183. Frank Brady, working from assumptions similar to Wimsatt's, provides a subtle account of the expectations many readers bring to what Brady terms "imaginative" and "memorial" works. See his *"Boswell's London Journal:* The Questions of Memorial and Imaginative Modes," in Jan

Fergus, ed., *Literature and Society: The Lawrence Henry Gipson Symposium* (Bethlehem, Pa.: The Lawrence Henry Gipson Institute, 1978), 33–47.

22. Ibid., 166. Wimsatt's argument here is roughly analogous to that of Roland Barthes in "L'Effet du réel," *Communications* 11 (1969): 84–89. See Martin Price's valuable discussion of Barthes's contention in *Forms of Life: Character and Moral Imagination in the Novel* (New Haven: Yale University Press, 1983), 35–36. Price's entire chapter (pp. 24–36) bears on the question of the fictive and the real.

23. Barbara Johnson, *The Critical Difference: Essays in the Contemporary Rhetoric of Reading* (Baltimore: Johns Hopkins University Press, 1980), 5.

24. Cohen, "Eighteenth-Century English Literature," 13.

WILLIAM R. SIEBENSCHUH

Boswell's Second Crop of Memory: A New Look at the Role of Memory in the Making of the *Life*

*P*eople familiar with Boswell's account of his first meeting with Johnson in the *Life* usually recall how Johnson rebuffs Boswell for an overfamiliar intrusion upon a conversation about David Garrick: "Sir, (said he, with a stern look,) I have known David Garrick longer than you have done: and I know no right you have to talk to me on the subject."[1] Neither this conversation nor the incident itself appears in the *London Journal 1762–1763*. The only hint of it there is a fragmentary note in the margin of the original manuscript: the letter *X* and the words "Mem Garrick refusing an order to Mrs. Williams and c."[2] Some twenty to twenty-five years later Boswell expanded this note into nineteen lines of dialogue and reflections.[3] Where did the specifics in the dialogue come from? Did Boswell simply invent them? Could he have remembered the incident and the dialogue accurately after nearly twenty-five years with only a somewhat cryptic note for a clue? Did he do so often? To try to answer such questions, I wish to revive the issue of the role played by Boswell's memory when he composed the *Life* by examining it in light of the enormous amount of research that has been done in the fields of human memory and perception in the years since Professor Pottle first applied such research to Boswell in his essay, "The Power of Memory in Boswell and Scott."[4]

Professor Pottle first raised the issue of the role of Boswell's memory some forty years ago and to my knowledge he has focused on it exclusively only once since then, in 1969 in an article written for James Clifford's edition of *Twentieth Century Interpretations of the "Life of Johnson"* ("The *Life of Johnson:* Art and Authenticity").[5] The basic argument of both articles is the same: that Boswell could remember the past with amazing accuracy; that his journalizing and indeed his whole life were a sort of continuous development of the ability and the skills needed to do so; and that the result is fundamentally different from fiction. The assumptions most fundamental to both articles are that substantial portions of Boswell's journals and the *Life* must have been reconstructed from memory after a lapse of weeks, months, and, in the case of the *Life,* years, and that many of the great conversations in the *Life* were never written up fully in the journals and therefore must have been reconstructed nearly completely in Boswell's memory at the time he wrote the *Life.* Professor Pottle is emphatic on this point. "In the *Life of Johnson,*" he tells us,

> the greater part of the extended Johnsonian conversations in which several speakers take part seems never to have been expanded in the journals at all. The only record Boswell had was frequently the rough notes written many years before. And even when he had before him a journal version which could have been transferred almost without change into the *Life,* one constantly finds additions which can only be explained, in my opinion, by assuming that even here he relived the scene as he copied it and recollected matter which had eluded him at the time he wrote the journal, or which he had then suppressed.[6]

In the essay written twenty years later Professor Pottle makes the same points: that the greater part of the extended Johnsonian conversations in the *Life* had never been expanded in the journals and that while composing from both rough notes and fully written journals Boswell regularly added "a second crop of memory gathered as he relived the matter he had copied."

Professor Pottle's inferences and information have been a matter of record for some years now, but I believe their implications have not been sufficiently pursued. What Boswell appears to have reconstructed in his memory is obviously not just a matter of factual details that are either accurate or not. If "the greater part of the extended Johnsonian conversations among several speakers" is involved, and if, as Professor Pottle suggests, relatively routine integration of a "second crop of memory" occurred during the making of the *Life,* then Boswell's memory must have been a major factor in the process of shaping the image of Johnson itself.

This raises a number of interesting possibilities. We are used these days to attributing the particular shape and implications of the image of Johnson in the *Life* to Boswell's art, to decisions made consciously or instinctively during what we might for convenience's sake call the composing process. It has become common to attribute changes or nuances in the portrait to artistic choice, and I have done so frequently. But what if it can be argued plausibly that some of the shaping we are familiar with, the frequent differences between a scene in the journal and the same scene in the *Life,* occurred in Boswell's memory—were done by his memory and then objictified by his art? What if what we might call "memory art" preceded—or superseded—literary art? Would we want to alter our estimate of Boswell's achievement? Would we be tempted to change our beliefs about the generic status of the portrait of Johnson? Would our critical perspective change at all?

An obvious place to begin to try to answer such questions is with the current view of how our memories work. It is common now to talk about three stages in the memory process: perception itself (the initial registering of sights, sounds, and other sensations), temporary storage of some of these perceptions in what is called "short term memory" (STM), and permanent storage of selected memories in what is called "long term memory" (LTM). It is now generally agreed that neither Boswell nor anyone else would have registered and recorded experiences indiscriminately, like a camera in a bank.[7] Each stage of the memory process is selective, and perception is a good example. We can only remember what we perceive in the first place, and because our minds are literally bombarded with sense impressions each moment, they filter them ruthlessly and exclude all but a few. This is a vital defense mechanism (like our ability to forget), for if we actually registered all the sense impressions we are exposed to, Pope would be right—we'd "die of a rose, in aromatic pain" (just as, if we remembered everything we recorded, our lives would be choked with memories we didn't want or need).

This process of selective registering and recording has a personal dimension. The filter that admits a chosen few sensory stimuli for possible storage in our memories is in some respects unique to each of us. It is conditioned by our particular interests, our life experiences, and our expectations. We notice and remember most easily things that we are looking for in the first place, things that we expect, or that our biases cause us to assume and focus on. Sometimes, as startling research with eyewitness testimony has shown, we imagine we remember things that weren't there at all.[8]

In the next stage, short term memory, a similar process of selection occurs. Most of the sensory stimuli our minds allow us to perceive are kept only briefly. Most items remain for about fifteen to twenty seconds, and we can juggle only six or seven items at a time. Short term memory is where we usually keep data like the telephone number we need to "memorize" only long enough to get it dialed correctly, or the number of the last check we wrote before we turned the page in our bank book, and so on. For our own protection we quickly jettison most of what we keep temporarily. In a given day only a small percentage will be retained in long term memory.

There is currently some debate about the degree of ultimate permanence of experiences stored in long term memory and also about their accessibility to us after long periods of time. About the general nature of long term memory, however, there seems to be broad consensus. It is, says Professor Elizabeth Loftus, "practically limitless, resembling a huge library with millions of books stashed away on the shelves."[9] Some decades ago some rather amazing evidence gathered in the process of electrical stimulation of the surface of the brain during surgery on epileptics suggested that no matter how deeply buried or for how long, memories we do store permanently can be recalled and possibly even relived. This view has been qualified since, but there is general agreement that memories can be stored permanently and most debate now centers around the issues of retrievability and changes in our memories while they are in storage.[10] For although there is compelling evidence that records can remain for years in our memories in their original state, there is also general agreement that we routinely alter permanently stored memories and can reshape them over time. To greater or lesser degrees we all apparently rewrite and update our own pasts.[11]

The relationship of all this to the making of the *Life of Johnson* should have begun to be obvious. And at this point, if we can agree to assume that Boswell's memory played an important role in the making of the final version of the *Life*, and if we accept, at least in general, the current view about how our minds work when we remember, then it seems to me that we need to ask some pointed questions. For example, in light of the clinical research done in the past twenty or thirty years, can we still believe that Boswell actually stored as much material about Johnson as he is supposed to have and then successfully retrieved it at the distance of so many years? How might Boswell's personality, experience, and expectations have affected his initial perceptions of Johnson? Or, how might the memories Boswell stored permanently have been altered over time? (That is, how much rewriting of his own past might Boswell have done?) And finally, how—if at all—do the answers to the first three questions affect our attitudes about Boswell's achievement in the *Life*?

To begin with, recent clinical work suggests strongly that indeed Professor Pottle's faith in Boswell's ability to record and retrieve Johnsonian memories is justified. Pottle correctly begins at the level of perception, since Boswell could retrieve only what he had stored in the first place.[12] And whole batteries of recent clinical research confirm what common sense already suggests: out of the welter of impressions we encounter daily we perceive and impress in our memories what we are most interested in. The degree to which an event, a fact, or a person will bite deep is in direct proportion to its importance to us, the intensity of our emotional involvement with it, and the degree to which we focus our attention upon it.[13] We do not need to accept Fanny Burney's rather cruel caricatures to tell us where Boswell's interests and attention most often lay when he was in Johnson's presence. Indeed, that persons of the historical stature and importance of Goldsmith, Burke, and Gibbon often have a shadowy and incomplete existence in many of the great conversations may be due to nothing more mysterious than the fact that Boswell was more often remembering than reflecting analytically upon information and research. His attention may never have been focused on them in the way it was on Johnson, and he would have had few if any concrete memories to reconstruct, because he had stored few concrete memories in the first place.[14]

Since permanent storage is linked so directly to interest, attention, and intensity of emotional involvement, there is surely little doubt that Boswell could genuinely have stored quantities of the kinds of Johnsonian memories that fill his journals and the *Life*. That next question, then, is, having stored such memories, how credible is it that he could actually have retrieved them in any state of completeness many years later with little more than a key word or phrase to build on? Professor Pottle claims that "Given the right kind of jog to his memory, Boswell had something that looks like total recall." When he did not have a fully written journal to rely on, Boswell's jogs to his memory were rough, often cryptic and abbreviated notes usually jotted down on odd scraps of paper. Cryptic and fragmentary as the notes were, however, they seem to have been the key to his ability to recall. As Professor Pottle explains, if Boswell "failed to make a written record soon after a series of events, he seems to have lost those events permanently, or at least to have no greater recall than the next person. But," Pottle argues, "given his written clue, and given time and patience, he could reconstruct accurately and in minute detail an account of practically everything that ever happened to him."[15]

Since stored memories are valuable to us only if we can retrieve and use them, our retrieval systems have become the objects of much interest and research. Though our ignorance of specifics—especially the biology of the storage and retrieval process—is great, there is consensus about how the system works in general.[16] Given the relative ease with which we can use our memories, it seems clear that we all have ready access to substantial amounts of information in LTM (or how would we remember where we parked our car, how to get to work, or how to find the house we lived in ten years ago?). Recent research suggests that to help us find stored items quickly we have in our minds an indexlike apparatus that is in fact cross-indexed by means of extremely sophisticated neural networks that provide a web of interlinked paths to particular memory records. We can retrieve a particular bit of information by seeking it along any of a number of different paths till we find a viable associative chain. This is what we do when, in trying to remember a person's name, we try, alternatively, to visualize him, visualize settings in which we commonly see him, recall particular events at which we were both present, and so on. We try various associative paths till we find one that leads to the information we want. If, by accident or design, adequate associative groundwork is laid when the memory is stored initially, if the retrieval paths are well formed, and especially if they are used often, then the details can usually be successfully retrieved even after quite long periods of time.

Given this model for retrieving permanently stored memories, Professor Pottle's inferences about what we would now call Boswell's retrieval system stand up rather well. According to current theory, the act of making even "cryptic and fragmentary" notes would have helped fix a given memory in Boswell's mind in the first place and would have established one (or probably more) retrieval paths. (The fact that Boswell could retrieve *only* material he had made written note of seems to confirm this dramatically.) Boswell's well-known lifetime habituation to this method of preserving items in his journals would have enhanced his ability to impress things in his memory, store them permanently, and recall them successfully later. Because the writing and rewriting would have constituted acts of both rehearsal and reenactment, they would enhance retrieval by firmly establishing pathways and multiple associations. Professor Pottle observes of Boswell's notes that "there appears to be no attempt to select what is important," suggesting that Boswell knew that one sort of hint would serve as well as another. Research now suggests that Boswell probably learned this from experience. As Professor Loftus emphasizes, "Almost anything can serve as a retrieval cue. A sight. A smell. A word. Flames pouring from a burning pot on the stove can bring to mind all we know about fires."[17]

Professor Pottle suggests that once Boswell had made his notes, the events they contained might be recalled at will, the fullness of the recovery depending less upon the interval of time than upon his patience and ability to concentrate his attention.[18] Interestingly, recent information suggests not only that this is an essentially accurate surmise but also that many of the strategies Boswell used when he composed the *Life* involve exactly the kind of mental acts that have been shown to stimulate the ability both to store memories and to recall them better. For instance, it is now clear that an important aid to our memories is the use of "landmarks," particular events in our lives that are especially important to us—birthdays, weddings, regular occurrences, and so on.[19] A moment's reflection reminds us how often in the *Life* Boswell organizes his material at and around landmarks in this sense. There is the year in which he first met Johnson, the fateful day itself; there are the formally announced annual moments when he can escape Scotland and return to Johnson's company, the first time at the club after his return, and so on. In the climactic movement toward the account of Johnson's death (at which Boswell was *not* present) he locates moments at which he was present as "the last time at the club," "the last time he visited Johnson," "the last time he actually saw him," and so on. That he does not always so organize the same material where it exists in fully written form in the journals suggests that because this use of landmarks often occurred as he was composing the *Life* it may not only have aided the clarity of recall, it may also have been a factor contributing to that "second crop of memory" of which Professor Pottle speaks.

Similarly with another common technique of Boswell's. The following is a list from the *Life* of the beginnings of a series of separate Johnsonian episodes between the dates 19 to 28 April 1778.

—On Sunday, April 19, being Easter-Day, after the solemnities of the festival at St. Paul's Church . . .
—Saturday, April 25, I dined with him at Sir Joshua Reynolds's . . .
—Found him at home in the morning . . .
—We went to the drawing-room, where there was considerable increase of company . . .
—On Tuesday, April 28, he was engaged to dine at General Paoli's . . . (III, 316–324)

Everyone will recognize here Boswell's habitual method of minimally anchoring the substantial conversations that often follow entries like these in space and time. A modern student of memory would recognize in this technique an analog of some of the methods commonly used to help people jog their memories or learn to increase recall.

One method is what is called the use of loci—the intentional association of things we want to remember with locations we are familiar with and can see in our mind's eye. Recall the place—the locus— which is easy and you can recall the items you have made yourself associate with it. Intentionally associate the one with the other and you can help fix items more firmly in your memory and make them more readily retrievable. I have not counted, but I suspect that the number of places in which the major Johnsonian conversations take place is relatively small, all of them quite familiar to Boswell. Whatever Boswell's conscious policies were when he composed the *Life*, it is hard not to imagine that the *effect* of even such nominal but habitual location of conversations in familiar named places did not work in the same way and that subsequent recall of the place did not aid in the recovery of secondary details.

The second method suggested by this list, though less definitely, is the use of scenes and the reconstruction of settings to help us remember the events that took place in them. At first glance this is a method that scarcely seems applicable in Boswell's case. His imagination was not visual, as Professor Pottle and others have pointed out. Though we may get an occasional detail like the "fine print of a beautiful female figure" that Wilkes archly pointed out to Johnson, we don't see many more rooms or scenes in Boswell than we do in Jane Austen. Boswell does, however, keep track of people, and in his notes he keeps track of subjects of conversations. "On Thursday, April 9," he tells us, "I dined with [Johnson] at Sir Joshua Reynolds's, with the Bishop of St. Asaph, (Dr. Shipley,) Mr. Allan Ramsay, Mr. Gibbon, Mr. Cambridge, and Mr. Langton" (III, 250). All will recognize here another of Boswell's habitual formulas, and having done so will, I hope, allow me to suggest that the names of people and notes of the subjects discussed may have acted as a jog to Boswell's memory in the same way that visual details help others. Indeed, in a familiar small group particular people could easily become associated with points of view and conversational topics habitual to them, so that those persons recalled conversation and vice versa.

Let me make a final, even more speculative suggestion. Two techniques sometimes used to help people increase their ability to keep items in their memories and recall them later are methods that require subjects to formally organize items they wish to remember or "weave them into a story." Usually when this has been the subject of clinical experiment it has been made a matter of mnemonic "tricks"— making up a crazy story that includes all the items on a shopping list, or often simplistic spatial and visual games played with items in a se- ries.[20] I do not mean to suggest direct parallels to Boswell here. But from the earliest days of his journalizing he had been habituating himself to organize his memories chronologically or dramatically; he was habituated to weaving his most important memories into a story. In short, he had for years been habituated to a whole spectrum of mental acts that clinical research and experiment now amply confirm to be directly related to our abilities to record and retrieve memories successfully. Thus, that Boswell was capable of the powers of retrieval he has been credited with is, I think, as believable as his ability to store the records in the first place. The final questions, then, are how did he remember them? and were they likely to have been altered substan- tially over time? Professor Pottle argues that Boswell's most remark- able feat "is that he combined the full recall of the savage or the mo- ron with the selectivity of the artist."[21] Without dubbing Boswell either a savage or a moron, we shall now turn to the question of the selectivity of Boswell's memory and the possibility of distortion.

The issue of selectivity involves both the question of how Boswell's initial perceptions would have been affected by his personality, expe- riences, and expectations and the question of how he might have re- written his own past at the time he was writing the *Life*. Some immedi- ate and obvious concessions must be made about the selectivity of Boswell's memory. If memory is an important factor in the making of the *Life*, then without question the perceptions and therefore the ini- tial memory records of Johnson that Boswell is likely to have stored permanently would have been of the events and statements that most directly reflected his own interests and fulfilled the expectations and confirmed the assumptions he had. When Boswell makes his famous comment that he got better at recording Johnsonian materials as he became more fully "impregnated with the Johnsonian aether" it seems simply a way of saying that his retention and recall increased as his interest and attention were heightened and as his expectations about Johnson became more precise and specific. Critics have been noting for years now that Boswell's portrait of Johnson is focused primarily on Boswell's own interests rather than on those of an imagined audience of future scholars. To the extent that this is true, it seems less likely due to faulty rhetorical or biographical choice than to the fact that the image of Johnson in the *Life* owes as much to Boswell's memory as to his researches.

The possibility that Boswell's memory records may have changed over time is more interesting. To get memory records of Johnson, Boswell had to recall his own past. Virtually all current research indicates that it is not only possible but common for us to rewrite our pasts when we remember. And apparently we can even change the memories themselves while they are in storage. The question we need to ask, therefore, is how altered—or unaltered—might Boswell's memories of Johnson have been?

Consensus among memory experts is that when we record a memory permanently we store what they describe variously as "fragments" or "bits and pieces of our experience." When we store these bits and pieces of experience, our minds apparently play an editorial role. The brain condenses them for us, says Professor Loftus: "It seems to edit the boring parts in order to highlight the interesting parts and cross-reference them for storage."[22] When we recall stored information and reconstruct a memory our minds are equally constructive. When we successfully remember an event, Loftus says, "We can usually recall only a few concrete facts or bits, and using these facts we construct other facts."[23] We fill gaps unconsciously with inferences supplied by common sense, by our expectations and biases, and sometimes by our present needs and desires. When the fragments of experience we retain have been integrated thus to make sense for us, they form what we call a memory. Furthermore, there is strong evidence that suggests that we can, in effect, update old memories, that we can rewrite them repeatedly in a continuously changing present. At present there is much debate about whether original memories, once altered, are changed forever, or whether successive new versions of a memory exist simultaneously with the old.[24] What seems clear, says Professor Loftus, is that "Whenever a memory for an event is called to consciousness, the potential appears to be there of substitution or alteration to occur ... we have a mechanism for updating memory that sometimes leaves the original memory intact, but sometimes does not."[25]

OBVIOUSLY SUCH EVIDENCE of the potential fragility and alterability of our memories provides grist for a Boswellian skeptic's mill. A completely skeptical—perhaps I should say "cynical"—scenario might offer a picture of Boswell giving to the airy nothings of the anxieties and neuroses of his later years a local habitation and the name of Samuel Johnson. But I believe that a moment's reflection and common sense will dispel such an image. The response of people who knew Johnson and were present at some of the scenes Boswell dramatizes does not suggest that his portrait of Johnson is either fantasy or a serious distortion. Either all of their memories were as bad as Boswell's and were altered in much the same ways or Boswell's memories were fundamentally true to the original. The image of Johnson in the *Life* is consistent enough with the image we get from Mrs. Piozzi, from Hawkins, and from Johnson's own works to suggest that whatever differences we sense are legitimate differences of inference and interpretation, the predictable results of what we might call different media of perception looking at the same object. In plainer English, the Johnson who seemed a "gross feeder" to Mrs. Thrale and whose appetite suggested to Boswell that "everything about his manner was forcible and violent" is the same Johnson—the stone in the midst of all.

When Boswell actually began to write the first draft of the *Life of Johnson* in 1786 he had at his disposal a multitude of Johnsonian records, some of which he had been accumulating since 1763 and some of which he had begun to solicit and gather soon after Johnson's death in 1784. He had his own records: his correspondence with Johnson, his fully written journals, and the fragmentary notes and cryptic phrases that served as the jogs to his memory. He also had the wealth of anecdote and copies of correspondence he had been collecting from others in preparation for his great undertaking.[26] The story of how all this material came together in his mind and took the final shape it did, the dynamics of the relationship between psychic pressures from the present and explicit data from the past, of the gray areas that may have mixed memory and desire—all this is a story still to be told, or at least attempted. Obviously, I shall not attempt it here.

Let me conclude, however, with the following, admittedly limited speculations.

When Boswell wrote the *Life* he was not working from memory in the way that we would be if we were suddenly pressed to name the third baseman for the Chicago White Sox in 1963 or to remember an essentially contextless incident from years ago. He was treading associative paths well worn to begin with, and his reconstructive imagination must have been controlled and guided by his own fully written records as well as the anecdotes of others. During the years when he was writing the *Life* his immersion in such a large body of concrete written records—many of them not his own—would almost certainly have continuously conditioned, shaped, and reinforced his already well-formed and highly specific expectations, so that when he did reconstruct scenes and events in memory he would have filled gaps and supplied "constructive facts" that were fundamentally consistent with his material of record and with the habits for Johnsonian recall he had developed in the course of twenty years. He would have constructed memories that "made sense" in these terms. Last-minute inventions, that is, would scarcely have been possible. As he was composing the first draft of the *Life* the relationship between the data and the memories was most probably reciprocal. If data conditioned and influenced memory, memory must also have influenced interpretive dramatization of data, Boswell's mind continually reconciling the one with the other. This might explain, at least in part, why the vision of Johnson the *Life* projects is so coherent in spite of the book's apparently loose and diffuse structure. This coherency may be as much the result of the forces at work on Boswell's perceptions and constructive memory as of any pattern of artistic choice. Or, in a work like the *Life*, it may be pointless to talk of biographical art or constructive memory as separable issues.

Is Boswell's portrait "slanted" or demonstrably "conditioned" by his memory? It seems certain that the assumptions, needs, and pressures Boswell felt at the time he composed the *Life* would have conditioned his memories to some extent. All men are mortal in this way. Boswell was a man. And so on. Without question Johnson meant different things to Boswell in 1786 than he did in 1763. In dozens of more or less subtle ways, their relationship was different and so were Boswell's

life and needs. Throughout the *Life*, in obvious ways, Boswell dramatizes the past in the context of the present; his vision of Johnson the
man is clearly the father of his vision of Johnson the child in the *Life*.
But we know a good deal now about the ways Boswell shaped and
reshaped his fully written record, and it seems most likely that the
pressures that influenced this treatment of his written records would
have acted upon him similarly when he reconstructed memories from
fragmentary notes. The strongest influences operating on Boswell's
reconstructive memory would have been pressure toward consistency
with his conscious perceptions of Johnson, certainly not toward invention or elaborate embroidery unchecked by his concrete external
records. Given what we know now about how our memories operate,
Professor Pottle's discussion of Boswell's reconstruction of Johnsonian
dialogue seems to me an accurate general description of the interpretive or constructive role Boswell's memory must have played in
the *Life*. The conversations we encounter are what Pottle calls "epit-
omes" or "miniatures." They are not verbatim except in "particular
sentences and in some brief passages of an epigrammatic cast." "The
crucial words," says Pottle,

> the words that impart the peculiar Johnsonian quality, are indeed *ip-
> sissima verba*. Impregnated with the Johnsonian ether, Boswell was able
> confidently to recall a considerable body of characteristic diction. Words
> entail sense; and when elements of the remembered diction were in bal-
> ance or antithesis, recollection of words and sense would almost auto-
> matically give "authentic" sentence structure . . . [and Boswell's intuitive
> sense of "Johnsonness" would] help him construct epitomizing sentences
> in which the *ipsissima verba* would be at home.[27]

I suggest that Boswell's fully written journals and other documents
were equivalents of the nuggets of *ipsissima verba*. It seems likely that,
as in the case of the extended conversations, Boswell's memory constantly helped him reconstruct the dramatic and interpretive contexts
that would be the equivalents of "epitomizing sentence structures" in
which his fragments of Johnson could be at home.

That Boswell's reconstructive memory may have been an important
factor in the making of the *Life of Johnson* is an issue that seems to me
to be ultimately separable from the affective dimension of his art. The
art may objectify the memories, but it neither creates nor controls

them. And in my view the most important legacy of Boswell's memory is neither its comprehensiveness nor its factual accuracy, though both are remarkable. The most important legacy of Boswell's memory is precisely the principles of selectivity that were peculiar to Boswell, the facts about his much maligned character that made him such a special medium of perception. While they may narrow our focus to subjects of interest and importance to Boswell, they also narrow our focus to some of his deepest psychic needs, needs that have nothing to do with his politics, or monarchical principles, or aristocratic prejudices— needs, I suggest, that a great many of us share. When he composed the *Life*, therefore, Boswell's memories provided an antidote not only to his own inadequacies, but to ours.

Notes

1. James Boswell, *The Life of Johnson*, ed. G. B. Hill, rev. and enl. L. F. Powell (Oxford: Clarendon Press, 1964), I, 395. Subsequent references to the *Life* are from this edition.

2. *London Journal 1762–1763*, manuscript original.

3. Professor Pottle, who helped me find this example in the manuscript of the *London Journal 1762–1763*, confirms that there is no evidence that Boswell ever expanded this note elsewhere until he began to compose the draft of the *Life* between 1784 and 1786.

4. Frederick A. Pottle, "The Power of Memory in Boswell and Scott," in *Essays on the Eighteenth Century Presented to David Nichol Smith* (Oxford: Clarendon Press, 1945), 168–189.

5. Frederick A. Pottle, "The *Life of Johnson:* Art and Authenticity," in *Twentieth Century Interpretations of Boswell's "Life of Johnson,"* ed. James L. Clifford (Englewood Cliffs: Prentice-Hall, 1970), 66–73.

6. Pottle, "The Power of Memory in Boswell and Scott," 176.

7. In this and the following discussion of the nature of human memory I depend heavily on three excellent sources, each of which provides a concentrated and highly readable summary of current work in the fields of memory, perception, neurology, and the cognitive sciences. These sources are Elizabeth Loftus, *Memory* (Reading: Addison-Wesley, 1980); George Ojemann and William Calvin, *Inside the Brain* (New York: Mentor, 1980); and Morton Hunt, *The Universe Within: A New Science Explores the Human Mind* (New York: Simon and Schuster, 1982).

8. See esp. Loftus, *Memory*, chapter 8, "The Power of Suggestion," 149–169.

9. Ibid., 15.

10. See Ibid., esp. 20–33, and see also Elizabeth and Geoffrey Loftus, "On the Permanence of Stored Information in the Human Brain," *American Psychologist* 35, no. 5 (1980): 409–420; and R. M. Shiffrin and R. C. Atkinson, "Storage and Retrieval Processes in Long-Term Memory," *Psychological Review* 76, no. 2 (1969): 179–193. For extended discussion of findings based on epileptic surgery, see Wilder Penfield and Phanor Perot, "The Brain's Record of Auditory and Visual Experience," *Brain* 86, part 4, (December 1963): 596–695; and also Ojemann and Calvin, *Inside the Brain.*

11. See Loftus, *Memory*, esp. chapter 7, "The Consequences of Imperfect Memory," 119–147.

12. Pottle, "The Power of Memory in Boswell and Scott," esp. 176–180.

13. See Ojemann and Calvin, *Inside the Brain*, esp. chapter 6, "Learning and Remembering: How Are Memories Recorded?" 55–67; and Loftus, *Memory*, chapter 2, "How Memory Works," 13–33.

14. Loftus, *Memory*, 13–33.

15. Pottle, "The Power of Memory in Boswell and Scott," 175.

16. For a brief but concise discussion of the biology of the memory process, see esp. Ojemann and Calvin, *Inside the Brain*, 64–67.

17. Loftus, *Memory*, 32.

18. Pottle, "The Power of Memory in Boswell and Scott," 175.

19. See Loftus, *Memory*, esp. chapter 9, "Computerizing Memory," 171–190.

20. Ibid.

21. Pottle, "The Power of Memory in Boswell and Scott," 175.

22. Loftus, *Memory*, 27–28.

23. Ibid., 40.

24. See esp. Loftus's discussion of the malleability of memory, 38–41.

25. Ibid., 47.

26. The obvious first source for information about the materials Boswell had available when he began to compose the *Life* is still Marshall Waingrow in his introduction to *The Correspondence and Other Papers of James Boswell Relating to the Making of the "Life of Johnson"* (New York: McGraw-Hill, 1969), xxi–li.

27. Pottle, "The *Life of Johnson*," 71–72.

DONALD GREENE

'Tis a Pretty Book, Mr. Boswell, But—

*W*hen was the golden age of English biography? I am inclined to answer, "We are in the midst of it." Consider the host of fine biographies that have appeared in recent years—Randolph Churchill and Martin Gilbert's still unfinished life of Winston Churchill, with its supplementary volumes of documentation; A. J. P. Taylor on Beaverbrook, James Pope-Hennessy on Queen Mary, John Grigg on Lloyd George, to mention some lives of public figures; Quentin Bell on Virginia Woolf, Peter Stansky and William Abrahams on George Orwell, Michael Holroyd on Lytton Strachey, Evelyn Waugh's sensitive life of Ronald Knox, Richard Ellmann's masterly biography of Joyce, to mention some literary ones. I have confined myself here to biographies of recently deceased individuals of the generation immediately preceding that of the biographer in order to draw a parallel to Boswell's situation in writing the *Life of Johnson*. But the list could be greatly expanded by including works where there is a greater time-span between biographer and biographee—John Brooke on George III, for instance; Geoffrey Faber on Jowett, Robert Blake on Disraeli, John Clive on Macaulay, and, most recently, the superb first installment of Joseph Frank's biography of Dostoevsky.

The point is that high standards for biography have been established and have come to be demanded of the would-be biographer. The dull, sloppy, whitewashing Victorian biographies described by Strachey, "with their ill-digested masses of material, their slipshod style, their tone of tedious panegyric," will no longer do. I will try to formulate some of the more obvious requirements with which a reputable modern biographer is expected to comply.

1. The work must be based, not on rumor or legend, but on the fullest and hardest available evidence. Every effort must be made to track down relevant records—official registrations of births, marriages, deaths, education, financial transactions, employment; letters to, from, and about the subject; diaries, newspaper items, conversations with those who knew the subject. The biographer must make himself familiar with everything written by his subject, from private memoranda to published volumes. If the subject devoted much of his attention to a particular branch of learning or a particular occupation, the biographer must acquire more than a superficial knowledge of it. No one with a mere smattering of twentieth-century British political history could produce a satisfactory life of Beaverbrook; no one less thoroughly versed than Waugh in Anglican and Catholic theology and church history could have produced an adequate life of Knox. And the biographer must make himself thoroughly familiar with the environment, physical, social, and intellectual, in which the subject lived at every stage of his life—if need be, going so far, as my teacher James Clifford has recently been doing, as to carry out extensive primary research into the sanitary arrangements in Gough Square, London, in the 1750s to satisfy himself, as he puts it, about just what happened to the contents of Samuel Johnson's chamber pot.

2. The evidence, when obtained, must be evaluated, always with a skeptical eye. The modern biographer will not, for instance, trust an older edition of a diary or a correspondence, knowing how older, and sometimes newer, editors will falsify them, but will seek out the original documents whenever possible. When the evidence is at second or third hand, he will ponder the reporter's reputation for reliability and will try to find out what the reporter's means were of knowing whatever it is that he retails. He will be vividly aware of how apocryphal anecdotes and *bons mots* attach themselves to well-known figures like Churchill and Johnson and be on the lookout for them. Part of every biographer's preparation ought to be a course of reading in the popular humor of his subject's time and earlier, so that he will recognize an old chestnut when attached to his subject and firmly eschew it (well,

perhaps occasionally, for light relief, allowing himself the luxury of recording something particularly *ben trovato* in a footnote, accompanied by a firm disclaimer). When attempting to analyze his subject's beliefs and values, he must carefully distinguish between the evidentiary value of his spoken and his written words.

3. When presenting his reader with excerpts from his evidence, he must be scrupulously honest. If what he is giving is his own paraphrase or adaptation of the primary source, he must not mislead his readers into thinking that it is anything else. If quoting an excerpt from a document, he must respect its context and not let his readers think it means more or less than what it means within that context.

4. The biography should be complete and continuous within the period it purports to be treating, whether this is the whole of the subject's life or only a portion of it. The reader should come away with a reasonably clear and coherent idea of how the subject occupied his time at all periods during the stated scope of the biography. It will not do to say, "Between the ages of nineteen and twenty-five, Orwell was a policeman in Burma. But since Burma is something which I know nothing about, and which would probably only bore the reader anyway, and furthermore, since Orwell did no writing there and we are primarily concerned with him as a writer, I shall skip over these six years and resume when Orwell returns to England and settles down at his typewriter." If, of course, there are gaps for which evidence is simply unavailable, the biographer must say so, and convince his reader that he has made an honest effort to uncover such evidence.

5. The canon of completeness and continuity, however, must not be taken to justify lack of discrimination between what is important and what is not. It would be wrong to pass over Orwell's Burma years in silence. At the same time it would be wrong to give every detail of his routine as a policeman during those years with the same emphasis as the details of his work as a writer. T. S. Eliot's letter rejecting *Animal Farm* for Faber and Faber and reports from other publishers' readers should be printed in full; a few significant samples from his superiors' reports on his police work in Burma (if available) would suffice. Very properly, a reviewer in the *Times Literary Supplement* (29 June 1973) complained of some recent biographies—chiefly American, one suspects—that "seem little more than literary data banks," in danger of

being "buried under heaps of accumulated rubbish. . . . One need not take five volumes to tell a story" (p. 735). If it seems important to make accessible to the reader the full documentary sources for the biography, it is surely better to print these separately, as Randolph Churchill and as Aleyn Lyell Reade (in his *Johnsonian Gleanings*) did, as "companion volumes," distilling from them a readable narrative, the biography proper, not resorting to the lazy method of faggoting one's data as they fall.

This is perhaps not very different from saying that a good biography should be well written. I quote the same reviewer, who is (rightly) praising Norman and Jeanne Mackenzie's biography of H. G. Wells: "A biography that could serve as a model to other practitioners in this difficult field. . . . Their treatment of Wells's life is full, but it is not inflated, and it is never boring; clearly the Mackenzies agree that the writing of biography is a narrative art, that it must have clarity and movement, and must be kept free of . . . congestions of unassimilated facts."

6. Finally, the biographer's attitude toward his subject. It is hard to deny that for a biography to be successful the biographer must feel a deep basic sympathy or attraction toward his subject. He must at least feel strongly (as one fears many academic biographers of minor literary figures don't) that his subject's life is important enough for him to go to all the labor involved in exhibiting it to the world. If he doesn't, the result will only be a dull "reference work." And a work whose aim is to depreciate its subject is not a biography but a polemic. Robert Gathorne-Hardy's biography of Logan Pearsall Smith, stressing the injustices inflicted by Smith on his biographer, is a fascinating and sometimes harrowing book to read, but it really tells us more about Gathorne-Hardy than about Smith, and was probably intended to do so.

The criterion of sympathy should not, of course, be allowed to prejudice the biographer's integrity. Indeed, if the sympathy is genuine, it will not. If you truly admire your subject, warts and all, you will not hesitate to paint the warts—he would be by so much less the person you admire, or "love," as Taylor tells us he loved Beaverbrook, on whose picture he lets plenty of warts remain.[1] "Nothing extenuate, nor aught set down in malice" remains as good a formula as any. Be prepared to argue with your subject when you think he was wrong and it needs to be said that he was. At the same time, remember that the reader didn't pick up the book in order to learn *your* political or religious or literary views, and will quickly find them boring.

A corollary: the biographer must be prepared to accept the fact that over the years his subject's views and personality may change and develop, and he must resist the temptation to present him as an unchanging monolith, imposing on him a factitious consistency—and, of course, distorting the evidence in order to do so.

THESE ARE COUNSELS OF PERFECTION, of course. They are a set of ideals that biographers have only recently set seriously before themselves. Even so "modern" a biographer as Strachey has been accused of grossly and wantonly violating the canons of honest transcription and strict evaluation of evidence, or concealing *parti pris* under a cloak of pretended impartiality (and he has also been powerfully defended against those charges). Is it then fair to apply such standards to Boswell? The answer must be, yes, it is. Macaulay, in his most famous journalistic *tour de force*, said the *Life of Johnson* was as much the first of biographies as Eclipse was the first of racehorses. I haven't looked up the statistics, but I would make a guess that Eclipse's time for the mile has long been beaten. We can continue to admire Eclipse for his achievement, but in a race between them it would be foolish to put one's money on him rather than on Secretariat or Seattle Slew.

This paper is a plea to students interested in Johnson to drop the foolish pretence that Macaulay's ranking still holds good—if it ever did. It does not detract from Johnson's reputation if we admit that, though his *Dictionary* was a mighty achievement, better dictionaries have since been produced. It does not damage Gibbon's when we read, in the words of an eminent modern historian, "To the literary mind, the great English historians may be Clarendon, Gibbon, and Macaulay. . . . Surely, they are worth reading and wrote splendid books, but they wrote in the prehistoric age and therefore lacked the opportunities we markedly lesser men enjoy. To the historian, the great English historians are Maitland and Namier."[2] It will not hurt Boswell's reputation—indeed, it may help it—if we stop trying to bolster it by the absurd contention that, as biography, the *Life* has unique merits that have never been equaled, and closing our eyes to the very plain fact that, by modern standards of biography, it has grave faults indeed; that in [1985] it is a most inadequate biography of Samuel Johnson. Its inadequacy has been made patent by the publication by such brave souls as Aleyn Lyell Reade, Joseph Wood Krutch, and James L. Clifford of biographies of Johnson that through their adherence to modern biographical standards, are far more competent than Boswell's, even though their writers sometimes feel a compulsion to apologize timidly to the shade of Boswell for their presumption— apologies that, as Edmund Wilson remarked in his review of Krutch, are entirely unnecessary. The continuing currency of the legend of the *Life*'s supreme excellence has gravely hindered the acceptance, even in academic circles, of Johnson as one of the very greatest of English writers. One needs only to chat for a few moments with one's colleagues teaching in other periods of English literature to recognize that, for most, Johnson is still the quaint old "personality," the figure of mild fun, that emerges most conspicuously from the *Life*, and very little more.

Assuming that the canons of modern biography that I have attempted to formulate have a modicum of validity (though I don't claim perfection for my formulation, I think most modern *aficionados* of biography would agree they have some), let us see how Boswell's *Life* measures up to them. By the first, assiduity in seeking out evidence, most will agree that it measures up quite well. A glance through Marshall Waingrow's excellent edition of *The Correspondence and Other Papers of James Boswell Relating to the Making of the "Life of Johnson"* (1969) convinces us of that. Boswell was not always successful—for instance, in securing Fanny Burney's valuable diary entries—but it is undeniable that he devoted an admirable amount of energy and persistence to hunting down evidence, especially in the form of reminiscences and anecdotes by acquaintances. Also, his acquaintance with Johnson's physical environment and his ability to communicate it—though perhaps not of the degree that Professor Clifford, say, demands of himself—are admirable; he has a keen eye for observing a scene and has given us many vivid and memorable vignettes.

Having granted this much, however, we must pause. For all

Boswell's work in accumulating evidence, the modern biographer would be expected to do much more, though, to be sure, with Johnson that "more" would be a back-breaking task, as Aleyn Lyell Reade, devoting his spare time for forty years to digging out the facts on which a sound account of Johnson's early life could be based, discovered. As for familiarity with the work of his subject and his intellectual milieu, one wonders just what percentage of Johnson's vast output of writing Boswell was really familiar with. The bibliography included in the *Life* is a patchy job, with inexplicable errors and omissions. It is probable that Boswell never read through the bulk of Johnson's copious journalism. True, it would have been a time-consuming operation to read through the several years of Johnson's reporting of parliamentary debates for the *Gentleman's Magazine*, and one is quite sure that Boswell, for whom time was running out anyway, never did. But a serious modern biographer, knowing how much the accomplishment of this task would add to the depth of his understanding of Johnson's grasp of contemporary political history, would never shirk it, and the result would be a much more accurate account of Johnson's political views than the shallow and misleading one found in the *Life*. Indeed, as I have complained elsewhere, Boswell's Scottish and Presbyterian upbringing often led to his failing to understand important nuances in Johnson's English politics and Anglican religion, and his misunderstandings of these matters, so important in Johnson's thinking, have been passed on to generations of readers. By comparison, Taylor's equipment, say, to deal with Beaverbrook's political involvements, or Waugh's to deal with Ronald Knox's religious life, are so splendidly professional as to make Boswell's look painfully crude.

On the second point, the skeptical evaluation of evidence, Boswell does not do too well. Again, Waingrow's volume does show a certain amount of laudable industry about checking and cross-checking. But sometimes Boswell fails disastrously. His willingness to rely on William Adams's report of the date of Johnson's leaving Oxford instead, as a competent modern biographer would, of on a first-hand inspection of college records, which Adams apparently misread, is a lamentable error: it is important in a man's life whether he spends three years in college, as Boswell reports, or only thirteen months. So great is the authority of Boswell's name, however, that the error, though corrected by Croker in 1831, continues to be reproduced in the most recent (third) edition of the most popular selection of Johnson's writing, widely used in colleges for the past quarter-century and bearing one of the most distinguished names in contemporary Johnson scholarship.[3]

What is even more disturbing is Boswell's apparent willingness to accept any "funny story" about Johnson anyone told him and insert it in his book, where it assumed the guise of gospel truth. Because of Boswell's undeserved reputation for accuracy as a biographer, this practice has had unfortunate consequences. The story of Johnson's reply to a rude boatman, "Your wife, under pretence of keeping a bawdy house, is a receiver of stolen goods," is one of the things most readers call to mind when they are told of Johnson's "rough tongue" and "conversational wit"—although E. L. McAdam found a version of the retort in the popular collection of humor, *Annals of Newgate*, current before Boswell was born.[4] James Clifford and Joseph Wood Krutch make solemn deductions about Johnson's psychological make-up from his alleged retort to Gilbert Walmesley about putting Irene in the ecclesiastical courts as the climax of her agonies—a quip found in jest books long before, with no reference to Johnson. We know whose authority Boswell relied on for this anecdote: Peter Garrick, well known as a raconteur. Apparently it seldom occurred to Boswell to question the authenticity of such chestnuts, and it might well have amused people like Peter Garrick to feed them to so willing a victim. Not long ago that vehicle of the best Johnson scholarship, the *Johnsonian News Letter*, averred that the author of a well-known limerick making fun of Berkeleyan idealism must have been inspired by a quip on the subject attributed to Johnson in the *Life*. He might have, but the quip itself, said to have been reported "by a gentleman" in one of those long sections of the "Collectanea" and "Johnsoniana" where Boswell fills up gaps in his chronological sequence where he has no biographical information to impart, stands a few paragraphs away from that of the retort to the boatman and was probably equally in the public domain. Such, again, is the continuing authority of the name of Boswell: something of the credulity of Boswell toward the anecdotes of a Peter Garrick seems to have been passed on in the form of the credulity of modern readers toward the anecdotes retailed by Boswell. Either that, or Johnson used to spend his days memorizing stale quips out of Joe Miller and then inflicting them on his friends, which seems unlikely. Careful work needs to be done on trying to detect and sort out the spurious ones; until this is done, a lingering shadow of suspicion will hover over many that, on careful investigation, may turn out to have excellent authority and over the host of popular articles about the "withering wit" of Johnson, "the great talker."

Which brings us to an even more damaging charge: gross misfeasance, or nonfeasance, of a biographer's first duty, to try to provide a reasonably complete and continuous narrative of his subject's life. In spite of the picture many readers have (how did it originate?) of Boswell spending most of his spare time throughout his adult life hovering behind Johnson with notebook at the alert, it has been calculated that Boswell was in Johnson's company on a total of only 425 days, and those only in the last twenty-two years of Johnson's life, with one-fourth of them during the tour of Scotland in 1773.[5] But many biographers have never met their subjects at all and yet turned out biographies containing no conspicuous gaps. What are we to say of one in which the whole account of one of those important twenty-two years, 1770, consists of (a) a short, hostile account of a political pamphlet published by Johnson during that year ("Even his vast powers are inadequate to cope with constitutional truth and reason"); (b) a short paragraph, dated during this year, quoted from his (published) *Prayers and Meditations*; (c) the reproduction of five short, businesslike letters from Johnson; and (d) the following: "During this year there was a total cessation of all correspondence between Johnson and me, without any coldness on either side, but merely from procrastination, continued from day to day; and as I was not in London, I had no opportunity of enjoying his company and recording his conversation. To supply this blank, I shall present my readers with some *Collectanea*, obligingly furnished to me by the Rev. Dr. Maxwell"—and then several pages of undated miscellaneous anecdotes, some of them, like the famous remark about a second marriage being "the triumph of hope over experience," sounding much out of character and suspiciously like a jest-book epigram.[6]

Presumably more happened to Johnson during the 365 days of this,

his sixty-first year, than his publishing one pamphlet, writing one diary entry, and sending five short letters. But what it was we shall never learn from Boswell's *Life*. The entry for 1780 is very similar (there is a larger number of letters). It is a sobering experience to go through these years in the latter part of the *Life*—eight out of the twenty-two—when Boswell did not come to London and meet Johnson; cross out the letters (of which Boswell's was an imperfect collection—Mrs. Piozzi had published the best lot), the inept and often misinformed critiques by Boswell of Johnson's writings, and the undated lists of sometimes dubious anecdotes; and discover that there is virtually nothing left. A modern writer who presented such an assemblage as a serious biography would be slaughtered by the reviewers. One can understand Croker's motive for trying to fill these huge gaps by interspersing bits and pieces of Hawkins, Mrs. Piozzi, and others throughout Boswell's text; and, for all Macaulay's disapproval, it is still only by means of doing something similar for himself that the modern student can get any kind of coherent picture of Johnson's later life, approximating in fullness that which Clifford and Reade have provided of his early years. Can Boswell not be bothered even to *attempt* some sort of connected narrative of Johnson's doings during that important time?

Apparently not. Although it is customary to say that the weakest part of the *Life* is the one-sixth of it dealing with the fifty-four years of Johnson's life before Boswell met him—and it has become customary to say it because it shows up so badly beside Reade's and Clifford's masterly treatment of those early decades—and that its glory is in the five sixths dealing with the last twenty-two years,[7] it appears that, from the point of view of serious biography (and from Waingrow's book on the making of the *Life*), precisely the opposite is true: the early part of Johnson's life, the pre-Boswellian years, is that on which Boswell may be said to have done serious research. It seems clear that for the last twenty-two years he virtually abandoned the idea of writing any sort of connected biographical narrative, but was willing to rest the success of the book on the edited extracts from his diaries reporting the occasions when he was in Johnson's company, interspersed with what letters he had, an attempt at a bibliography (often with tedious and inept critical comment by Boswell), and the aforesaid collections of undated anecdotes.

AND OF COURSE it *was* a success—an overwhelming one. What caused its success we all know: the excerpts from Boswell's journals[8] and to some extent the letters from Johnson to Boswell (certainly not those from Boswell to Johnson). But why call such an assemblage a biography? It is hardly—in the last five-sixths—even an attempt at one. It should be called what it is, *Memoirs of James Boswell, Concerning His Acquaintance with Samuel Johnson,* with the not very important additions mentioned. Even Eckermann (whose book, in the seven years it covers, provides us with far more *biography* of his subject than Boswell does in the last twenty years of his, since Eckermann kept in much closer and more constant touch with him than Boswell, in distant Edinburgh, did with Johnson) was content to call it only *Conversations with Goethe,* and it is regularly and properly consigned to the genre *Tischreden* ("table talk") along with Luther's, Selden's and Coleridge's—*not* biography. The biography of those last eventful and important twenty years of Johnson's life, for which so much more evidence is available than for the first fifty, has still to be written. One hopes that Professor Clifford, whose qualifications for that task no one—certainly not Boswell—has ever equaled, will be able to do something about them.[9]

As *Gespräche* Boswell's achievement is another matter, and I shall turn to it presently. But as a biography, when one takes the trouble to analyze what actually appears in the pages of the *Life,* it seems startling that students have commended its structure and praised the subtlety of its organization.[10] The organization of the bulk of the work—the nearly five-sixths of it covering the last twenty-two years of Johnson's life (and in any other biography this imbalance would be regarded as a gross fault)—could hardly be more elementary. It is divided mechanically into annual installments (of widely varied lengths, depending solely on how much recorded conversation Boswell has available to stow into each). Most installments begin monotonously with a sketch of Johnson's literary production (so far as Boswell is aware of it) for the year: "In 1770 he published a political pamphlet . . ."; "In 1771 he published another political pamphlet . . ."; "In 1772 he was altogether quiescent as an author . . ."; "In 1773 his only publication was an edition of his folio Dictionary. . . ." Sometimes there is an attempt at elegant variation, as "The first effort of his pen in 1775 was . . . ," or, as in 1774, where he begins with a quotation from Johnson's New Year's Day diary entry. But of the twenty-one annual installments between 1763 and 1783 inclusive, thirteen begin with the sledgehammer "In 1769," "In 1770," "In 1771," and another two with the variant "Early in 1764." Though the opening topic of the installment is sometimes varied (four begin with a statement about Johnson's health, physical or mental), Boswell seems to find security in returning to the familiar pattern of the catalog of writing and obviously rejoices when he is able to extract no less than three such openings from the *Lives of the Poets:* for 1779, "This year Johnson gave the world a luminous proof that the vigour of his mind . . . was not abated;[11] for this year came out the first four volumes of his 'Prefaces . . .'"; "In 1780 the world was kept in impatience for the completion of his 'Lives of the Poets'"; "In 1781 Johnson at last completed his 'Lives of the Poets.'" It is with a certain relief that one reaches Boswell's triumphant final variation on the pattern: "And now I am arrived at the last year of the life of Samuel Johnson."

Having, as it were, divided his desk top into twenty-two neat squares (I am speaking of the bulk of the work, the post-1763 part), Boswell proceeds to sort out his materials and methodically drop them by chronology into their proper compartments: first, the yearly installment of Johnson's literary production (with commentary by Boswell); the year's quota of the letters Boswell has at his disposal (often with copious explanatory annotation, especially when the letter has anything to do with Boswell's personal or family affairs)[12]; a sprinkling of entries reprinted from *Prayers and Meditations* (published six years earlier); sometimes a quasi-judicial opinion on some legal problem that Boswell had asked Johnson to write out,[13] then the major ingredient, the large chunks of entries from Boswell's diaries, which, unfortunately, are not available for eight of the squares, leaving them looking woefully empty. There is a particularly bad gap right in the middle of the composition, 1770 and 1771. It is interesting to observe the devices to which Boswell resorts to fill some of these gaps. Into 1767 goes Boswell's carefully preserved account (copyrighted) of

Johnson's meeting with George III—it fills six of the eight pages devoted to that year. Maxwell's assorted anecdotes, as we saw, helped to fill 1770; another collection of miscellaneous "Johnsoniana" from Bennet Langton goes into 1780 (which he also helps to fill by reprinting, from his rival Mrs. Piozzi's volume, Johnson's long letter about the Gordon Riots). But even after such efforts, there are still nearly empty years left—1764 with 6 pages, 1765 with 9, 1771 with 7, 1774 with 12—by contrast with the fat ones when Boswell met Johnson during his spring visits to London and sometimes went on expeditions with him: 1776 with 107 pages, 1778 with 100, 1777 with 82. Can it really be maintained that 1775 (77 pages) is six times more important a year in Johnson's life than 1774 (12 pages)? If not, how can we defend the book against the charge that, as a biography, it is an incompetent piece of work, except, of course, by the usual defence offered by partisans of Boswell that the criteria by which the worth of other biographies is judged are not, for some metaphysical reason, to be applied to Boswell's *Life*? Would it not be simpler and honester simply to say, "The *Life* is not to be judged by the criteria applicable to other biographies, because the *Life* is not a biography"? If such a work were to be published today, an experienced reviewer of biographies might surmise that it was the work of a tired and timid man, with little talent for organization and aware of the fact, unwilling to abandon a project he has publicized widely, but frightened of the immensity of the task he has set himself and clinging desperately to the rock of simple chronological order. And this, if one reads the dreary journals of Boswell's later years and the correspondence between him and his gadfly Malone, pretty well describes the actual situation.

This, I know, is dire heresy. I am now going to utter a direr one (Macaulay will spin in his grave, and some recent Boswell scholars may spin here on the surface of the earth): what useful function does the *Life* now serve for the serious student of Johnson? Would it not be better to break it up into the component parts that Boswell so perfunctorily strung together, to extract the parts deriving from the journals and publish them separately as *Boswell's Conversations with Johnson*, following the example of Eckermann? Does not whatever artistry Boswell contributed to the *Life* consist in them alone, and would not that artistry be enhanced by this procedure? There would be no need to print the letters, which are available—better edited than in the *Life* and in the full context of Johnson's correspondence—in Chapman's edition. So are the extracts from the *Prayers and Meditations* in McAdam's. A better record of Johnson's career as a writer will be found in the Courtney bibliography, supplemented by many recent studies of Johnsonian writings of which Boswell knew nothing. The "legal opinions" Boswell extracted from Johnson will presumably be published, along with Johnson's other legal writing, of which there is much, in some later miscellaneous volume of the Yale edition, and the demand for them meanwhile is not likely to be great.

Would the student not be better served if the *Life* were, so to speak, repealed in this way? What would be lost in the process? The biography of the pre-1763 years has long been obsolete; it has been superseded by Clifford's *Young Sam Johnson* and the sequel, *Dictionary Johnson*. The undated anecdotes should remain in suspense until their authenticity has been more fully investigated. We should of course lose Boswell's critiques of Johnson's writings, his confidences about the state of his own soul, his windy commentary on Johnson's political and religious views. There are not many, I think, who would weep if what Leopold Damrosch recently called these "less appealing aspects of Boswell"[14] were consigned to the dustier shelves of the library stacks for perusal by the occasional specialized graduate student or antiquarian. We should *not* have lost the biography of Johnson's last twenty years, since, when the aforesaid subtractions have been made, there is virtually nothing left to lose—almost nothing not already available in Hawkins, Mrs. Piozzi, and others. To repeat, the biography of those important last two decades still needs to be written.

The more obvious other contraventions by Boswell of the criteria I tried to formulate for good biography are not unknown. His breaches of the criteria of discrimination and relevance have been a subject of complaint from Macaulay onward: his tiresome intrusions of disquisitions on the history of the Boswell family; the state of the famous Boswellian hypochondria (which Johnson too found excruciatingly boring); the Boswellian justifications, against Johnson's protests, of slavery and polygamy; the distortion of Johnson's political and religious views by assimilating them to his own. The complaint James Clifford makes at the beginning of *Young Sam* is familiar and justified:

in the *Life* Johnson is always an old man. To preserve the patriarchal image, Boswell unscrupulously suppressed evidence that might disturb it, evidence that we know, especially since the publication of Waingrow's volume, to have been available to him: the fact that he was not as faithful to Tetty's memory as Boswell makes out, but during her last illness used to fondle Mrs. Desmoulins on his bed, and later planned a second marriage; that as a young man he engaged in a ferocious bout of drunkenness with Hector; that Boswell cleaned up the occasional use of profanity in his speech—much the same kind of Victorian cleaning up poor Mrs. Hawthorne is laughed at for having done to her husband, but which seems not to impair modern Boswell-olatry. The book is *not* well written—Boswell's prose is often tedious, trite, and insufferably unctuous.

Finally, the question of the attitude of the biographer to his subject. I once suggested[15] that, far from being the naive worshipper of Johnson he used to be thought, Boswell manifests a good deal of no doubt unconscious hostility to the father figure he substituted for his own rejecting father. Like a Canadian missionary of whom Sinclair Lewis once devastatingly wrote, "He was always forgiving the Indians for being Indians," Boswell is always forgiving Johnson for being Johnson. In his account of the *Dictionary*, he has to concede, "A few of his definitions must be admitted to be erroneous. . . . His definition of *Network* has often been quoted with sportive malignity, as obscuring a thing itself very plain. . . . His introducing his own opinions, and even prejudices . . . cannot be fully defended." Yet, "Let it . . . be remembered that this indulgence does not display itself only in sarcasm to others, but sometimes in playful allusions to . . . his own laborious task." Of Johnson's *The False Alarm*, "That it endeavoured to infuse a narcotick indifference, as to publick concerns, into the minds of the people, and that it broke out sometimes into an extreme coarseness of contemptuous abuse, is but too evident. It must not, however, be omitted, that when the storm of his violence subsides, he takes a fair opportunity to pay a grateful compliment to the King, who has rewarded his merit." There is the notorious "dark hints" passage, where Boswell magnanimously points out that "like many other good and pious men, among whom we may place the Apostle Paul," Johnson was "sometimes overcome" by his "amorous inclinations" (there is not the least evidence of his having been so "overcome").

Many such examples of what I once described as the "technique of damnation by inadequate defence" can be found in the *Life*. One effect of this technique is that the first instinct of naive younger students is to react hostilely themselves against the bullying dogmatist who requires so much extenuation. Another more ominous is that older "general readers" cherish Boswell's quaint "Doctor Johnson," perhaps as assuaging (to quote myself again) "a deep emotional need for some older, publicly honored figure whom one can bolster one's shaky ego by patronizing; a surrogate father." It is worth remembering that Johnson, like other sensible holders of honorary doctorates, detested having that label inflicted on him, and Boswell was well aware of the fact; nevertheless thoughout the *Life* the "Mr. Johnsons" of the journals are replaced by "Dr. Johnsons." Popular biographies, which once concentrated on "Johnson the great Clubman," the eccentric conversationalist, have recently concentrated instead on "Johnson the great neurotic," and this development has sometimes been hailed as a movement away from the domination of Johnson studies by Boswell's *Life*. Perhaps. Much material illustrative of Johnson's troubled emotional life can certainly be collected from his own writings, though the number of great writers whose own deep "neuroses" are liberally manifested in their writings is legion. But I am not certain that the primary inspiration for such works still does not come from Boswell's many dark, and not so dark, "hints." At any rate, the reason for the popularity of those works may be, as before, that readers (to quote Swift on the reception by his friends of the news of his last illness) can "hug themselves, and reason thus, / It is not yet so bad with us."

To repeat: the modern scholar who uncritically goes along with Macaulay's praise of the work as a *biography* is in a difficult position. Its true merit—and this is certainly no novel suggestion—lies in Boswell's reports of his meetings with Johnson; and these constitute not, by modern standards, a biography but, as with Eckermann, a Memoir, a "Conversations with," *Gespräche*, Table Talk, *Tischreden*. And in this genre—a rare one—it must rank very high indeed. If this is allowed, I am happy to go along with Macaulay's praise, and repeat, with a slight modification, "Homer is no more decidedly the first of epic poets, Shakespeare the first of dramatists, than Boswell is the first of composers of *Tischreden*. Eclipse is first, the rest nowhere." Well, not quite. Eckermann comes a close second, though he lacks Boswell's élan. Eckermann's reports sometimes drag in a way Boswell's seldom do; and that may well be because Eckermann is a more faithful reporter —is a better biographer—than Boswell.[16]

For *Tischreden* are not biography, and it is imperative the distinction be kept. For the serious biographer, the canon given in the most recent biography of Luther must apply:

> Over the years . . . scribes compiled volume after volume of Luther's talk, now graced with the name *Table Talk*. The remarks are often quoted nowadays, but careful students should remember that they were spoken over a glass of wine or beer, and not only are they rather private, but also they are often highly coloured and have passed through many hands. *No comment at table is accepted by a Luther scholar as authentic unless there is corroboration for its substance in Luther's writings.* This is not to say they were not said, and said in a form very near to what is recorded, for many of the sayings crop up in similar forms at different times at different hands: it is only to say that they can be no more than corroborative evidence.[17]

Boswell's reports of Johnson's sayings in the *Life* are not biography: they are material for the biographer, material that the biographer must scrutinize carefully when he uses it. As they appear in the *Life*, we all know, they are heavily (and silently) edited versions of Boswell's earlier jottings—edited so as to add color, heighten their dramatic effect, emphasize the traits of the Boswellian "Johnson" not sufficiently illustrated, in Boswell's opinion, in the original form of the report. Adverbs ("frowning," "gesticulating") are added, parenthetical speculations on the state of Johnson's mind are inserted, and there is a liberal sprinkling of superfluous "Sirs." Elsewhere I have called attention to Boswell's addition, in his account of Johnson's explaining to Goldsmith the legal maxim "The King can do no wrong," of such expressions as "majesty" and "the king is supreme; he is above everything," to make Johnson's "Toryism" seem closer to his own,[18] and I protested that, though the reader may be more entertained by the revised than the original version, anyone attempting a serious study of Johnson's political views would be guilty of a gross breach of scholarly method if he used the revised rather than the original report.

Indeed, current Johnsonian scholarship is well aware of this trap. Ever since the earlier forms of Boswell's reports began to be available with the printing of the Malahide papers in the 1920s, careful Johnson scholars have invariably turned to them, rather than to the *Life*, as the most authentic evidence available. The latest stage in this process has been Marshall Waingrow's publication of much of the nonjournal material from which Boswell constructed the *Life*, with its dozens of passages annotated by Waingrow as "Not used" by Boswell in the *Life*, or "Deleted," or "Omitted." It should not be thought paradoxical that the result of the labors of the galaxy of Boswell scholars like Waingrow and Pottle over the decades has been to render the *Life* more and more obsolescent as time goes on. No scholar would now dream of using as biographical evidence of Pope or Fanny Burney their letters or diary entries in the form edited by themselves, tidied up, rewritten, bowdlerized, now that the reconstructions of the originals by George Sherburn and Joyce Hemlow are available. Nor will a sane modern scholar be satisfied with the tidied up, bowdlerized, and rewritten Johnson of Boswell's *Life* when a form at least closer to the original is available in his "private papers." To adapt what Housman said about manuscripts "corrected" by a later scribe or editor, give us the raw materials and we will mix our own Johnsonian salad, rather than buy Boswell's ready-made one. It may be pleasant to some tastes; for many others, the Boswellian seasoning seems to overpower the flavor of the original ingredients.

WHERE DOES ALL THIS LEAVE the *Life of Johnson* today? At least one student of Boswell is happy to abandon any claim it may have to being serious biography and to applaud it as a work of fiction—the highest fiction, to be sure: "Of all the subjects of all biographies, Johnson virtually alone lives for us in a way comparable not to Napoleon or Lincoln or Frederick the Great but to Hamlet or Sherlock Holmes."[19] Other Boswellians, however, are not yet ready to go so far, nervous, perhaps, that however much enjoyment the Baker Street Irregulars and similar groups may obtain from devoting their time and energy to the minutiae of Sherlock Holmes's feats, many intelligent people will still feel that the study of Lincoln or Napoleon may in the end be a more profitable occupation, and that Samuel Johnson—in the toughness of his personality, the scope of his achievement, his significance for the human condition—bears somewhat more resemblance to Lincoln than to Conan Doyle's entertaining detective.

Such scholars struggle valiantly to have it both ways: Boswell's Johnson is both great art and also the authentic Johnson. This proposition has always been difficult to accept. If Boswell is reproducing the authentic Johnson, then whatever artistry his figure displays must redound to the credit of Johnson, not Boswell. Conversely, if the figure that appears in the *Life* is an artistic creation of Boswell, then he is *ipso facto* not the Johnson who was born in Lichfield in 1709 and whose bones lie buried in Westminster Abbey. One argument along these lines is that with which Marshall Waingrow concludes the introduction to his excellent book: "No matter how many new facts are brought to light, Samuel Johnson will always be somebody's hypothesis. And none has pleased so many or is likely to please so long, as Boswell's." But the Richard III who has pleased the greatest number and the longest is undoubtedly Shakespeare's. And the Richard III whom the latest biographer or historian constructs from the laborious accumulation of new facts gathered since Shakespeare's time is undoubtedly still the hypothesis of that biographer or historian. All the same, some hypotheses are better than others, and if the next biographer of Richard III who comes along, swayed by Waingrow's reasoning, decides to adopt the Shakespearian one, on the ground that this is the one that has pleased the most people for the longest time, we should stare at him in amazement.

As Leopold Damrosch puts it, "Beyond the precincts of the kinds of literature which criticism has learned to interpret in satisfying detail—the drama, the lyric, and so forth—lies a wide variety of works which owe at least part of their 'success' to literary qualities, but which do not lend themselves very easily to the usual categories by which the critic explains and justifies his admiration," and he cites Boswell's *Life* as one which falls into that classification.[20] Yes, indeed, literary critics, especially recent admiring critics of the "artistry" of the *Life*, need to be reminded that in the vocabulary of Johnson and Boswell the word "literature" included many other forms of writing than what we call "imaginative literature," and that there are other species of criticism of a book than merely "literary criticism." The excellence of a treatise on physics, say, is not determined solely by its author's display of brilliant imagination or striking prose (or mathematical) style. If, on investigation, its conclusions turn out to have been based on inaccurate measurement or on sloppy or cooked experiments, no literary or imaginative skill will save it from the contempt of those qualified to pass judgment on it.

"Imaginative literature" is one thing, biography and history are another. They have a different end, which is most simply stated by the use of a somewhat old-fashiond term, the discovery of the truth. It was a word that Johnson did not hesitate to use. In his own fine review of a biography (an autobiography, to be precise, that of Sarah Churchill, duchess of Marlborough) he comments on the difficulty of ascertaining the truth about her career at the heart of affairs in the reign of Anne. The duchess has every motive to give a version of events distorted so as to exalt her own reputation. Yet who except those in an insider's position like the duchess's have the knowledge of what actually went on behind the scenes? "The man who knows not the truth," he writes, "cannot, and he who knows it, will not, tell it: what then remains but to distrust every relation, and live in perpetual negligence of past events, or, what is still more disagreeable, in perpetual suspense?"[21]

But such Pyrrhonism (or Marxism) is not Johnson's final answer. One should certainly apply scholarly skepticism to such accounts as the duchess's, he agrees. Yet such skepticism "quickens [the student's] discernment of different degrees of probability, animates his search after evidence, and perhaps heightens his pleasure at the discovery of truth, for truth, though not always obvious, is generally discoverable." That, to be sure, was written nearly two and a half centuries ago. Yet G. R. Elton, perhaps the most eminent British historian now writing, concludes the first chapter of his fine essay on his own discipline, *The Practice of History*, with these words: "It is not the problems they [historians—and, one might add, biographers] study or the lessons they teach that distinguish the historical sheep from the goats but only the manner of their study, the precision of their minds, and the degree to which they approximate to the ultimate standards of intellectual honesty and intellectual penetration. *Omnia veritas.*" It is interesting that Professor Elton thought it expedient, when addressing modern readers, to clothe that last word in the decent obscurity of a learned language. Yet I do not see how any scholar who sets himself up as a practitioner or critic of biography can do other than say, "Amen."

There is, I think an aesthetic side to truth. A piece of admitted fiction, *Tom Jones,* say, or *Clarissa,* can delight later generations as much as earlier, whatever historical or biographical research may discover in the interim. Some scholar may find, for instance, that Fielding modeled Squire Western on some country acquaintance of his, or that Richardson projected his own internal repressions into Clarissa. Such information, however useful to the task of the biographer of Fielding or Richardson, need not—should not—affect our aesthetic, our literary critical, response to those works. Tom and Clarissa and Squire Western exist only in the world of the imagination and in the text of the novel: no evidence from outside the text can modify the terms of their existence. It adds a fillip to our enjoyment of Maugham's *Cakes and Ale* when we realize that Edward Driffield has many affinities with Thomas Hardy and Alroy Kear with Hugh Walpole, and the psychological analysis of those characters in the novel may conceivably provide valid and useful insights for biographers of Hardy and Walpole. But the knowledge of those affinities—or, indeed, the knowledge that, on the contrary, the characters are grossly libelous and malicious travesties of Hardy and Walpole—should in no way interfere with our delight in reading the novel.

It would be different, I think, had Maugham entitled the book *Memoirs of Thomas Hardy and Hugh Walpole* and given his characters those names; that is, published it as a biography instead of a novel. When we learned that the conversations in the book were gross distortions of those that actually took place, that much of the innuendo about the private lives and moral characters of those figures cannot be supported by research, that the literary criticism of their writings found in the book is inept, that the book was in fact written with hostile bias, then I doubt that we could read it with the same pleasure or attribute to it the same excellence. As a novel, as admitted fiction, it is an honest book; if presented to us as biography, as alleged truth, we should feel that the author was being dishonest with us, and that feeling would prevent us from enjoying the brilliance of the construction and the word play. If the Sherlock Holmes stories were presented as a factual biography of Dr. Joseph Bell of Edinburgh, 1837–1911 (or whoever the real medical man was who is supposed to have given Conan Doyle the inspiration for his character), I imagine they would not now be held in such high esteem.

Perhaps part at least of the problem lies in the quantity of historical evidence still available about the original of the fictionalized biographical subject. Too much is no doubt still available in biographical dictionaries to make it plausible that Dr. Bell nearly met his death in the Alps at the hands of Professor Moriarty or was taken in by the beautiful Irene Adler. King Macbeth and Prince Hamlet (of Saxo Grammaticus) are historically so nebulous, however, that Shakespeare is at liberty to do with them what he pleases. Richard III is more equivocal; most spectators know and care about the historical Richard so little that their knowledge seldom gets in the way of their enjoyment. For the Company of the White Rose, however, a small but devoted group of students of the historical evidence about the last Yorkist king, one imagines that Shakespeare's play can hold little aesthetic merit.

Far too much is known about the historical Samuel Johnson for his existence to be forgotten, while the fictional character in Boswell's *Life* survives. Ironically, there once existed a similar artistically constructed and equally fictional James Boswell. No more brilliantly written account of Boswell has ever appeared than that in Macaulay's notorious review of Croker, a piece reprinted innumerable times and used in schools all over the world as an illustration of how effectively English can be written:

Boswell was one of the smallest men that ever lived. . . . Johnson described him as a fellow who had missed his only chance of immortality by not having been alive when the *Dunciad* was written. Beauclerk used his name as a proverbial expression for a bore. . . . He was always laying himself at the feet of some eminent man, and begging to be spit upon and trampled upon. . . . Servile and impertinent, shallow and pedantic, a bigot and a sot, bloated with family pride, and eternally blustering about the dignity of a born gentleman, yet stooping to be a talebearer, an eaves-dropper, a common butt in the taverns of London.[22]

The magnificent vilification rolls on, page after page. It is certainly more readable, more gripping, more memorable, put together with more artistic skill than Professor Pottle's sometimes ponderous biography of Boswell or Boswell's own long-drawn-out self-psychoanalyses.

Yet the determined uncovering by Professor Pottle and his helpers over the decades of a mass of information about the historical Boswell has produced a very different picture. They rightly point out that the Boswell so revealed is more complex, more interesting, more rewarding than the Macaulayan Boswell, however brilliant that construct. And, also rightly, they insist that the Macaulayan Boswell, however much delight he has given the reader, should be discredited and abandoned, and their view has prevailed. How paradoxical that, at the same time, they insist that the Boswellian Johnson, however different from the historical one, however heightened and over-simplified, should be preserved because of its artistic excellence! Is Boswell's artistic skill in the creation of a fictional character so much greater than Macaulay's that Boswell's artifact should be retained and admired (to the neglect of the historical Johnson) while Macaulay's is to be relegated to the dustbin and the historical Boswell carefully reconstructed from the huge mass of papers Boswell left for posterity? If God, who created the historical Boswell, has proved so much greater an artist than Macaulay, who created the fictional one, is it not conceivable that, in creating the historical Johnson, God likewise demonstrated himself a greater artist than even James Boswell?

Statistical Appendix

Johnson once wrote to little Sophia Thrale, urging her to work hard at her arithmetic, "A thousand stories which the ignorant tell and believe die away at once when the computist takes them in his grip." One story that has not yet died away is the firmly believed one that James Boswell spent a large part of his life tagging after Samuel Johnson with pen and notebook in hand, taking down every word he said. One still encounters such expressions as "Boswell, who knew Johnson better than anyone" and "as the ever-present Boswell reported." Those aware even of the elementary facts that Boswell's home was in Edinburgh—four hundred miles from Johnson's London—and that he came down to London only infrequently—a few weeks in each of fourteen of the twenty-two years after he had made Johnson's acquaintance—are sometimes inclined to emend the latter expression to "the seldom-present Boswell."

In the hope that a visual presentation may help to correct such misapprehensions, Figure 1 portrays the last twenty-two years of Johnson's life. Each square represents a day in each of those years, a total of 7,884 days between the date when Boswell first met Johnson, 16 May 1763, and that of Johnson's death, 13 December 1784. (In addition, Johnson had lived 19,599 days, from 18 September 1709 to 15 May 1763, before Boswell met him.) Squares with a black circle represent the days in which Boswell, in his *Life of Johnson* and *Journal of a Tour to the Hebrides*, mentions having been in Johnson's company. The block of 101 consecutive days in the autumn of 1773 represents the tour that Johnson and Boswell took through Scotland, recorded in the *Journal of a Tour*. Other blocks of consecutive dates, in 1776, 1777, and 1784, represent jaunts the two men took to Oxford, Lichfield, and Ashbourne. (Boswell is able to fill up virtually the whole of the biographical section of the *Life* for 1777 with an account of his eleven-day jaunt to Ashbourne.) Many of the other days so recorded, however, receive short shrift in the *Life*. For instance, of one day all we have is "At Streatham, on Monday, March 29, [1779,] at breakfast he maintained that a father had no right to control the inclinations of his daughters in marriage." Many entries merely record Boswell's attendance at meetings, often dinner parties, at which Johnson was present: for instance, in 1784, "On Sunday, May 9, I found Colonel Vallancy, the celebrated antiquarian and engineer of Ireland, with him. On Monday the 10th, I dined with him at Mr. Paradise's, where was a large company; Mr. Bryant, Mr. Joddrel, Mr. Hawkins Browne, &c. On Thursday, the 13th, I dined with him at Mr. Joddrel's, with another large company; the Bishop of Exeter, Lord Monboddo, Mr. Murphy, &c."

In the latter part of the *Life* especially Boswell's records become quite erratic. "I have preserved no more of his conversation at the times when I saw him during the rest of this month [May 1784], till Sunday, the 30th of May, when I met him in the evening at Mr. Hoole's," he writes, and, in April 1781, "For some time after this day I did not see him very often, and of the conversation which I did enjoy, I am sorry to find I have preserved but little. I was at this time engaged in a variety of other matters, which required exertion and assiduity, and necessarily occupied almost all my time." On the latter passage, his editor L. F. Powell writes, "Boswell is here disingenuous. He met Johnson at least five times between 21 April and 8 May, and the matters which engaged his attention were not of so serious a nature as he implies. He was in fact at this time extremely dissipated. . . . On the 7th of May he called on Johnson, who greeted him with the admonition, 'I hope you don't intend to get drunk tomorrow as you did at Paoli's.' "

Many scholars, beginning with Boswell's early editor J. W. Croker in 1831, have remarked what a surprisingly small amount of time Boswell and Johnson spent in each other's company. As well as the 327 days I list in Figure 1, P. A. W. Collins[23] makes a generous estimate of other meetings noted in Boswell's journals that either did not get into the *Life* or are subsumed under miscellaneous undated accounts (which I indicate in Table 1 with a plus sign), and, "by an extremely rough form of extrapolation," would bring the probable total of days of meeting to 425. This seems to be about as high an estimate as one can arrive at. But it is still only a small fraction of the nearly eight thousand days of Johnson's life during his last twenty-two years after he had first met Boswell.

Table 1, an approximate analysis of the content of Boswell's *Life of Johnson*, is based, as note 7 points out, on the Modern Library Giant Edition of the work, which, unlike later scholarly editions, has few footnotes added by later editors and therefore gives a fairly accurate idea of the actual Boswellian content. Figure 2, based on this, is a graph recording the strange variations in length of the sections of the *Life* dealing with the individual years of Johnson's later life and the fact that their length varies almost in direct proportion to the amount of time Boswell spent in Johnson's company. This must pose a problem for those scholars who extol the "artistry" of Boswell's composition. Did Johnson's activities in 1782 really contain less than a third of the artistic interest of those in 1781 and 1783, and those in 1774 less than a fifth of those in 1775? Or did Boswell possess such artistic intuition that he timed his visits to London so as to coincide with the periods of greatest artistic potential in Johnson's life? Was it because he foresaw their artistic sterility that he decided not to come down to London in the years 1774 and 1782?

FIGURE 1
Days in Johnson's life on which meetings between him and Boswell are mentioned in Boswell's *Life of Johnson* and *Journal of a Tour to the Hebrides*. Figures after the date of each year stand for the number of days on which such meetings are recorded and the total number of days in the year.

1763 (20/365)

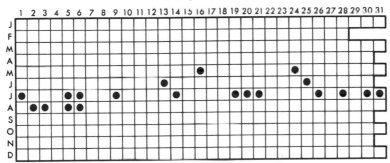

1766 (2/365)

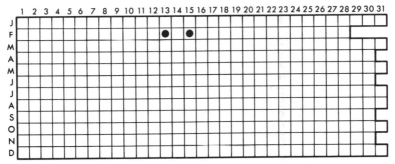

Continued on next page

FIGURE 1—*Continued*

1768 (5/366)

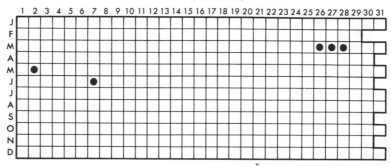

1769 (9/365)

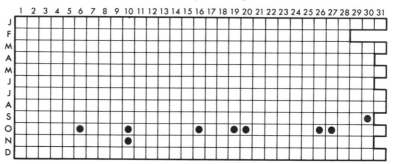

1772 (14/366)

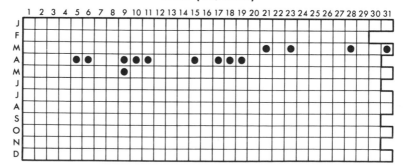

136

FIGURE 1—*Continued*

1773 (116/365)

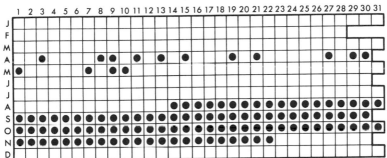

1775 (20/365)

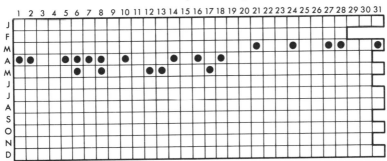

1776 (27/366)

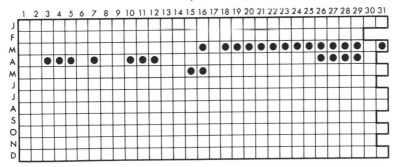

Continued on next page

FIGURE 1—*Continued*

1777 (11/365)

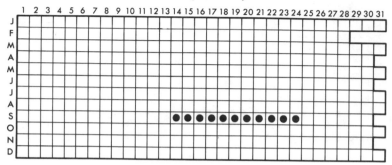

1778 (31/365)

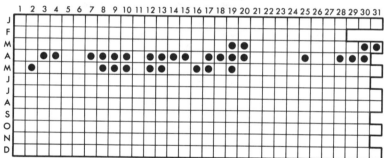

1779 (18/365)

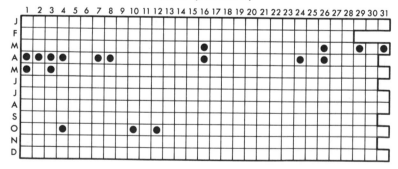

FIGURE 1—*Continued*

1781 (14/365)

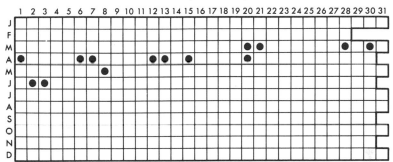

1783 (14/365)

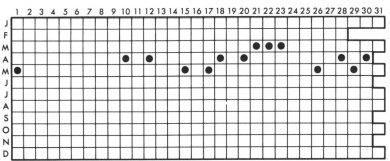

1784 (26/366)

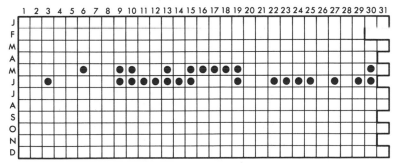

TABLE 1
The Content of Boswell's *Life of Johnson,* 1763–1784

A. Number of pages dealing with year indicated.
B. Number of pages occupied by accounts of meetings between Boswell and Johnson.
C. Number of days Boswell reports he and Johnson met (broken down by month).

Year	A	B	C	D		E	
1763	55	44	20 (May, 2; June, 2; July, 12; August, 4)	1	2.5	1	0.5
1764	7	0	0	1	0.5	0	0
1765	9	0	0	1	0.5	0	0
1766	18	5	2 (February, 2)	5	5.5	1	2.5
1767	10	0	0	3	2.0	0	0
1768	12	9	5 (March, 3; May, 1; June, 1)	3	1.0	1	0.5
1769	25	22	9 (September, 1; October, 7; November, 1; +)	3	1.5	0	0
1770	16	0	0	5	2.0	0	0
1771	7	0	0	4	2.0	3	1.5
1772	40	28	14 (March, 4; April, 9; May, 1)	5	2.0	3	1.5
1773	43	29	15 (April, 11; May, 4)	10	4.5	2	1.0
1774	14	0	0	17	10.5	4	2.5
1775	77	38	20 (March, 5; April, 10; May, 5)	21	12.5	7	4.0
1776	108	73	27 (March, 14; April, 11; May, 2; +)	19	15.5	3	2.0
1777	82	38	11 (September, 11)	19	14.5	17	14
1778	101	82	31 (March, 4; April, 18; May, 9; +)	10	5.5	7	6.0
1779	32	19	18 (March, 4; April, 9; May, 2; October, 3; +)	9	4.5	6	5.5
1780	40	0	0	12	7.0	6	6.0
1781	69	30	14 (March, 4; April, 7; May, 1; June, 2; +)	13	5.0	1	1.5
1782	19	0	0	21	13.0	1	0.5
1783	62	24	14 (March, 3; April, 6; May, 5)	21	9.5	1	0.5
1784	121	37	26 (May, 10; June, 16)	74	32.0	4	2.0
Total	967	478	226	277	144.5	68	52.0

Source: Modern Library Giant Edition (New York, 1931).

D. Number of letters by Johnson printed, and pages occupied by those letters.
E. Number of letters by others printed, and pages occupied by those letters.
F. Main additional material in year (pages).

F

Account of Anna Williams, 1; of Sheridan, 2; of Goldsmith, 3; Cock-Lane ghost, 1

The Club, 1.5; J's habits, 2; attack on Hawkins and Piozzi, 1; from *Prayers and Meditations*, 2

The Thrales, 3; *P&M*, 2; Shakespeare edition, 2

Goldsmith's poems (J's help), 1; P. Langton, 1.5

Interview with George III, 5.5; poem by Cuthbert Shaw, 0.5; Thomas Hervey affair, 1

Undated anecdotes (Maxwell), 11.5; *P&M*, 0.5; comment on *False Alarm*, 1

P&M, 1; *Falkland's Islands*, 1; J as M.P., 1

Legal opinions for Boswell, 6.5

Legal opinions for Boswell, 5

J's Paris notebook, 10; Paris anecdotes, 2; anecdotes (Burney), 1; J and Scots, 5; Oxford diploma, 1

Legal opinions, 5; Goldsmith epitaph, 2; Auchinleck entail, 2; B on Horace, 2; *Monthly Review*, 1

Dodd papers, 6.5; legal opinion, 1.5

Undated anecdotes (Langton), 20; Gordon Riots, 2

Variant readings and commentary, *Lives of Poets*, 22; legal opinion, 2; Corbyn Morris cited, 1

Poem on Levet, 1

Undated anecdotes (Bowles, Mickle, etc.), 19

Anecdotes (Astle, etc.), 8; attack on Piozzi, 5.5; J's projected works, 4; imitations of J's prose, 5; "dark hints," 1.5; prayers, etc., 1.5; J's will, 4; Essex Head club, 0.5; poem on Lade, 0.5; accounts of J's last days (Nichols, Hoole, etc.), 15; iconography of J, 4; funeral and monument, 2; Boswell's summary of J, 4

FIGURE 2
Distribution by Year of Content of Boswell's *Life of Johnson, 1763–1784*

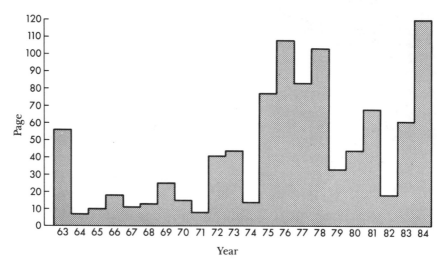

Notes

" 'Tis a pretty book, Mr. Boswell, but you must not call it a biography." The great classical scholar Richard Bently, when presented with a copy of Pope's translation of the *Illiad*, is supposed to have remarked, " 'Tis a pretty poem, Mr. Pope, but you must not call it Homer."

This essay is a revised and expanded version of an article printed in the *Georgia Review* 32, no. 1 (Spring 1978). Its earlier history is somewhat curious. It was originally prepared for delivery at a Modern Language Association seminar on biography, and some photocopies of the typescript were distributed in advance to members of the seminar. The night before the meeting of the seminar, however, I was struck down (by Boswell's ghost?) with a mild heart attack and of course could not attend. The following year, Professor F. A. Pottle of Yale, *Boswellianissimus*, who had obtained one of the photocopies, devoted much of his presidential address at the annual meeting of the Johnson Society of Lichfield to an attack on it, which was published in the *Transactions of the Johnson Society* (1974): 6–19. Few scholarly papers have been thus honored by the appearance of a printed reply before they themselves had been either delivered or published. Later, however, I discovered an earlier publication on the subject by Professor Pottle ("James Boswell, Journalist," in *The Age of Johnson*, ed. F. W. Hilles [New Haven: Yale University Press, 1949], 15–25). The first volume in the Yale edition of Boswell's journals was to appear in 1950, and in this article Professor Pottle, their general editor, was concerned to praise Boswell's journals at the expense of the *Life*, the competence of which he there attacks for some of the same reasons I do—plus a few that had not occurred to me. I take the liberty below of supporting some of my statements by quotations from Professor Pottle's earlier article.

Much of the material in the statistical appendix is reprinted, by permission, from *Modern Language Studies* 9, no. 3 (Fall 1979): 128–136. Some small corrections have been made in the figures appearing in Table 1.

1. Richard Ellmann was chid by a reviewer for recording too faithfully Joyce's consumption of alcohol. Ellmann's retort was a noteworthy expression of the good biographer's philosophy: "It is . . . your reviewer, not I who finds some romantic impropriety in the fact that artistic grandeur can live with human weakness" (*Times Literary Supplement*, 11 December 1959, 725).

2. G. R. Elton, *The Practice of History* (New York: Crowell, 1967), 4.

3. *Samuel Johnson: Rasselas, Poems, and Selected Prose*, ed. Bertrand H. Bronson (San Francisco: Rinehart, 1971; first pub. 1952), xxix. The erroneous date (1731) appeared for many decades in Macaulay's article on Johnson in the *Encyclopaedia Britannica* and was recently printed again in the article on Johnson in the *Funk-Wagnalls New Encyclopedia* over the initials of Lionel Trilling.

4. *Times Literary Supplement*, 21 July 1961, 449; see also 13 October 1961, 683.

5. A detailed study of the content of the *Life* and *Journal of a Tour to the Hebrides* is given in the statistical appendix, pp. 132–142.

6. Johnson indeed once seriously contemplated a second marriage, though Boswell suppressed this information. This is one of the anecdotes in the *Life* that worried Ronald Knox, whose fine ear for prose found it "curiously not characteristic Johnson. Or, to speak more accurately, not characteristic Boswell-Johnson. All these last five quotations were 'communicated' to Boswell by friends, not heard and reported by him." Knox's own language is cryptic: he does not overtly accuse the quotations of being unauthentic, but congratulates Boswell on having included so few of "those flashy pieces of comment upon life which used to go by the name of epigrams, but in these last few years have been very regrettably labelled 'wisecracks,'" and instead "concentrated on the more proper fruits of his friend's genius, the unquestionable Johnsoniana" ("Dr. Johnson," in *Literary Distractions* [London: Sheed and Ward, 1958], 84–85). Others included in his list of "questionable" Johnsoniana are "I never take a nap after dinner but when I have had a bad night, and then the nap takes me" and "There is less flogging in our great schools than formerly, but then less is learned there, so that what the boys get at one end they lose at the other." The kind of saying Knox would have thought of as "characteristic Johnson," illustrating "his ready habit of providing illustration, on the spur of the moment, for the point he wanted to enforce" (p. 91) is probably exemplified by the one admired by Auden, which he says even Goethe was not up to: "Sunday should be different from other days: people may walk but not throw stones at birds" (Auden, *Forewords and Afterwords* [New York: Random House, 1973], 147). The quotation is from the *Journal of a Tour to the Hebrides*, 20 August 1773.

7. My calculations of space, here and below, are based on the Modern Library Giant edition of the *Life*. Since it has little annotation, its pages of text are approximately of the same length throughout—and, conveniently for mathematics, it runs to exactly 1,200 pages. The years from 1709 to 1763 occupy the first 233 pages of the volume, and those from 1763 to 1784 the remaining 967.

8. "If any man who has read a good many of the great English biographies sets himself to answer the question: 'What is it that gives the *Life of Johnson* its unique distinction as literature?' I can imagine him in the end returning only one answer: 'The conversations'" (Pottle, "James Boswell, Journalist," 15).

9. The hope was not to be realized. Professor Clifford died 7 April 1978.

10. "The construction of the *Life*, for example, is remarkably unartificial. Boswell adopts a mechanically chronological scheme, which, with the year 1740, settles down to an annual review, each section baldly headed by the year and Johnson's age in that year. Within this loose and accommodating framework are inserted, with relatively few editorial exclusions, all Johnson's letters that Boswell could come at [etc.]" (Pottle, "James Boswell, Journalist," 15).

11. Why this apologia? Who had charged that Johnson's mental powers might be failing? Boswellian undercutting often takes the form of such unnecessary defense against accusations that would not have occurred to the reader if Boswell had not put them in this mind.

12. "To put the matter in the mildest way, the inclusion of this largely unselected mass of correspondence represented a biographer's easiest choice" (Pottle, "James Boswell, Journalist," 16).

13. "In the last year of Johnson's life, just before the death, Boswell interrupts the thread of his narrative to insert 'specimens of various sorts of imitations of Johnson's style,' which come at that point for no better reason than that he had promised (in a part of the book already printed) to get them in somewhere, had so far found no really appropriate place, and now had to do it by force. And nearly all readers, I think, will agree that Johnson's opinion on Boswell's legal cases would better have gone in an appendix" (ibid., 16).

14. See Note 20.

15. "Reflections on a Literary Anniversary," *Queen's Quarterly* 70 (Summer 1963): 198–208.

16. Eckermann's book is certainly one of those things responsible for Auden's judgment that "[Goethe's] life is the most documented of anyone who ever lived; compared with Goethe, even Dr. Johnson is a shadowy figure" (*Forewords and Afterwords*, 131).

17. James Atkinson, *Martin Luther and the Birth of Protestantism* (Baltimore: Penguin Books, 1968), 323–324, my italics. In an account of a meeting with Max Beerbohm, Edmund Wilson reported, "I was surprised to discover that Max did not care for Virginia Woolf's novels. He had a good word only for her criticism, and he did not seem enthusiastic about that." When Leonard Woolf read this, he produced a letter from Beerbohm to Virginia Woolf, about "*The Common Reader*, a book which I have read twice, and have often dipped into since, and rate above any modern book of criticism." Wilson comments, "Any report of a conversation is likely to be somewhat unreliable, since the reported may give way to a mood and the reporter may misinterpret" (*The Bit Between My Teeth* [New York: Farrar, Straus, and Giroux, 1965], 50–51 n.). It used to be argued that Boswell was uniquely endowed with "total recall" and thus immune to such fallibility, but the evidence for this contention left something to be desired. And Boswell did not always obey the first law of the table-talk reporter, which is surely to stay alert at the table. At a dinner in Scotland, where another guest reported Johnson as having denounced George III as "an idiot," Boswell only records, "I was so indolent as to let almost all that passed evaporate into oblivion." The cause of Boswell's oblivion on such occasions is fairly obvious.

18. *The Politics of Samuel Johnson* (New Haven: Yale, 1960), 292–293.

19. William R. Siebenschuh, "The Relationship between Factual Accuracy and Literary Art in the *Life of Johnson*," *Modern Philology* 74 (February 1977):

288. Mr. Siebenschuh concludes his article, "Donald Greene once called Johnson a 'character in Boswell's book,' and this is perhaps the shrewdest criticism and the highest praise that it has been given." I wrote Mr. Siebenschuh thanking him for the "plug," but pointing out that I had not intended the remark as praise.

20. "The *Life of Johnson*: An Anti-Theory," *Eighteenth-Century Studies* 6 (Summer 1973): 486.

21. *Gentleman's Magazine* 12 (March 1742): 128–31. Reprinted in some nineteenth-century editions of Johnson's works.

22. Macaulay, *Critical and Historical Essays,* ed. F. C. Montagu (New York: Putnam, 1903), 1:366.

23. In *Notes and Queries* (April 1956): 163–166.

FREDERICK A. POTTLE

The Adequacy as Biography of Boswell's *Life of Johnson*

Some forty years after Boswell's *Life of Johnson* was published, Macaulay pronounced it incomparably the best of biographies;[1] Carlyle, writing at the same time, rated it "in worth as a book beyond any other product of the eighteenth century."[2] I do not know that anyone else has ever gone the length of Carlyle, but Macaulay's judgment was generally accepted by critics and literary historians and has since reigned as a truism. Of late, however, radically depreciatory objections have been advanced, culminating in a serious proposal that the work be "repealed" as no biography at all.[3] What are the causes and grounds of this revolt, and is it likely to prevail?

One main cause no doubt has been that formalist revolution, loosely called the "New Criticism," that emerged some fifty years ago and has ended by discrediting the use of biography and diachronic literary history in the teaching of literature except where necessary for explaining historical allusions. Strictly speaking, the New Critics' objection to biography of authors is not to biography as a mode of literature but to biography as a substitute for, or a diversion from, the writings of the subject of the biography. A New Critic should theoretically be able to accept the traditional judgments that some biographies are literature and that Boswell's book is the greatest of literary biographies, but even if he did I suspect that he would place the *Life of Johnson* pretty far down in his list of literary priorities—in the spirit, let us say, of Dr. Leavis's dictum that Fielding deserves a place in literary history but that life is not long enough to permit giving much time to him.[4] Actually, the fear of the usurpative power of biography causes the more extreme New Critics to disparage the mode altogether. The history of an author's life, they assert, is totally irrelevant to that author's writings and can only get in the way of them.

Equally important as the cause of the reassessment of the worth of Boswell's book has been the recovery of Boswell's private papers close on to fifty years ago and their subsequent publication. Not everyone has reacted to those events with pleasure. Some Britons were piqued because the papers went to America; some scholars and journalists on both sides of the Atlantic found Colonel Isham's method of publication flamboyant and pretentious; many good people everywhere were shocked and offended by the subsequent trade publication of *Boswell's London Journal*. Readers who were settled in a comfortable conviction that Boswell as author was merely parasitic on Johnson found it preposterous to be asked to read more than a dozen large volumes of Boswell's private journal and to weigh his claims to be considered an important writer quite apart from Johnson. Some Johnsonians were disturbed by the amount of attention that was being paid to Boswell, feeling it not only unjustified but also as somehow a derogation of Johnson's claims. Scholars were aroused and unsettled by the emergence of a mass of totally unexplored documents of obvious literary and historical interest, documents that it will take at least a century to assimilate. The new papers show completely and in minute detail just how Boswell gathered his materials and how he went about writing his book. The *Life of Johnson* is now perhaps the most fully documented large work in world literature. When it became possible beyond all hope to follow the shaping process of Boswell's hand, scholars at first turned their attention more to process than to product, to taking apart rather than to judging as a whole. Boswell's papers, in short, provide large opportunity for skeptical analysis of his book, and some scholars have been taking advantage of it.

Professor Donald Greene appears to be more of a literary historian of the old school than a New Critic, but his attitude in this instance could be taken as a classical case of what I have called the fear of the usurpative power of biography. A deep student of the works of Johnson, he considers Johnson to be a very great writer indeed, and he

148

thinks that it is mainly Boswell's *Life* that keeps this judgment from being generally accepted. "The good," he says, "is enemy of the best." The *Life of Johnson*, in his opinion, is indeed a work of art, a minor masterpiece, but it is really more about Boswell than about Johnson. It consists essentially of conversations on casual topics. The quantity of factual information it provides is much too small to justify its being given the name of biography, and there is much inaccuracy in the factual matter that is presented. The character of Johnson that it embodies is diminished and caricatured (the "Toby mug Johnson," he calls it), but it is entertaining and easy to grasp and has accordingly been embraced by the ordinary reader, unwilling to face the formidable reality he would find in Johnson's own writings.[5] Greene has recently given his argument a firmer base by providing a series of careful definitions of what he considers the minimum requirements of acceptable biography to be.[6]

Greene's demonstration of general inaccuracy in the *Life* may cause fair-minded readers to conclude that the book must in fact be reasonably accurate if his list includes all the mistakes an expert opponent can assemble. The *Life* does contain one serious error: Boswell, by depending on the information of Dr. Adams, head of Johnson's college, went badly wrong as to the length of Johnson's residence at Oxford. Otherwise, considering the great length of the book and the quantity of factual information it contains, it seems captious to bring a charge of general inaccuracy against it. At first blush the charge of thinness of narrative detail will likewise seem captious to anyone who really knows the book. Boswell was almost pedantic about the need of circumstantial detail in biography, and circumstantial detail implies temporal grounding. ("I have sometimes been obliged to run half over London, in order to fix a date correctly.")[7] His use of double dating ("Wednesday, May 15, 1776") for nearly all the conversations in the book indicates his care for precision in a matter where it might seem to be of little importance. Boswell's life of Johnson was much fuller in narrative detail than any previous English biography had ever been; indeed, the commonest contemporary charge against it was that it gave too much small detail. Aleyn Lyell Reade devoted a lifetime of research to Boswell's narrative of Johnson's earlier years, subjecting it to the minutest kind of scholarly scrutiny, but indicated his sense of small pickings by giving to his own collections the title of *Johnsonian Gleanings.*

By failing to mention the many letters of Johnson to Boswell that Boswell prints, Greene exaggerates the thinness of narrative information in the years after the two met. Boswell's plan, stated by himself at the beginning of the *Life*,[8] was to let Johnson tell his own story so far as was possible. Since the two men lived apart, they naturally tended to report personal news every time they wrote. Yet Greene is quite right in maintaining that full *coherent* narrative was not Boswell's principal aim. Chronologically arranged reports ("innumerable detached particulars")[9] on selected events of Johnson's life were essential to his method, because he felt that only by locating Johnson firmly in time and place could he convey the sense he had of Johnson's being a real and living man, a fact and not a fiction.

This is not the first time that Boswell's handling of the aspect of time in the *Life* has been called in question. He professes to relate "all the most important" events of Johnson's life "in their order,"[10] and, you will remember, gives his book an ostentatiously chronological arrangement, breaking it into annual sections with the year and Johnson's age in that year at the top of every page. Yet the *Life* almost completely lacks narrative tension: one is never impelled to skip ahead to see how the story is coming out. George Saintsbury's remarks on this, which he made in the early 1890s, are acute and helpful. The *Life,* he suggests, has in general experience proved to be a book for dipping into rather than for continuous straightforward reading. One may dip in anywhere, may move either forward or backward, will generally end by reading the entire book, and may repeat the performance. Saintsbury himself had read it all several times. But he allowed himself to doubt whether this lack of narrative tension did not indicate a structural fault in Boswell as compared with Lockhart (his favorite), who tells a story that one wants to follow and wants to follow in just the order in which Lockhart laid it out.[11]

Saintsbury's test, it will be seen, is literary: the story of a biography ought to be so constructed as continually to hold one's attention. Greene's test is not literary but scholarly. By his definition a biography must give its readers "a reasonably clear and coherent picture of how the subject occupied his time at all periods during the stated scope of the biography." Boswell, he now admits, was reasonably assiduous in seeking out evidence for the earlier part of the *Life* before he met Johnson, but from the point at which Boswell himself enters the story (Greene still maintains) he simply does not provide enough narrative detail to entitle his book to be called a biography.

All theoretical discussions of biography would be greatly clarified if the concept of "chronology," pure and simple, were set over against the concept of "biography." I have long insisted that every major author, besides (ideally before) having a biography, should have both a biobibliography and a chronology. I shall not go into detail here about the biobibliography, but may perhaps cite as a humble example my own *Literary Career of James Boswell*. The object of such a book is to fix the canon of an author's works; provide such technical descriptions of editions and issues as is necessary for the establishment of a sound text; collect whatever can be recovered concerning the origin, progress of writing, and publication of each work; and give at least a selected list of contemporary reviews. By attentive study of a biobibliography a biographer can decide what he is to say about the historical aspect of his subject's writings. The existence of a sound and thorough biobibliography will help him to avoid pedantry and disproportion and at the same time will keep him from separating the "man" from the "author."

The work that first opened my eyes to the value of chronologies for all major authors was the *Chronologie critique de la vie et des œuvres de Jean-Jacques Rousseau* by L.-J. Courtois (1924). For a comparable work on an English author, I can point only to the fine *Wordsworth Chronology* (1967), by Mark L. Reed, now published only to the year 1799. A chronology records specific events of an author's life by year, month, and day, like a calendar diary, with full references to the sources. Events are listed without connection (no narrative), and the style is as terse and abbreviated as clarity permits. A chronology may argue at length over the proper date of an event, but it avoids value judgments. It is a purely *factual* record. A Johnson chronology on the same scale as Reed's chronology of Wordsworth would soon establish itself as the work most frequently consulted by Johnson specialists. Do you want to know where Johnson was on a given day and what he was doing? A literary biography is of necessity badly set up to answer the question. Even if it gives the information (it may not, though the information would admittedly be useful to a scholar) it may give it without precise date or out of chronological order. A chronology will answer such factual questions much more quickly and certainly than a biography can. And it will list many, many useful details that you will not find in any biography that aspires to be art, to be itself literature.

How much chronological detail a biography shall contain depends on the character of the subject. Sir Walter Scott lived a life as exciting as a fiction from beginning to end, and Lockhart consequently presented a good deal of chronological detail for all periods of Scott's life. The details naturally cohered into a story, a story with strong narrative tension. But Johnson's life, after he settled in London as a bookseller's hack and occasional author on his own account, is not enough of a story to interest anybody but a Johnsonian specialist. After he received his pension, most of the daily events of his life became trivial and repetitive. I do not mean, of course, that they cannot be made rewarding and even charming as represented by occasional concrete examples, only that they cannot all be recorded seriatim. A life of Johnson, if it is itself to be literature, must have other than narrative organization.

In declaring that a group of modern biographers has given fuller and more coherent accounts than Boswell of how their subjects occupied their time at all periods of their lives, Greene is no doubt right, but I think he exaggerates the situation through being a specialist in Johnson and not in Churchill, Lloyd George, Beaverbrook, Orwell, Strachey, and Joyce. If he knew those men as well as he knows Johnson, I suspect that he would in every case be aware of very considerable periods of life and activity concerning which the biographers he praises are quite silent. Lockhart is justly praised for the fullness of his narrative, but I know Scott well enough to assert that Lockhart is almost completely silent about no less than half of Scott's existence during the years of his greatest fame. Scott's appointment as one of the Principal Clerks of Session in Edinburgh required his personal attendance in the Court of Session during five days of every week through six months of every year. Just precisely what did he do during all that time? Could I, for example, go to the Register House in Edinburgh and find masses of court records in Scott's hand? You will look in vain to Lockhart for an answer, though of course he knew it perfectly well because he was a Scot and had himself practiced in that same court. I am not blaming him, though as a Scott scholar I should find the information very interesting. It was enough for Lockhart's purpose as a literary biographer to indicate that Scott's Session job was responsible, carried a good salary, dealt at the administrative level with the keeping of records, and was utterly routine. To have gone into much greater detail would have been to write for specialists.

Greene, I think, suffers from specialist's syndrome. Specialists generally tend not to care very much for literary biographies of the subjects of their specialty. Information, yes: Greene wants to know not merely Johnson's works but every minutest fact about him. He does not, however, wish anyone else to shape the information imaginatively for him; he wants to form his own idea of how Johnson looked and acted and spoke. But he is very much aware at the same time of the literary character of Johnson, the towering mind that emerges from Johnson's own writings, and he wants that aspect of Johnson always to dominate the other in the public consciousness. He wants it so much that he has come to wish the personal Johnson—all the vivid details of Johnson's appearance and gestures and talk—to be laid aside and forgotten, at least by everyone except people like himself who can be counted on to hold the two aspects properly together. What he wants is not a literary life of Johnson but a chronology.

Professor Ralph W. Rader has recently cast a flood of light on this whole problem of alleged structural defects in Boswell's work. He begins by recognizing and stating the basic distinction between literary biography and biography that is content merely to provide information. He also gets down to fundamentals as regards the diagnosis of literary faults, remarking sensibly that nothing alleged to be a structural fault in a literary work is really so if thoughtful readers do not react to it as a fault while reading. Critics who have formulated lists of faults of structure in Boswell have mostly done so because an inadequate or a misapplied theory forced them to, not because as readers they felt anything of the sort. The theory they have been applying is one that would be proper for a play or a novel. Rader's own theory of the structure of the *Life* seems to me by far the aptest that has yet been advanced. The *Life*, he says, lacks narrative tension because Boswell knew that he did not have a story to tell. The organizing principle of the book is a massive idea or image of Johnson's human character, existing as a whole only in Boswell's mind but ruling the book from beginning to end. This image is developed in time by what, taking a hint from Rader, I may style "the method of redundancy"; that is, by the exuberant repeated etching in of similar but not identical characterizing detail. The developed image in the book is, as Boswell insisted, "a Flemish picture." Johnson's unattractive traits are fully and vividly presented, but always within an enveloping overall impression of wisdom, magnanimity, and goodness.[12]

I should like to expand this theory a bit by a reflection of my own. If time is not the organizing principle of Boswell's book, why does he make it so prominent in his scheme? I suggest that he employed the annals of Johnson's life as a firm but shifting frame for developing his character of Johnson. His chronology has often been called "mechanical," and indeed it is mechanical. If a time-scheme is important for your book but is not its main organizing principle, what better method can you devise than to handle it mechanically?

Professor Leopold Damrosch has been moved by Rader's theory to publish what he emphatically calls "an anti-theory."[13] He insists that he is not out to repeal the *Life;* on the contrary he admires the book greatly and wants it to go on being admired. Like Greene (and probably echoing him) he grants that it is a masterpiece but doubts that it is the world's greatest biography. First, he contends, it has faults of tone and (in spite of Rader) defects of organization and structure. It is not a fully realized work of art; it can and should be admired as an extraordinary performance without being judged as possessing coherent form. Second, it lacks "that deep and full insight into a man's mind which the greatest biographies are able to convey." I like this essay very much, but am bound to say that it shows a basic misapprehension of Rader's theory and attacks its misapprehended version with a breathtaking amount of *petitio principi.* Rader's tone might perhaps encourage a reader to think that he considers the *Life* utterly without defect, but in fact he carefully restricts his discussion to alleged defects of proportion, lack of narrative connection and development—in short, to alleged defects of temporal structure. Acceptance of Rader's theory does not demand agreement with him at all points: one may think him right on the whole though disagreeing with him on particulars. And Rader does not in effect say, "In a factual work like Boswell's, anything goes." The sentence that Damrosch selects as summarizing Rader's argument actually deals with writers of factual narrative other than Gibbon and Boswell.

Damrosch feels that it was simply a defect of structure for Boswell to depict the character of Johnson as unchangingly that of a mature, indeed of an old, man. To have devoted half the book to the last nine years of Johnson's life, he asserts, leads to an unfortunate emphasis on the old, the fussy, the querulous Johnson. He thinks that Boswell's remarks on Johnson's works show no imaginative grasp of Johnson's literary achievement; indeed, that Boswell gave merely peripheral attention to the nature of Johnson's literary powers. "Who would guess," he questions, "that the often querulous and blustering figure of the later years was engaged in writing the *Lives of the Poets,* with their wonderful fluency and penetration?" Finally, he charges Boswell with continually intruding his own opinions, which are seldom memorable, in language that is at times pompous and laboriously elegant; indeed he feels that the pretentious "public Boswell" imparts a pervasively disagreeable tone that seriously impairs the quality of the book.

I have not read enough biographies in enough languages to be able to assert as my own judgment that Boswell's *Life of Johnson* is the greatest of all biographies, but I do consider it the greatest of those I have read. I have never considered it flawless and have always thought the art that it displays, except in the conversations, to be robust rather than highly finished. On the conversations Boswell lavished minute and subtle attention; in other matters his solutions have seemed to me successful but frank and direct rather than graceful. I used to think that I had to make the conventional strictures on his handling of his narrative, but Rader has convinced me on that score. While I should not like to commit myself to the defense of every single detail of Boswell's handling of his chronological scheme, I now feel the narrative to be more than adequate for grounding the book's brilliant character of Johnson. Of course, for purposes of historical research, the *Life* has to be supplemented by many, many other books, but its character of Johnson remains perennially self-sufficient and valid.

It may well be thought that the most serious charge that both Greene and Damrosch bring against Boswell is that he did not do justice to Johnson's literary personality. I am not myself convinced on this point. An author does certainly have a literary personality (the personality you would infer from his works even if you knew nothing whatever about his personal history) and a human personality (the personality you would know if you were familiar with him as a man even if you had not read a line of his writings), and the two are by no means identical. Furthermore, neither can be wholly inferred from the other. Biography, as Boswell defined it, quoting Johnson who was quoting Thuanus, strives to "lay open to posterity *the private and familiar* character of [a] man whose candour and genius will to the end of time be *by his writings* preserved in admiration."[14] Biography deals primarily with the human personality: it gives a history of the subject's life and character or, better, of his character as developed by a history of his life. One may properly demand of a biographer that his history of the human character of his subject be reconcilable with that subject's literary character, but one may not demand that the character dominating the biography shall be the literary character. If it is wrong to substitute biography for literary criticism, it is just as wrong to substitute literary criticism for biography. Though Boswell shows no particular distinction in extended literary criticism, I do not feel that he was incapable of entering fully into Johnson's works. In spite of his own occasional self-indictments for illiteracy, he was widely read in good literature and made shrewd and generally sound literary judgments. Indeed, his judgments in several cases accord more with those of present-day critics than Johnson's do. Johnson's writings were well known and generally accessible, and Boswell could assume that Johnson's literary character was forever preserved by them, whereas much of his private character would be forever lost if he did not bestir himself. He undoubtedly had, and met, an obligation to call Johnson's writings constantly to the attention of the reader as the principal cause of his fame and to make glancing but pregnant critical remarks about them, but we should be glad that he did not stuff his book with literary criticism. Literary criticism is a very datable commodity. It would be untrue to call its changes of interest mere fashions, but they are certainly modes. When we accuse a critic of the past of inability to enter imaginatively into a piece of literature, we generally mean that he does not remark on the aspects of it that are peculiarly visible to our historical mode. If a biographer is a Johnson (that is, a critic whom one reads for the powerful way he makes judgments, not necessarily for the judgments themselves), he may venture on extended literary criticism. If he is not, he will inevitably strew his book with dead patches as shifts of sensibility alter the focus of criticism.

Damrosch admits that most of what he calls defects in the *Life* were due to no bad choices on Boswell's part but were insuperable limitations in the material accessible to him. One fault he does attribute to Boswell himself is that of not being more rigorously selective in his handling of the embarrassingly abundant materials of the last nine years. By that time Johnson was old, ill, and failing and of course should have been shown so, but by printing so much of symptoms and drugs, petulancies and irritations he thinks Boswell exaggerates the aspect of "the old, the fussy, and sometimes actually tedious Johnson." It would have been helpful if Damrosch had named some of the biographies he was prepared to place above Boswell's. When one rates a book for excellence one should rate it against other actually existing books, not against an admittedly impossible norm. No biographer in history can ever have been able to treat with equal fullness all the periods of the life of a contemporary who lived to be seventy-five years old. Authors of genius compensate for limitation at one point by originality and brilliance at another. If Boswell conceived his main responsibility to be character and not chronicle, and if Johnson's character remained essentially unchanged from youth to old age (which seems really to have been the case), then an abundance of material from the later years was as useful for Boswell's purpose as the same amount of material evenly distributed would have been. The argument that the *Life* would be improved by removing from Johnson's letters some of the mention of drugs and symptoms surely deserves consideration (Boswell undoubtedly did suppress elsewhere several vivid bits of characterizing evidence because he thought they would etch some trait too deeply) but I do not think that I want the record of Johnson's old man's petulancies and irritablenesses softened. It is fused with a record of wise and benevolent and keen-witted sayings, and is Boswell's way of demonstrating dramatically that although

Johnson's body deteriorated sadly, the deeper traits of his character remained unchanged. Damrosch's paradox was a paradox of historical fact: the often querulous and blustering figure of the later years *was* engaged in writing the *Lives of the Poets,* with their wonderful fluency and penetration. Reynolds performed the same service as Boswell, but he had to do it in a series of portraits, not one. The same Johnson looks out of all of them, but the one I should most cherish as my own is the last one, with its fallen lip and its suffering indomitable eyes.

Damrosch finally charges Boswell with unwarranted intrusion of his own opinions into the *Life* and with making matters worse by imparting an annoying tone to these intrusions. For the private Boswell of the journals, with their expressive simplicity, he feels real and constant affection; by the public Boswell who is often pompous and laboriously elegant he is often repelled. This is an acute and original judgment, and I cannot but agree with it. Damrosch thinks it hardly worthwhile to bring in the concept of a persona, but as a persona I certainly see this public Boswell. He is Mr. Hypochondriack, who for six years held forth on assorted topics in the *London Magazine.* Sententiousness, as I have said elsewhere, does not suit Boswell; waywardness does.[15] A very large part of these annoying intrusions first appeared in the second edition of the *Life;* they originated partly in Boswell's desire to help the sale of that edition by announcing additions, partly in his horror and alarm at the unrolling events of the French Revolution. If I were allowed to make what I personally consider the best text of the *Life of Johnson,* I would ruthlessly excise most of these sententious addenda.

To conclude. In my opinion, the attempt seriously to degrade the reputation of the *Life of Johnson* for faults of structure and proportion will not prevail. Rader's theory, probably somewhat qualified, will gain general acceptance, and when it is agreed that the *Life* is structurally a character, the charge of inadequacy in the narrative will evaporate. The debate as to whether the book, being a character, deserves to be called a biography could, like any other semantic argument against prevailing usage, go on forever. I consider it quite empty except insofar as it helps to develop the important and neglected concept of a chronology. Because of the strong tendency of the present age to depreciate biography as a mode of literature and to convert it into literary criticism, and furthermore because of its laudable desire to make the literary personality of Johnson better known, I expect to hear a good deal more about the perfunctoriness and externality of Boswell's dealings with Johnson's works. I have expressed my own dissenting opinion on that score. In my opinion, the most cogent and permanently valid charge now being brought against the *Life* is Damrosch's last one. Boswell does talk too much in his own person upon matters on which his opinion is neither necessary nor useful, and he does so in a tone that present-day readers sometimes find annoying even when his judgments are unexceptionable. Why has the distinction between Boswell's two styles, apparently so obvious, not been marked before? It is because the publication of Boswell's journal in the present century has given us an education in Boswell's better literary personality. In the journals, where he is invariably tentative, self-doubting, and unpretentious, his opinions strike one as generally interesting, often charming, often acute. As I have remarked elsewhere, some of the aspects of Boswell's private style had to wait for Lamb and Hazlitt to make them public.[16] We are using private writing of Boswell's to criticize his public style, just as Macaulay used Johnson's letters to depreciate his books. The charge against Johnson's *Rambler* style is now less often heard than it used to be, but the charge against Boswell's public style is not likely to wane. I have no doubt that the *Life of Johnson* will always be rated Boswell's greatest literary performance, but I think the future may well agree that it was in his journals that he did his best writing.

Notes

This essay is based on a presidential address delivered in Guildhall, Lichfield, on 21 September 1974. It was first published in the *Transactions of the Johnson Society* (1974): 6–19.

1. Review of J. W. Croker's edition of the *Life* in *Edinburgh Review* 54 (August–December 1831). Collected as "Essay on Boswell's *Life of Johnson*," in Macaulay's *Critical and Historical Essays Contributed to Edinburgh Review*, 3 vols. (London, 1843).

2. Also a review of Croker in *Fraser's Magazine* 5 (May 1832): 386. Collected

as "Biography: Boswell's *Life of Johnson*," in Carlyle's *Critical and Miscellaneous Essays*, 4 vols. (London, 1839, etc.).

3. See n. 6.

4. F. R. Leavis, *The Great Tradition* (London, 1948), 11–12.

5. D. J. Greene, "Reflections on a Literary Anniversary," *Queen's Quarterly* 70 (Summer 1963): 198–208.

6. D. J. Greene, " 'Tis a Pretty Book, Mr. Boswell, But—," xeroxed typescript circulated at the Seminar on Biography and Autobiography of the Modern Language Association, December 1973. This paper repeats and considerably enlarges on the arguments of the article in n. 5. My remaining references to Greene are to this more recent statement of his views.

7. *Life*, "Advertisement to the First Edition."

8. Seventh paragraph from the beginning.

9. As in n. 7.

10. *Life*, eighth paragraph from the beginning.

11. "Some Great Biographies," *Macmillan's Magazine* 66 (May–October 1892): 99. Collected in Saintsbury's *Collected Essays and Papers 1875–1920* (London, 1923), vol. 1.

12. "Literary Form in Factual Narrative," in *Essays in Eighteenth-Century Biography,* ed. P. B. Daghlian (Bloomington, 1968). "Flemish picture" is from *Life*, III, 191.

13. "*The Life of Johnson*: An Anti-Theory," *Eighteenth-Century Studies* 6 (Summer 1973): 486–505.

14. *Life*, fifteenth paragraph from the beginning, my italics.

15. *James Boswell, the Earlier Years 1740–1769* (New York, 1966), 129.

16. Ibid.

DONALD GREENE

Boswell's *Life* as "Literary Biography"

When I was invited to reply to Professor Pottle's attack on an early version of my essay, I was not very enthusiastic about the proposal; this controversy has been going on for a long time, and Professor Pottle may well be as weary of it as I am. Still, the issues involved are important enough to warrant a continuation of the argument. I seem to have lost the typewritten draft that he worked from. I don't think, however, that the later form of my essay, as printed above, differs greatly from the original. There are a few additions, such as the quotations from Professor Pottle's early article downgrading the *Life* in favor of the *Journals*. But since he concludes his presidential address to the Johnson Society "The future may well agree that it was in his journals that he [Boswell] did his best writing," he will surely not object. (I have always maintained that Boswell's *Journal of a Tour to the Hebrides* is a far better piece of biography than the *Life*.) There is also the statistical appendix, giving a visual demonstration of how relatively little time Boswell actually spent with Johnson. But the main points in my argument are the same in both versions, and I will comment briefly on how they are dealt with by Professor Pottle.

As, unfortunately, too often happens in literary controversy, many of Professor Pottle's strictures are simply *ad hominem*, sometimes rather naively so. If I am not a New Critic, who despises biography, then I must be a mere chronologer. Apparently I am incapable of any intermediate position. I "suffer from specialist's syndrome" (why this animus against specialists? if any modern literary scholar is entitled to the appellation "specialist," surely it is Professor Pottle) and so "tend not to care much for literary biographies of the subject of my special-ty." (Despite which defect, I managed to be of some assistance, kindly acknowledged, to the late Professor James Clifford in composing his fine biographies of the young and the middle-aged Johnson. But per-haps these are not "literary biographies" in Professor Pottle's sense, and perhaps Clifford too was a mere chronologer, suffering from spe-cialist's syndrome. It seems odd that in Professor Pottle's critique he makes no mention of Clifford's way of doing Johnsonian biography as a possible alternative to Boswell's.) I "have come to wish the personal Johnson—all the vivid details of Johnson's appearance and gestures and talk—to be laid aside and forgotten." What I want "is not a liter-ary life of Johnson but a chronology." My "test" of a biography "is not literary but scholarly." (Are the two qualities antithetical? Is schol-arship a detriment to "literary" investigation? Surely the greatest praise is due to Professor Pottle's own high standard of scholarship in his work on Boswell.)

How Professor Pottle acquired so intimate a knowledge of what I want in literary studies, I don't know. I think we met only once, when, as a graduate student, I was introduced to him at a Johnsonian cele-bration and expressed my sense of the honor I felt at meeting him. I was later invited, and gratefully accepted the invitation, to contribute an essay to a festschrift honoring him. To his strictures quoted above, I can only reply that, when I complete the biography of Johnson's later years that I hope will form not too unworthy a continuation of Clifford's work, its readers will see that (1) I do care for literary biog-raphies of the subject(s) of my specialty(ies), and (2) it will be some-thing more than a bare, mechanical, undiscriminating chronology of trivia. Professor Pottle must have missed section 5 above of my at-tempt to formulate criteria of good biography, where I reject the idea of biography as a "literary data bank . . . buried under heaps of accu-mulated rubbish," and write: "The canon of completeness and con-tinuity . . . must not be taken to justify lack of discrimination between what is important and what is not. It would be wrong to pass over Orwell's Burma years in silence. At the same time it would be wrong to give every detail of his routine as a policeman during those years with the same emphasis as the details of his work as a writer"—just as Professor Pottle says that it would have been wrong of Lockhart to give every detail of Scott's work as a Clerk of Session.

Still, I think that a conscientious biographer *should* try to gather as much information as he can about the doings of his subject, if only so as to be in a position to decide what is important and what less so, what to include and what to leave out. Professor Pottle is less than gracious to the late Aleyn Lyell Reade, whose monumental *Johnsonian Gleanings* he terms "small pickings." (And, incidentally, the subject of Reade's research was not "Boswell's narrative" of Johnson's earlier years, but those years themselves, a good deal of which Boswell knew little about or got wrong.) It was Reade's work that made possible Clifford's *Young Sam Johnson,* now the definitive biography of Johnson's early years; no competent teacher would send a student to Boswell's rather than to Clifford's account of that period of his life. Clifford used to lament that for his biography of the middle years, *Dictionary Johnson,* there had been no Reade to devote his spare time for decades to searching the records of those years.

As for "all the vivid details of Johnson's appearance and gestures," I do not wish them to "be laid aside and forgotten" (when did I ever say or write such a thing?), but I, and many others, do think they have formed much too prominent a part of the "image" of Johnson that Boswell and his successors have constructed, and should be kept in proper perspective. The details of Alexander Pope's appearance and physical habits were quite as "vivid" as Johnson's. Johnson devotes four brilliantly written short paragraphs to them, out of the 446 paragraphs of his "Life of Pope," which seems to be about the right proportion. Although, as Johnson recognizes, Pope's physique may afford clues to his writing and his general psychology, it is not for the possession of such "vivid" physical traits that Pope is remembered and warrants being the subject of serious biography. Nor is Johnson.

On the matter of Boswell's accuracy, Professor Pottle calls attention to Boswell's "care for precision," especially in dating, in the *Life:*

> Boswell was almost pedantic about the need of circumstantial detail in biography, and circumstantial detail implies temporal grounding. ("I have sometimes been obliged to run half over London in order to fix a date correctly.") His use of double dating ("Wednesday, May 15, 1776")

for nearly all the conversations in the book indicates his care for precision.

To anyone who, like myself, has experienced the difficulty of trying to piece together from the *Life* and the *Journals* an accurate list of the dates on which Boswell was in Johnson's company, this is more than a little ironic. Boswell may have been concerned for such precision, but he very often didn't achieve it. There are numerous places in the Hill-Powell edition of the *Life* where Powell, in his page headings, has to correct the date given in the text of the *Life,* sometimes (also ironically) noting as his authority for the correction "Pottle, *Private Papers of Boswell.*" In the *Life,* Boswell writes that in 1778 "On Wednesday, March 18, I arrived in London," whereas his journal shows him to have arrived on Tuesday, 17 March. In the same year Boswell writes, "On Saturday, April 14, I drank tea with him," and Powell notes, "Saturday was April 18" and corrects the headline accordingly. In 1783, "On Monday, April 29, I found him at home"; footnote, "The correct date is Wednesday, April 30. *Boswell Papers,* xv. 206." And a dozen more of the same—so much for Boswell's careful double dating.

Then there are the places where Boswell lumps together a number of meetings during a month without specifying the individual dates, though often these dates seem to have been available in his journals. Here is the passage in the *Life* that follows the account of a meeting with Johnson on 20 April 1781:

> For some time after this day, I did not see him very often, and of the conversations which I did enjoy, I am sorry to find that I have preserved but little. I was at that time engaged in a variety of other matters, which required exertion and assiduity, and necessarily occupied almost all my time.

On this, Boswell's editor, L. F. Powell, normally the mildest of commentators, cannot resist an acid note:

> Boswell is here disingenuous. He met Johnson at least five times between 21 April and 8 May, and the matters which engaged his attention were not of so serious a nature as he implies. He was in fact at this time extremely dissipated. . . . From the entry for the 29th we learn that it was on the 22nd that he got drunk at the Duke of Montrose's. . . . He met Johnson on the 28th at the Academy dinner, and again on the 30th. On

1 May after finding himself unfit, through drink, for an engagement, he
"ranged"; the next day he dined with Johnson; on the 5th he had an
interview with Lord Bute, before and after which he was "very wild"; on
the 7th he called on Johnson, who greeted him with the admonition: "I
hope you don't intend to get drunk tomorrow as you did at Paoli's."
Boswell Papers [ed. Pottle], xiv. 204–17.[1]

Precision? Accuracy?

Such slips are perhaps not too important, so long as there are scholars around like Powell and Pottle to correct them. Much more serious
is Boswell's distortion of Johnson's spoken words, or dubious attribution or even apparent invention of them. I call attention to some of
these in my essay above. I'd like here to dwell in particular on two of
Boswell's reports that have had a most powerful and damaging effect
on the "image" of Johnson.

One is "The woman's a whore, and there's an end on't," Johnson's
supposed verdict on Lady Diana Beauclerk, née Spencer, who had
been divorced by her first husband, Lord Bolingbroke (whose brutal
treatment of her made her the object of much sympathy) for adultery
with Topham Beauclerk, whom she then married. Many students of
mine, and other acquaintances, have said that they were put off Johnson by such unrelenting bigotry. But when one begins to think about
it, the remark seems somewhat out of character. Johnson, in *Ramblers*
170 and 171 (1751), had written a most moving and sympathetic account of the unhappy life of a prostitute, the victim of an unjust society. (And he had printed a similar plea for sympathy for prostitutes,
written perhaps by his friend Joseph Simpson, in *Rambler* 107.) Beauclerk, the other "guilty party" in the divorce case, remained one of
Johnson's dearest friends. Some months after the supposed remark,
we find Johnson writing with apparent friendliness and with a seemingly affectionate abbreviation of her name, "Poor Beauclerk is so ill
that his life is thought to be in danger. Lady Di nurses him with very
great assiduity." After Beauclerk's death in 1780, Johnson writes, "He
has left his children to the care of Lady Di,"[2] and expresses no disapproval of the action.

For all my growing distrust of Boswell's reporting, I had, like most
others, accepted the remark without question—it is (unfortunately)
one of the best known "Johnsonian" quotations. It was only recently,

in connection with another scholarly project, that it occurred to me to check its origin in Boswell's journals. What does one find there about Boswell's authority for the attribution of the remark? When we turn to *Boswell for the Defence, 1769–1774*, edited by W. K. Wimsatt, Jr., and F. A. Pottle, we are told (p. 194) that on 7 May 1773 Boswell break-fasted with Johnson and the Thrales in Southwark, and an argument ensued about the divorce and remarriage (which had taken place five years before). We do not know the exact nature of the argument, but the editors tell us that "Johnson was 'angry.' 'Go to Scotland! Go to Scotland! I never heard [you] talk so foolishly.'" "For which," they add, "Boswell in the *Life* manuscript has Johnson say: 'My dear Sir, never accustom your mind to mingle virtue and vice. The woman's a whore, and there's an end on't.'" Boswell "*has Johnson say*"?

There was a time when some Boswellians would have argued that this was one of the many spectacular feats of Boswell's miraculous endowment of "total recall," which retained every detail of an incident, every word of a conversation, after no matter how long a lapse of time. That is to say, when preparing the manuscript of the *Life* fifteen years after the event, Boswell looked at his journal notes, snapped his finger, and said, "How silly of me! Now I recall that what Johnson actually said was not what I wrote down at the time, 'Go to Scotland! I never heard you talk so foolishly,' but 'My dear Sir, never accustom yourself, etc.'" About all one can say regarding this is what the great Duke of Wellington, at the height of his fame, is supposed to have said to someone who approached him on the street and addressed him, "Mr. Jones, I believe": "If you can believe that, you can believe anything."[3]

Later Boswellians, such as Professor Rader, would probably argue instead that the expression is no doubt fictional but that it is a splendid addition by Boswell to the "image" of Johnson—much better than what a mere unimaginative "informative" biographer would have set down. (And, of course, it also helped the image of Boswell to suppress one of Johnson's not infrequent blasts at Boswell's "foolishness.") To most people it would seem to be a very unpleasant addition. But for Professor Rader and others, if the historical Johnson differs from the Boswellian one, so much the worse for the historical Johnson.

Since Professor Pottle in his presidential address applauds Pro-

fessor Rader for having solved the vexed question of alleged deficiencies in the structure of the *Life* by "recognizing and stating the basic
distinction between literary biography and biography that is content
merely to provide information," I should like to take as my second
example a passage from the *Life* that Professor Rader quotes with
admiration in the essay to which Professor Pottle alludes. This is in
illustration of his praise of "Johnson's speech—edited and pointed by
Boswell to preserve and heighten its Johnsonian essence" (but is the
"Johnsonian essence" really in need of such "heightening"?):

> "He seemed to take a pleasure in speaking in his own style," says Boswell;
> "for when he had carelessly missed it, he would repeat the thought trans-
> lated into it. Talking of the Comedy of 'The Rehearsal,' he said, 'It has
> not wit enough to keep it sweet.' This was easy; he therefore caught
> himself, and pronounced a more rounded sentence; 'It has not vitality
> enough to preserve it from putrefaction.'" Pure style, pure pleasure—
> but as always in Johnson, the style is the man.

If, of course, Johnson said it. This "translation" into "his own style"
was seized on by Macaulay as the text for a vehement denunciation of
"Johnsonese"—sesquipedalianism. But we might ask, just where and
when did Boswell hear Johnson make that "translation"? He lists it, in
the *Life,* under the year 1776 as one of "particulars which I collected
at various times." The facts—assuming that we're interested in facts—
seem to be these.

On 18 August 1768 Helfrich Peter Sturz, a German scholar in the
entourage of King Christian VII of Denmark, who was paying a state
visit to England, was brought by George Colman the elder to Streatham to meet the Thrales and Johnson. Sturz left a long and interesting account of the meeting, which included this exchange: "Colman
mentioned the 'Rehearsal,' as a once admired masterpiece, which no
one now could be bothered to read. 'There was too little salt in, to
keep it sweet,' said Johnson."[4] A metaphor from pickling meat: a
strong infusion of salt (i.e., wit) is needed to preserve it or it will go
bad. And indeed, to most readers of *The Rehearsal* today, the real wit-
ticisms seem few and far between; most of the jokes in it are pretty
dull.
Where was Boswell on 18 August 1768 when this exchange took

place? Was he one of the company at Streatham? No, he was in Scotland, as usual.

Five years later, in the Blue Room at Streatham Place, Mrs. Thrale and Johnson had a long chat about writers—Steele, Gray, Swift, Richardson, and others. "This conversation passed on the 18: of July 1773 & I wrote it down that night, as I thought it particularly interesting." Part of what Mrs. Thrale wrote down was this:

> We talked of Dryden—Buckingham's Play said I had hurt the Reputation of that Poet, great as he was; such is the force of Ridicule!—on the contrary my Dearest replies Doctor Johnson The greatness of Dryden's Character is even now the only principle of Vitality which preserves that Play from a State of Putrefaction.[5]

Here the discussion is not about the amount of "salt" or "wit" in the text of the play but about its topicality. In the earlier comment, the lack of salt has *caused* it to putrefy; in the later, the continued interest in Dryden, the central character of the play, has *preserved* it from putrefaction; that is, if anyone still enjoys reading it, it is because of the references to Dryden in it, not because of its wittiness. In no sense is the later comment a "translation" of the earlier one because the conclusions reached are different: the imagery is different, one from the kitchen, the other from a biological or medical laboratory.

And where was Boswell when the second comment on *The Rehearsal* took place? In the Blue Room at Streatham? No, he was back in Edinburgh again. It is true that when Boswell was putting the *Life* together the second comment was available to him in Mrs. Thrale-Piozzi's *Anecdotes,* published in 1786. The earlier one was not yet in print in English (though it was in German, in 1779); it might of course have been circulated orally by Mrs. Thrale or Colman. But where and when did Boswell or anyone else hear Johnson deliver the two comments in quick succession, with the concrete "salt" of the first being flattened to the abstract "wit," and with the whole point of the second being destroyed by the change of preservation into lack of preservation? There is no other record that I know of in Johnson's conversation or his revisions of his writings of his inflating the vocabulary of a statement merely in order to make it more polysyllabic. In the words of the little girl in the *New Yorker* cartoon whose mother is urging her to eat her nice broccoli, I can only retort that if this is "literary biography," I say it's spinach, and I say ———. The reader can finish the quotation.

No one yet has systematically tried to list all such instances in the *Life* of what, at best, can be called inaccurate reporting and, at worst, conscious or unconscious fakery. But it badly needs to be done. The obvious person to do it is Marshall Waingrow; but I don't envy him his task, as he nears the end of his great project of editing the manuscript of the *Life*, of noting all the passages in it for which no source can be traced in the *Journals* or in memoranda by others who were present at the time when a Johnsonian quip was supposed to have been uttered.

Professor Rader's plea, seconded by Professor Pottle, for recognition of a genre called "literary biography" that is distinct from "biography that is content merely to provide information" boils down simply to a plea to legitimize falsification by biographers. Would the plea not equally justify as "literary biography" such a work as Irving Stone's *The Agony and the Ecstasy: A Life of Michelangelo*, which its author frankly calls a novel? If not, just where is the dividing line to be drawn between it and Boswell's *Life*?

It is not a plea that is likely to succeed. Professor Pottle does not address himself to the first point I make in my essay: that the excellent biographies now being written are composed on very different principles from Boswell's. As I write, the fifth volume of Martin Gilbert's biography of Winston Churchill, dealing with the early years of World War II, has just appeared to great acclaim. So has a new enlarged edition of Richard Ellmann's biography of Joyce, which one reviewer describes correctly as "A work of exacting scholarship which is also a humane and liberating document" and another as "The greatest literary biography of the century." Clearly the latter—novelist and critic Anthony Burgess—defines "literary biography" in a way very different from Professors Rader and Pottle.

I doubt that Ellmann and other serious biographers in the future are ever likely to be persuaded by Professors Pottle's and Rader's arguments to abandon their commitment to exacting scholarship and revert to Boswell's methods. Professor Pottle argues for the high literary quality of the *Life* on the grounds that, like Saintsbury, one can pick it up at any time, open it at any place, read in it desultorily ("dip into it"), and lay it down again without qualms. This seems an odd way to recommend the literary value of a book. It is the kind of praise that might be given to, say, *My Years with Noël Coward*, by his valet, or *Chats with Somerset Maugham*, by a casual acquaintance—in short, *ana*. It would not be given to Ellmann's *Joyce,* where one starts at the beginning, is at once gripped by the fascinating story and the skill with which it is told, reads on continuously, and finds it hard to put down. And one reads it with the conviction that one is coming as close as it is possible to come to the truth of the reality of a complex and fascinating human being who was a great artist. "History will always take stronger hold of the attention than fable," wrote Johnson, contrasting Dryden's second Saint Cecilia's Day ode with Pope's. "The passions excited by Dryden are the pleasures and pains of real life, the scene of Pope is laid in imaginary existence. Pope is read with calm acquiescence, Dryden with turbulent delight; Pope hangs upon the ear, and Dryden finds the passes of the mind."[6]

But thanks to Boswell and his fans, the "double tradition" of Johnson, described and deplored by Bertrand Bronson more than thirty years ago, is alive and well and likely to remain so for a long time. Thanks to such dubious anecdotes as "The woman's a whore, and there's an end on't," we have the arrogant, noisy, obese bully pictured by Charles Addams in a recent *New Yorker* cartoon (captioned "Doctor Johnson Gets Off a Good One"), declaiming to a group of utterly bored denizens of a tavern, "So I say, 'You have Lord Kames. Keep him, ha, ha, ha, ha!' "[7] Thanks to the story of Johnson's "translating" into "his own style," we have the recurrent attempts at supposedly humorous "Johnsonian" polysyllablism, such as one in *Punch* a short time ago.[8] No doubt this construct of "literary biography" will continue to amuse as many as that equally "artistic" construct Sherlock Holmes (whom I can enjoy as much as anyone, just as Johnson occasionally enjoyed "relaxing his mind" with *Tom Thumb*). Some of us, however, even though stigmatized as "scholarly specialists," will get more genuine aesthetic pleasure out of the deeply understanding observations on the problems of the human condition found in Johnson's works and the splendidly varied and sensitive language in which they are written, and will feel that while we are doing so we are engaged on a higher plane of "literary" artistry. Clifford's and my attempts to write a biography of the man capable of this will never, I suppose, be ranked in the same high class as Ellmann's. But it is Ellmann's methods and standards of biography we have been trying to follow, not Boswell's.

Notes

1. Boswell, *Life of Johnson*, ed. G. B. Hill, rev. L. F. Powell (Oxford, 1934), IV, 491–492.

2. Johnson, *Letters*, ed. R. W. Chapman (Oxford, 1952), nos. 374, 655.

3. Another famous remark the authenticity of which I have begun to wonder about (though it has nothing directly to do with Johnson) is the often quoted one that Boswell attributes to Oliver Edwards, "You are a philosopher, Dr. Johnson. I have tried too in my time to be a philosopher, but, I don't know how, cheerfulness was always breaking in." In Boswell's journal account of the meeting with Edwards, written up apparently ten days after it took place, all the other details given in the *Life* are there—but not this one (*Boswell in Extremes*, ed. C. McC. Weis and F. A. Pottle [New York, 1970], 293–296). Boswell goes on to say that he was fond of repeating the remark to his friends, who greatly enjoyed it. No doubt they did. But where did it come from? Why, if it is so memorable, is it not to be found in the journal?

Still another last-minute *trouvaille*. No "saying" of Johnson's is more often quoted than that given in the *Life*, III, 178: "Why, Sir, you find no man, at all intellectual, who is willing to leave London. No, Sir, when a man is tired of London, he is tired of life; for there is in London all that life can afford." According to Boswell's journal (*Boswell in Extremes*, p. 171), all that Johnson said on this occasion was "You find no man wishes to leave it."

4. Sturz, *Schriften* (Munich: Wilhelm Fink, 1971; facsimile of the 1779 Leipzig edition), p. 4: "Colmann nante den Rehearsal als ein ehemals bewundertes Meisterstück, das man jezt nicht mehre zu lesen im Stande sei: there was too little salt in, to keep it sweet, sagte Johnson." In a footnote, Sturz gives a translation into German of Johnson's English, which emphasizes the metaphor from the preservation of meat: "Er war nicht gesalzen genug, um sich lange zu halten"—"It had not been salted enough to keep it for long." The *Monthly Magazine* (March 1800) gives an English translation of Sturz's account of his meeting with Johnson.

5. *Thraliana*, ed. Katharine C. Balderston, 2d ed. (Oxford, 1951), 172.

6. Johnson, *Lives of the Poets*, ed. G. B. Hill (Oxford, 1905), 3:227.

7. 18 October 1982, p. 45.

8. 23 March 1983. Howard Weinbrot reprints the piece in the November 1983 number of the *Newsletter* of the Johnson Society of the Central Region with the comment, "From time to time one hears that the old myth of ponderous old Sam Johnson of big-word fame is dead and buried. If only it were so."

JOHN J. BURKE, JR.

But Boswell's Johnson
Is Not Boswell's Johnson

*W*hat does the phrase "Boswell's Johnson" mean? Or, better, what should it mean? This seems an increasingly urgent question for those concerned with both writers. The phrase can seem harmless enough as a simple grammatical construction. What is it but a possessive and a noun? Yet often there is acid in the phrase and some philosophical sting. For when the phrase makes a philosophical statement, it denies that there is any objective truth in the assessment of human affairs, or at least any human capacity to arrive at it if it does exist. Behind all claims for objective truth lie the snares of prejudice, subjective biases, and blind spots—in this case, Boswell's. *Esse est percipere* is the axiom. Perception is in the saddle and rides mankind. And biography—one person writing about another— is no more than a form of fallible human perception. Another common usage of the phrase intends to tell us that the Johnson portrayed in Boswell's *Life* must stand as no more than equal to—no better than, if no worse than—the Johnson portrayed by Sir John Hawkins in his *Life* or by Mrs. Piozzi in her biographical sketch, to name only the chief rivals for our attention.[1] A recent twist in the argument over whether any one biographer's version of Johnson ought to take precedence over any other is the claim that, neither Boswell's Johnson, nor Hawkins's Johnson, nor Mrs. Piozzi's Johnson, but the Johnson being reconstructed by the collective efforts of modern scholars is the Johnson that should command our attention, as if modern commentary on Johnson were itself a seamless web.[2] All of this has, understandably, shaken our confidence in what was once thought to be the supreme example of the art of biography. The question that needs to be asked is, are the debunking meanings implied in the phrase "Boswell's Johnson" truly justified?

As a practical matter, we do not live with the consequences of either philosophical skepticism or epistemological egalitarianism. We believe there is such a thing as truth in the assessment of human affairs, though not that it is easily attained. We also believe that some people get closer to objective truth than others. That is why Boswell has traditionally been granted pride of place among Johnson's biographers.[3] Given the increasing sophistication of the attacks on that pride of place, I believe the time has come to reopen the case for Boswell's Johnson. I want to do that by examining the steps Boswell took to guard against the superficial subjectivity he has been charged with. Such an examination will show, I believe, that his portrait of Johnson is a rich and sophisticated blend of objective and subjective content, a kind of achievement in biography that cannot be dismissed or easily surpassed.[4]

First of all, Boswell's Johnson is to a significant degree Johnson's Johnson. Boswell was well aware of Johnson's argument for the superiority of autobiography in *Idler* 84. He acknowledges at the beginning of his *Life* that if Johnson had written his own life "the world would probably have had the most perfect example of biography that was ever exhibited."[5] By biography Boswell clearly meant what we mean by "autobiography." Moreover, his concession here is not a concession to any inherent superiority in autobiography but a concession to Johnson as an autobiographer.

Boswell framed his biography with the claims of Johnsonian autobiography in mind. He stated his intention clearly in a letter to Temple dated 24 February 1788: "I am absolutely certain that *my* mode of Biography which gives not only a *History* of Johnson's *visible* progress through the World, and of his Publications, but a View of his mind, in his Letters, and Conversations is the most perfect that can be conceived, and will be *more* of a *Life* than any Work that has ever yet appeared."[6] His *Life of Johnson* gives us just that view. Johnson speaks for himself in quotations from his diary entries, from his prayers, from his meditations, and in 344 letters, largely new or unfamiliar material whose purpose was to reveal the private man. Hawkins quotes generously from Johnson's writings, too, but he typically quotes from published writings already familiar to the public.[7] Boswell wisely avoids this mistake in the *Life*. The kinds of quotations, the length of the quotations, and the timing of them are all indications of Boswell's tact as a writer and of his understanding of his task. The contrast between himself and Hawkins in this regard could hardly be more telling.

Boswell is also more unusual and effective as a biographer in making use of information Johnson had directly communicated to him. This remains his permanent advantage over modern biographers working in libraries. For "upwards of twenty years" he had numerous opportunities to observe and record those "evanescent" and "volatile" details that, in Johnson's own words in *Rambler* 60, alone "give excellence to biography."[8] Boswell's advantage allows him to tell us, in spite of Hawkins's and Mrs. Piozzi's declarations to the contrary, that Johnson did not as a three-year-old child compose the verses on a duck; the verses were rather composed by his father and passed off by him as the work of his precocious son (I, 40). He is also able to use what he learned from Johnson to record some startling contrasts in perception. The Reverend William Adams remembered Johnson while at Pembroke as a "gay, frolicksome fellow" who was "caressed and loved by all about him," and believed it was "the happiest part of his life." Johnson, on the other hand, remembered himself as being "mad," "violent," and "miserably poor" and said his "frolick" was actually "bitterness" (I, 73). He was also able to correct inaccuracies. Sir John Hawkins had carelessly repeated the apocryphal story that Johnson's quarrel with Lord Chesterfield began when he was snubbed by Chesterfield in favor of Colley Cibber.[9] But Boswell, with Johnson's authority, was able to deny that there was any basis at all to the story about Cibber and to say that the quarrel should rather be attributed to Chesterfield's "continued neglect" (I, 256–257). This kind of authoritative information is not accessible to modern scholars separated by time and distance from the subject of their inquiries. This can only be obtained by someone who lived in close social intercourse with his subject, though only by one sufficiently diligent and inquisitive to elicit the kind of information that makes the difference between colorful legend and less glamorous but still pointed truth.

Boswell's other achievement—his record of Johnson's conversations (surely the most volatile and evanescent of any of the materials of biography)—also cannot be duplicated. Too much has been said about this feature of Boswell's biography to dwell on it at any length, but a few points may need to be emphasized. First, Boswell does not claim that his record was either perfect or complete. Quite the contrary. He regrets on occasions that he failed to record certain incidents or remarks because he was indolent or busy with other matters. Moreover, he openly admits that he had to learn how to record conversations and that his techniques improved only gradually over time as he absorbed more and more of the "Johnsonian aether" (I, 421). Frederick Pottle once made the unfortunate argument that Boswell boswellized Johnson even when recording conversation.[10] But even if Pottle is correct—which I do not concede—the boswellizing had to be subtle, very subtle. For one thing we know that Johnson read in Boswell's journals and even made a few corrections (III, 260; V, 307) but was otherwise content to let Boswell's record stand, thereby giving us a tacit guarantee of its authenticity. Second, many of the people who are quoted in the *Life* were still alive when it was published, and it is hard to conceive of how they would have let Boswell's record stand without contradiction if they had believed there were any serious distortions, subtle or not. The protests, such as they were, were confined to complaints about the accuracy of what he had recorded. Those who were uncomfortable in Boswell's presence after the publication of the *Tour* and the *Life* were uncomfortable not because he had distorted what they had said but because he had recorded accurately what they had said, something they did not want as part of the public record, often for obvious reasons.[11]

A second guarantee of the objectivity of the *Life* is, oddly enough, that part of it which is often taken to be evidence, *prima facie*, of its subjectivity: Boswell's portrait of himself. The Boswell of the *Life* has been the source of many complaints whose point can be summed up as "too much Boswell, too little Johnson." If the *Life of Johnson* was not actually a pretext for writing his own autobiography, he was at least using it as a platform for parading himself before the public. Whatever the merits of such complaints, they miss an important point: there is method to it. Even the most primitive comparison of the Boswell of the journals and the Boswell of the *Life* can only lead to the conclusion that the two are very far from identical.[12] The autobiography in the *Life* is clearly not autobiography in the usual sense, Boswellian or otherwise. That is because the autobiography in the *Life* serves another purpose, the purpose of establishing the *Life* as an objective document.[13]

Boswell's inclusion of so much material about himself is a refusal to hide behind a contrived fictional objectivity and thus a check on any tendency to falsify the conditions under which this biography was composed. By focusing attention on the special set of circumstances that gave rise to the *Life,* it helps to keep the relationship between Boswell and his readers an honest one. The writing of this life depended upon a personal relationship, a relationship that had to triumph over many obstacles, especially those of chronology and geography. Boswell was not acquainted with Johnson before 16 May 1763, and he tells us so. Boswell, tied up with commitments in his native Scotland, could not be with Johnson during the important weeks that preceded his death, and he tells us so. One thing easily forgotten amidst the quibbles about how much time Boswell did or did not spend in Johnson's company during the last twenty-one years of his life is that the chief source for this information is Boswell himself.

Another gain from Boswell's portrait of himself involves one of the touchiest issues surrounding the publication of the *Life* in 1791. Many of the figures portrayed in the *Life* were still alive and less concerned about the portrait of Johnson than the portraits of themselves. We have letters from Bishop Percy, for example, pleading with Boswell to omit any mention of himself, even as the source of anecdotes. Percy was willing to let Boswell use the material he had given him, but he feared that public mention of his name would expose him "to ridicule from the non-importance of the Particulars."[14] Boswell resisted Percy's repeated requests for anonymity, understandably, since his portrait of Percy could hardly be described as having a dark, uncharitable cast. It may not be altogether flattering, but it certainly is kindly, and we know that Boswell thought well of Percy.[15] Nevertheless, we learn from Sir William Forbes that publication of the *Life* "had hurt the Bishop so much, that it was with difficulty he could be prevailed on ever to speak to him again; or even to come to the Literary Club when Mr. Boswell was present."[16]

But Percy and the others who were portrayed in a less than glamorous light had to acknowledge that Boswell did not spare himself. If Boswell told of painful quarrels between Johnson and his other friends, he also described quarrels just as painful between himself and Johnson. If they were shown being tossed and gored for all to see, Boswell also showed himself being tossed and gored. This did not escape the notice of contemporary readers of the *Life*, nor has it escaped the notice of modern readers with much less of a personal stake in such moments being brought to public attention. The very fact that such unsparing moments are there eases our suspicions about this being an art whose purposes are merely self-serving and enhances our willingness to accept it as an objective record.[17]

Perhaps most important of all, Boswell's portrait of himself keeps on reminding us that he and Johnson, though they held many similar views, were still quite distinct persons. Boswell tells us that Dryden was, apart from Shakespeare, Johnson's favorite poet. But Dryden's poems rarely drew a tear from Boswell, so he can only summon up the most dutiful admiration for a poet of "strong reason" rather than "quick sensibility" (IV, 45). He reports that Johnson always expressed a low opinion of Swift's merits, but he makes it clear that he does not share that estimate (II, 318–319; IV, 61). Johnson thought that Goldsmith wrote better history than Robertson. Boswell thought the reverse was true (II, 236–237). Johnson detested slavery; Boswell defends it at length (III, 200–205). Boswell's constant airings of his own contrasting views are not just occasions for expressing his own sense of self-importance, but important means for allowing readers to mark the boundaries between his own personality and that of Johnson, a way of reinforcing objectivity by dwelling on subjectivity.

But Johnson and Boswell did, after all, share much in common. True friendship in the Johnsonian sense, as Jean Hagstrum has shown us, is a *concordia discors,* a spiritual knot that allows for differences but not basic incompatibility.[18] These two men shared a passion for literature, an engagement with ideas, a zest for society and conversation, melancholic temperaments, and numerous views on matters social, political, and religious, though we have been told, with some justice, that the similarities of their views on politics and religion are not as close as they might at first seem.[19] If I had to register my own complaint about the *Life,* it would be Boswell's tiresome obsession with the subject of male succession, surely a topic in which he was more interested than Johnson. But even here I hesitate about labeling the repeated references to this topic an instance of the sin called "boswellizing." There is evidence that suggests that Johnson might have been more taken with the subject than I like to think. The references to the subject in his letters following the unexpected and tragic death of the nine-year-old Henry Thrale come readily to mind as an instance quite independent of anything Boswell had to say.[20] What can be found in Boswell can change our minds on other matters too. If we can judge by what has been omitted from the numerous modern abridgments of the *Life,* the exchange of letters between Boswell and Johnson concerning the legal arguments Boswell was preparing for court is one of the most dispensable (read "boring") parts of the *Life.* Yet the pioneering work of E. L. McAdam, Jr., and the recent work of Thomas Curley have changed our views on this matter. We are learning that Johnson was far more interested in the law and the workings of the law than many of us have ever suspected.[21] The exchange of letters may not be to our tastes, but the growing evidence is forcing us to admit that it reveals a significant objective component in Johnson's character and is much more than an example of Boswell's obsession with himself.

A more genuine controversy can and does surround what can only be called Boswell's "experiments," those moments when Boswell consciously manipulated his subject to provide materials for the *Life.* Whether or not they represent authentic science, the underlying motive that prompts them was clearly shaped by the scientific spirit that was in the air. The Johnson-Wilkes meeting is paradigmatic: let's bring together the Toriest of the Tories and the Whiggiest of the Whigs and see what happens.[22] The tour of Scotland and the western isles in 1773 is another of these experiments on a grander scale: what will happen if we take Johnson far away from his familiar London setting? For every successful instance of this we can detect the faint remains of many others that were not, such as Johnson's first meetings with General Oglethorpe or with Paoli or in the picture of Gibbon's tight-lipped prudence at meetings of the Club. In fact, Boswell's tendency to fashion such experiments—not quite a habit, but close—brought about Johnson's famous rebuke when Boswell expressed his wish to see Johnson and Catharine Macaulay together: "Don't you know that it is very uncivil to pit two people against one another?" (III, 185).

The defense of this practice—insofar as it can and should be defended—is largely an obvious one. It brought to light aspects of Johnson's character that were either hidden or obscured even from those who thought they knew him best but knew him mostly in familiar roles, such as the literary monarch expounding from his tavern throne. We are inclined to forgive Boswell his manipulations because the results of his experiments were largely happy ones. Johnson managed to turn the tables on those who, thinking they knew his height and breadth, expected crushing rudeness to Wilkes or little but grouchy complaints about the primitive conditions of a land and a people he supposedly disdained. Boswell can be said to have forced his contemporaries, as he forces us, to see more of Johnson the man than we might otherwise have seen and thus he enlarges our understanding of *his* contributions to the *Life of Johnson*.[23] They are instances when the phrase "Boswell's Johnson" is literally accurate and genuinely meaningful. Paradoxically, or perhaps ironically, they are rarely the Boswell's Johnson that is the object of Boswell's critics.

Often, in fact, his critics are aiming their fire at a Johnson that is not Boswell's at all, though he is the Johnson of the *Life*. For the Johnson of the *Life* is truly the work of many hands besides Boswell's.[24] Boswell's activities as a gatherer of information about Johnson are well documented. He worked as diligently as he did because he recognized that certain limitations would keep him from being as good a biographer as he wanted to be. He clearly needed help from those who had known Johnson before he first met him in 1763. But he also needed help from those who were with him in the last twenty-one years of his life, since it was not possible for him to be in Johnson's company for more than 425 days or so.[25] We know that he sought Bishop Percy's help as early as 1772 when he tried to compile a complete list of all that Johnson had written. We know that he interviewed Edmund Hector and Bennet Langton to find out more about Johnson as early as 1776. The advertisement for the *Life* appended to his 1785 *Tour* acknowledges "many valuable communications" from others that enabled him to make the *Life* more complete, and he mentions nine names: "The Rev. Dr. Adams, the Rev. Dr. Taylor, Sir Joshua Reynolds, Mr. Langton, Dr. Brocklesby, the Rev. Thomas Warton, Mr. Hector of Birmingham, Mrs. Porter, and Miss Seward" (V, 421). It is not clear whether the names are arranged in order of what appeared to Boswell as descending importance at that time, but questions would later arise about the value of Lucy Porter's contributions and certainly about those from Anna Seward.[26] The others are among the most important contributors to the *Life*. Much the same thought was in Boswell's mind when he wrote to the Reverend William Bowles of Wiltshire on 14 June 1785, trying to coax information from him:

> In the Great Literary Monument which I am ambitious to erect to the memory of our illustrious departed Friend, I wish that those who are able to bear an honourable part, should each have a pillar inscribed with his own name. To speak without a metaphor the World is to have Dr. Adams's Communication Mr. Malone's Communications Dr. Brocklesby's Communications etc. etc. etc. etc.[27]

Careful study of the *Life*, it seems to me, vindicates Boswell's claim that the *Life* was constructed from the testimony of a large number of Johnson's friends and acquaintances, though Boswell himself remained the principal architect. It is inconceivable that Boswell's own consciousness as he fashioned his portrait of Johnson would have remained unaffected by what he heard and learned from the many others he consulted. This feature of the *Life* more than any other blunts suggestions that the *Life* is simply one man's version of Johnson, because Boswell's Johnson is not just Boswell's Johnson, literally or rhetorically.

The literal record concerning the composition of the *Life* is amply documented in Marshall Waingrow's edition of the *Correspondence*, but more attention needs to be paid to the way the rhetoric of the *Life* deliberately reflects its composition. That the Johnson of the *Life* is not dependent solely on the observations of Boswell is evident to any careful reader. The dedication to Sir Joshua Reynolds is an obvious first step toward establishing the objectivity of the portrait that will follow. The dedication reflects Boswell's warm regard for Reynolds and his gratitude for Reynolds's many contributions.[28] It also invokes Reynolds's help, rhetorically, as a guarantor of the record he presents. Reynolds's own intimacy with Johnson was well known, and he is listed as a kind of silent witness in a large number of the scenes Boswell records.[29] Clearly Reynolds was satisfied that what Boswell reports is what he also saw and heard.[30] In this way Reynolds implicitly as well as explicitly objectifies Boswell's portrait of Johnson.

The authority of others is invoked time and again and in several forms. Others are in fact the source of a significant number of the famous *bons mots* and anecdotes that are thought to be Boswell's Johnson, and we are told this in the *Life*. Edmund Hector supplied the picture of Johnson as a boy being carried on the backs of his grateful schoolfellows (I, 47), while the story about Johnson astonishing his college tutors on his first day at Pembroke by quoting Macrobius was from the Reverend William Adams (I, 59). The story of Johnson doing penance for his earlier disobedience to his father by standing in the rain at the marketplace in Uttoxeter was from the Reverend Henry White (IV, 373), while the keyhole view of his tumultuous fondness for Tetty in the marriage bed was from David Garrick (I, 98). His oft-quoted quip that a second marriage was "the triumph of hope over experience" came from the Reverend William Maxwell (II, 128), while his famous witticism on epitaphs, that "in lapidary inscriptions a man is not upon oath," came from Dr. Charles Burney (II, 407). That Johnson insisted his marriage with Tetty was "a love-marriage upon both sides" was recorded on the authority of an amused Topham Beauclerk (I, 96). It is true that these are all from Boswell's *Life of Johnson,* but it is not accurate in these instances to speak of "Boswell's" Johnson. Such are instances, not of Boswell's Johnson, but of Hector's Johnson, Adams's Johnson, White's Johnson, Garrick's Johnson, Maxwell's Johnson, Burney's Johnson, and Beauclerk's Johnson.

A few of the contributions are so substantial that they are set off as separate sections. They function as the eyes and ears of Boswell when circumstances or chronology made it impossible for him to be present. Thus, Thomas Warton is allowed to recollect Johnson's conversations from the 1750s during his visits to Oxford in his own words, even though Warton's contribution "is not written with the same care and attention" he "usually bestowed on his compositions" (I, 271–274).[31] Sir Joshua Reynolds supplied an account of Johnson's trip with him to his home county of Devon in 1762 (I, 377–379). Charles Burney, who in addition to his own acquaintance with Johnson also saw him frequently at the Thrales', is also allowed a section for his recollections of Johnson's *bons mots* (II, 407–410). The Reverend William Maxwell, who was acquainted with Johnson from about 1754 until some time before his return to Ireland in 1775, provides an extended memorandum dealing mostly with Johnson's sayings and doings in the 1750s. But no one, with the possible exception of Sir Joshua Reynolds, was more important than Bennet Langton.

Langton's role in the composition of the *Life* illustrates in an especially pointed way that Boswell's Johnson is also the Johnson of others and why we can see the Johnson of the *Life* as an objective phenomenon. Langton's own relationship with Johnson was in its initial stage fully independent of Boswell.[32] Though he was only about three years younger than Boswell, Langton had first met Johnson while still in his teens. Boswell tells us that the meeting occurred "soon after the conclusion of [Johnson's] Rambler" (I, 247), but it probably happened in the autumn of 1754, about a year and a half after the conclusion of the *Rambler*, with the aid of Dr. Robert Levet, by then a member of Johnson's household.[33] In any event, a close bond soon formed between the two, if we are to judge from the written evidence. In a letter to Langton dated 6 May 1755, Johnson said, "I have very seldom received an offer of Friendship which I so earnestly desire to cultivate and mature."[34] Mature it did through thirty years, for Langton was to be attending to him faithfully in late 1784 as he lay on his deathbed. In another letter dated 16 June 1781, some twenty-six years later, Johnson seems to be consciously echoing the language of the earlier letter when he speaks of their friendship as one "not only formed by choice but matured by time."[35]

Langton's value to Boswell as he set out to compose the *Life* is in part apparent from the dates. He had been friendly with Johnson during the middle years, a period of Johnson's life forever sealed off from firsthand observation by a biographer who valued firsthand observation above all. During those years Johnson had taken Langton with him to visit Richardson (IV, 28). Langton had been there when Johnson was completing the *Dictionary* that would make him famous. Later he would entrust to Langton's keeping the copy of the letter to Lord Chesterfield he had dictated to Baretti some time after the event (I, 260). Langton had been able to watch as Johnson composed an *Idler* essay (I, 331), and he had even been invited to contribute an essay to the series (I, 330). And, of course, he along with Beauclerk had accompanied Johnson on the famous frisk (I, 250). Clearly, Langton had much he could tell a biographer of Johnson keenly aware of the limitations on his own knowledge of those middle years.

But Langton's value to a biography of Johnson was not limited to events before 1763. From 1763 to 1784, when Boswell was traveling on the Continent or back in Scotland, Langton was often in London and often in the company of Johnson.[36] In 1764 Langton was one of the founding members of the Club (I, 477–478); Boswell would be admitted in 1773 (II, 239–240). In 1767 Langton was present when Johnson gave an account of his visit with King George III in the queen's library (II, 41). Langton attended to Johnson during his severe illness in the mid 1760s, and he was in almost constant attendance upon him during the weeks before his death.[37] During another illness in 1784 he had acted the part of confessor when Johnson, believing that he should straighten out matters with his Maker, had asked for a list of his faults; it was Langton who then received a tongue-lashing for having suggested that Johnson was "sometimes" too rough on people during conversation (IV, 280–281).[38] In so many words, Langton's closeness to Johnson under so many different circumstances over such a long period of time made his value to Boswell almost beyond calculation.

But his value would not have been what it was had he not also been Boswell's friend, for the relationship was truly triangular. Boswell first mentions Langton in his journals in an entry dated 7 June 1768, an entry that suggests some kind of previous acquaintance but not much more than that.[39] But the elements were there that could lead to friendship. Apart from their mutual attachment to Johnson and general love of literature, they were both from the landed gentry and therefore from a similar kind of social background. Moreover, Langton was Tory and High Church—"up to the Eyes," according to Mrs. Thrale.[40] Their friendship solidified noticeably in 1772 when Langton, who had married the widow of a Scottish peer in 1770, came to Scotland to visit with his new wife's relatives and friends. During that time Boswell was warm and attentive. His journal records twenty-one occasions when they were in each other's company.[41] After this they began their own correspondence.[42]

Langton's contributions to the *Life* appear in different forms. Some, such as the report of his first meeting with Johnson (I, 250) or his account of Johnson composing an *Idler* essay in Langton's room at Oxford a half-hour before the post (I, 331), Boswell used at the time and place they occurred.[43] He also reports three occasions when Johnson left London to visit Langton: a visit to his ancestral home in Lincolnshire early in 1764 (I, 476–477), to Warley Camp in Essex in the summer of 1778 when Langton was with the militia (III, 360–362), and for thirteen days in July of 1783 to Rochester in Kent where Langton had recently bought a home (IV, 233). Only the account of Johnson's visit to Warley Camp is entirely in Langton's own words, but there is little that is especially memorable in any of them, except possibly to learn that Langton's father went to his grave believing that Johnson was of the Romish communion because of the way he talked (I, 476). Such visits are inherently less interesting than Johnson's journey with Boswell to faraway Scotland and the remote western isles and even less interesting than his journey to Devonshire with Reynolds in 1762 and his journeys to Wales in 1774 and France in 1775 with the Thrales. But they are not without value, pedestrian as they may be. For one thing, they reveal an important dimension in Johnson's character. Despite his reputation as the preeminent Londoner, he did in fact leave his tavern throne, in part because he believed in the value of travel.[44] Travel, because it exposes one to the unfamiliar, to what is new and different, enlarges the understanding. If anything seems basic to Johnson's character, it would have to be that kind of restless intellectual curiosity. Such moments also show that Johnson was able to mingle with people outside of his settled habits and to adapt to new situations with some success.

There was, however, one stumbling block to their literary relationship. Langton did not have "the habit" of writing, as Boswell puts it delicately in the *Life* (IV, 1). What survives of what he did write amply justifies Johnson's characterization of him as "muddy" (II, 362). Apparently Langton found writing difficult and so avoided it whenever he could.[45] If Boswell wanted what he could contribute to the *Life*, he had to get it by way of detailed interviews where he did most of the writing.[46] And that is what happened on 15 April 1776 and 11 November 1786. Once Boswell did get Langton talking, he uncovered a wealth of material. This led him to compare the Johnsoniana he extracted from Langton to the treasures uncovered by archaeologists when they dug beneath the fields of ancient Herculaneum (IV, 1–2).

A goodly portion of what Boswell collected from Langton he presents in the year 1780 (IV, 1–33) apart from any chronological arrangement. This was a year when he had no chance to be with Johnson, so he offers as a substitute what Langton recollected from thirty years of friendship with Johnson. Langton had a good memory when primed, but he tends to recollect, as one might expect, in terms of vivid moments from a timeless past. Nevertheless, we learn from Langton much about Johnson that we might not otherwise have known. We learn, for instance, about his opinions of classical Greek writers (IV, 2), as we might expect, given Langton's well-known interest in Greek. Somewhat more surprisingly, we learn that Johnson thought highly of the plays of Farquhar (IV, 7), something that might give pause to those who think him guilty of too much high seriousness as a critic. There are reports of complimentary remarks about Beauclerk (IV, 10), Tom Davies (IV, 13), and Edmund Burke (IV, 19–20, 26–27) that show Johnson's affection and regard for these friends. There are also examples of Johnson's wit. When the publication of an abusive attack on Reynolds had worried and upset his friends, he restored the group to its senses by asking to have it read aloud and then asking rhetorically after it was concluded, "Are we alive after all this satire!" (IV, 29). And there is the more famous story of the man who brought his brother to see Johnson, promising him that once his brother started talking he would be very entertaining, to which Johnson simply replied, "I can wait" (IV, 21). There are also the stories that have passed into myth and legend, such as Johnson's comments on his own faults as a writer, "too wordy," when he reread one of his *Ramblers,* and "I thought it had been better" when *Irene* was read out loud at a gathering some years after it had been published. Some of these are favorite stories from Boswell's *Life,* and understandably so. But it is well to remember that they are not examples of Boswell's Johnson, but of Langton's Johnson.[47]

Focusing on the relationship between Langton and Johnson has critical value. It is looking at the *Life* through one of many possible windows, and what we can see through this one window should increase our admiration for Boswell's ability to weave so many different strands into a dense, complex whole while still doing justice to each strand. The friendship between Johnson and Langton was one of the strongest and truest (*"Sit anima mea cum Langtano"* [IV, 280]), yet it, too, had its ups and downs. And one of the more remarkable elements in Boswell's portrayal of that friendship is his inclusion of some unpleasant moments, something that gives little comfort to those who want to convince us that Boswell "sentimentalizes" his portrait of Johnson in the *Life.*[48] We are told that Langton liked to introduce religious questions into open discussions, a tendency that annoyed Johnson, who feared what might happen. On one occasion in May of 1773 Johnson rebuked Langton in very angry terms for trying to introduce the doctrine of the Trinity as a subject for discussion. Langton was hurt by Johnson's rebuke and left London in what Johnson described as "deep dudgeon" (II, 265). After that the two were on very cool terms for almost eighteen months. Johnson announced their reconciliation in a letter to Boswell dated 27 January 1775: "Langton is here: we are all that ever we were" (II, 292). Clearly, when Langton suggested in June of 1784 that Johnson was sometimes too rough during conversations he was speaking from firsthand experience. Boswell also reports conversations between himself and Johnson, when Langton was not present, in which Johnson criticized him for his poor management of household finances (III, 222, 300, 317, 348) and ridiculed him for making out a will that favored his sisters and so violated the principle of male succession (II, 261–262).

Some will obviously find in such moments a lapse of good taste or a violation of decorum. But the requirements of good taste or decorum are all too easily used to compromise the higher purpose of biography, that of telling the truth, the whole truth. Moreover, what constitutes good taste or an appropriate decorum varies, sometimes wildly, from individual to individual and from age to age. My own inclinations are to credit Boswell in this regard. By including such unpleasant material he reassures me that his basic commitment in the *Life* is to telling the whole truth as best he knew it. Johnson may have been a great and a good man, but he was not above talking about people behind their backs, a very human kind of pettiness that coexisted with other, far more admirable qualities.[49]

Boswell's picture of the relationship also allows for its subtleties. There are, for instance, clear indications that Langton saw Johnson's faults just as clearly as Johnson saw his. Langton's contribution to the *Idler* papers, No. 67, composed when he was only twenty-two, provides an early clue to this.[50] The essay gently pokes fun at sages (read Johnson) who recommend that the young (read Langton) commit themselves to a "settled [read rational] plan" of study. It goes on to point out the limitations of such rational schemes, noting that the best of what we do is often done "fortuitously" and that we are frequently most productive when, instead of following the schemes of sober reason, we yield to "warm inclination." Langton is certainly jibing at one of Johnson's favorite dogmas and at one of his favorite roles, that of philosopher and guide for the young. He may have been young, but he was clearly capable of standing up to his Imlac. The fact that *Idler* 67 was brushed up and published by Johnson in his *Idler* series is certainly one instance in which Johnson did betray "good humour" and also an indication that he was large enough to recognize the merit of some well-aimed criticism.[51]

Another instance of this dimension of their relationship is captured vividly in the Boswellian record. On Friday, 8 May 1778, Johnson and Boswell had dined at Langton's house. After dinner, when Langton had to leave for a while, they became reconciled after an earlier quarrel and then resumed their usual flow of conversation, and Langton soon rejoined them.

> Mr. Langton having repeated the anecdote of Addison having distinguished between his powers in conversation and in writing by saying "I have only nine-pence in my pocket; but I can draw for a thousand pounds;"—*Johnson.* "He had not that retort ready, Sir; he had prepared it before-hand." *Langton:* (turning to me.) "A fine surmise. Set a thief to catch a thief." (III, 339)

Clearly, Langton suspected, probably with good reason, that Johnson on occasion prepared some of his conversational *bons mots* in advance.

A careful look at the Johnson-Langton-Boswell relationship has another value when we ask another question: how was Langton treated in the biographies of Johnson by Boswell's chief rivals, Mrs. Piozzi and Sir John Hawkins? The answer—to the discomfort of Boswell's detractors—can only be one that does credit to Boswell. Apart from listing Langton as one of the original members of the Club, Mrs. Piozzi has but one mention of Langton in her *Anecdotes:* Johnson "had the greatest possible value for Mr. Langton, of whose virtue and learning he delighted to talk in very exalted terms."[52] It could be argued in Mrs. Piozzi's behalf that hers was never intended to be a full-scale biographical treatment of Johnson. But a reduction of Johnson's long-term and very close relationship with Langton to a single mention does much to tell us that her biographical record is less than satisfactory on more counts than just her infamous inaccuracies.[53]

The case of Hawkins's *Life* is more complicated, but only slightly so. Unlike Mrs. Piozzi's *Anecdotes,* his *Life of Samuel Johnson* was intended to be a full biographical treatment of his subject, so direct comparison with Boswell's *Life* can hardly be unfair. There are a few more references to Langton in Hawkins' *Life,* but not many more.[54] We are told he was one of the original members of the Club, and he is mentioned eight times in the weeks preceding Johnson's death, and that includes the contretemps over Johnson's stolen diary. The other references are consistent with the record provided by Boswell and Mrs. Piozzi: "Johnson had now [in the early 1760s] considerably extended the circle of his acquaintance, and added to the number of his friends sundry persons of distinguished eminence: among them were, Sir Joshua Reynolds, Mr. Edmund Burke, Mr. Beauclerk, and Mr. Langton. With these he passed much of his time, and was desirous of being still closer connected." But other than telling us about Langton's *Idler* essay and informing us that he brought back a copy of the *Dictionnaire* as a gift for Johnson from the French Academy, that is it. What makes the stinginess of reference to Langton even more astonishing is that Hawkins was, from all that we can tell, on very good terms with him, and there are clear indications that Langton supplied him with information.[55] What then are we to make of the claims that Hawkins's *Life* deserves at least as much of our attention as Boswell's?

It has been suggested that we might learn more about the subjective biases in Boswell's *Life* by examining his deliberate omissions.[56] It is true that Waingrow's edition of the *Correspondence* reveals more than a few interesting omissions, but none that could not be defended on reasonable grounds. Some are simply dubious. William Bowles claimed that Johnson "knew how to mend his own stockings to darn his linen or to sew on a button on his cloaths. 'I am not (he would often say) an helpless man.' "[57] But Boswell eliminated this anecdote from Bowles in proof, probably because, given what he had seen, he was not convinced it was true.[58] Sometimes Boswell seems to have objected to the phrasing or the implications of the phrasing of a possible contribution. James Beattie had reported that Johnson had told him he was often unwilling to go to church because "shocking impious thoughts" were almost constantly passing through his mind.[59] True, Boswell did not use Beattie's anecdote as such, but its point is covered in another way. Boswell quotes Johnson as saying, "Everything which Hume has advanced against Christianity had passed through my mind long before he wrote" (I, 444). This allows for a more dignified Johnson, one who had considered and then rejected impious thoughts rather than one who was constantly at their mercy. Edmund Hector told Boswell that Johnson, while living with him in Birmingham, "would sometimes steal an hour and read but had a vanity in concealing that he ever studied. It was all to be from his own mind."[60] Again, though Boswell did not use Hector's observation as such, he captures the sense of it in his own more carefully nuanced observation that Johnson could be induced "from his spirit of contradiction, or more properly his love of argumentative contest, to speak lightly of his own application to study" (I, 446). This is a more flexible interpretation, one that allows for competing impulses of vanity and honesty in Johnson's character rather than something suspiciously like the determined hypocrisy suggested by Hector's phrasing.

The deliberate omission that has received the most attention is the famous (or infamous) interview with Mrs. Desmoulins marked "*tacenda*." It is said that Boswell deliberately ommitted her story, which reveals a Johnson almost overpowered by his sexual drives, because of its delicate nature and because it conflicted with the sentimental picture Boswell wanted to draw of Johnson's marriage.[61] But such conjectures, it seems to me, assume that Boswell was completely convinced that Elizabeth Desmoulins was an entirely reliable informant. Given the picture we have of her from other sources, this is not necessarily a safe assumption.[62] Even if it was, Boswell almost certainly would have felt compelled, given its explosive nature, to find independent corroboration before using it in the *Life*. Given these considerations alone, it is hardly surprising that he did not use it. There is no need to look for a dishonest motive here.

It should not be overlooked that he did include unflattering information when it met his test for reliability. So, when puzzling over the unusually close and warm relationship between Johnson and the Reverend John Taylor, Boswell reports what he learned from Reynolds: Johnson had mentioned to Reynolds that Taylor had told him he was to be his heir (III, 180–181). Boswell introduces this matter gingerly and seems reluctant to endorse something that seems, on the surface, so much at odds with what he knew about Johnson. Whatever Johnson's faults, the determined pursuit of material advantage was not among them, and certainly not at the price of sycophancy. Yet Reynolds's authority persuades him to include what he might rather have omitted. None of these instances will settle once and for all whether Boswell blamably bent the rules of biographical truth to further other ends, but I think the cases made against Boswell for willfully suppressing information inconvenient to the "image" of Johnson he supposedly wanted to project are weaker than they have been made to seem.

One criticism that is not weaker is the observation that the *Life* fails to act as a bridge between Johnson the man and Johnson the writer. It may not be fair to require biography to function as a means to an end, to point beyond itself, toward literature. Yet somehow many of us expect the biography of a literary figure to do just that, though we know from experience this does not happen. It is easy enough to notice how many readers are satisfied that they know what they want to know about Johnson after reading the *Life* and so never move on to explore in any depth what it was that won Johnson the respect and admiration of so many of his contemporaries, not least of whom was Boswell himself. It is also a commonplace experience for the few who do move beyond Boswell to experience Johnson the writer to be surprised and exhilarated by his extraordinary power, only to reflect later on how poorly prepared they were for this experience by reading the *Life*. I'm not sure what accounts for that gap, but I'm sure that it is there. I have felt it myself, and others have assured me that they have had a similar experience. But if Boswell's *Life* fails to lead us to Johnson the writer, I don't know of another biography of Johnson that succeeds where it has failed, nor for that matter do I know of the biography of any writer that succeeds at this task.

It may be worth noting that Boswell was composing for an audience he could assume was reasonably familiar with Johnson's works, those who already knew the writer but wanted to know more about the man. One of the recurring refrains in the *Life* is the initial shock of those already acquainted with the writer when first meeting the man. Typically they had formed an idealized portrait of the "author of the *Rambler*" or of the mighty "Dictionary Johnson" in their heads. When they first encounter the huge, lumbering, disheveled figure they are shocked almost into wordlessness, only to be reassured they had not completely lost their senses when the figure begins to talk. Boswell's audience knew the writer before they knew the man, but we know the man before we know the writer. In that sense, Boswell can hardly be blamed for writing a book well suited to the circumstances of his world but not so well suited to ours. There is a gap, and a gap that has been made larger by time. This gap, I believe, is best filled by informed criticism, not by biography.[63]

If Boswell's *Life* fails on that count, it succeeds and succeeds magnificently on another count, one more suited to the nature of biography: its portrait of Johnson the man. It is a rounded, rich, dense, complex portrait, one that defies paraphrase or formula, one measure of its greatness. In its world the fact that Johnson was a great writer is necessarily only part of his humanity, a much wider phenomenon. It is filled with facts and information about Johnson, and its accuracy and fullness have stood up remarkably well to almost two hundred years of exhaustive scrutiny. Such discoveries as there have been of factual errors and areas where Boswell's knowledge was incomplete or altogether lacking do constitute one point on which later generations can, if they choose, claim that they have improved on the work of an earlier one. But constant reminders that Boswell left Johnson at Pembroke eighteen months longer than he should have, or that he failed to find all of Johnson's letters, or that he misunderstood Johnson's fear of insanity do not add up to a case for serious doubt about its value as a document, much less for dismissing it altogether.[64] Nor are such failings an adequate way of estimating its success, because its success is rooted in the aesthetics of biography, not its science.

Boswell's *Life* succeeds aesthetically because it succeeds in achieving an aim quite different from that of science. That aim is to engage us imaginatively with Samuel Johnson the man, to induce an emotional response of warmth and affection, to help us feel what Boswell himself and so many other of Johnson's friends and acquaintances felt toward him.[65] And let's make no mistake about it. Boswell did love Johnson, not in any kind of pure untroubled way that belongs only to the world of fairy tales, but in a rich, complex human way that does not exclude anger, irritation, jealousy, and even subtly undercutting him on occasions.[66] According to Hester Thrale, Boswell was the only one who really did love Johnson.[67] But it is clear that others, like Bennet Langton, also did, despite the all too predictable ups and downs of human relationships. Moreover, there can hardly be any doubt that, if we exclude its romantic sense, Hester Thrale once loved Johnson too, before their relationship went sour.[68]

It is the aim of Boswell's *Life* to show that Johnson was in his own way a lovable man, that he valued the love and affection of others and loved them in return. That is why Boswell's portrayal of his relationship with Johnson is not overdone. It is entirely functional. Their relationship is charged with feeling; from the dramatic moment in 1763 when Johnson says, "with warmth," "Give me your hand; I have taken a liking to you" (I, 405) to the final moment on 30 June 1784 when, with the air charged with foreboding of Johnson's approaching death, they "bade adieu to each other affectionately" (IV, 339). Boswell intends his relationship with Johnson to be emblematic, a pattern and a focal point from which we can observe Johnson establishing similar kinds of relationships with various kinds of people. This kind of relationship, based on mutual feelings of affection, is ex-emplified in Johnson's relationship with Sir Joshua Reynolds, Bennet Langton, Dr. Richard Brocklesby, Edmund Burke, Robert Levet, Anna Williams, Frank Barber, and numerous others. Certainly an es-pecially powerful moment is captured in a scene where Johnson comes to the deathbed of Catherine Chambers, a woman who had come to live with his mother in Lichfield about 1724 and who had been all but a member of the family for forty-three years.[69] Boswell allows, indeed wants Johnson to tell it in his own words.

> I then kissed her. She told me, that to part was the greatest pain that she had ever felt, and that she hoped we should meet again in a better place. I expressed with swelled eyes, and great emotion of tenderness, the same hopes. We kissed, and parted, I humbly hope to meet again, and to part no more. (II, 42–44)

Then Boswell adds the following:

> By those who have been taught to look upon Johnson as a man of harsh and stern character, let this tender and affectionate scene be candidly read; and let them then judge whether more warmth of heart, and grate-ful kindness, is often found in human nature. (II, 44)

Bertram Davis has astutely observed that Hawkins's *Life of Johnson* was the kind of book it was because of what had come before it and that it in turn directly shaped the kind of book Boswell's *Life* be-came.[70] Not only do I think this is correct, I think it is the key to any just appraisal and satisfying interpretation of Boswell's *Life*.[71] His quarrel with his chief rivals was not in its essence a quarrel over fac-tual accuracy or over method or industry, but a quarrel with the emo-tional tones of their respective biographical portraits. His first re-corded comments after reading Mrs. Piozzi's *Anecdotes* are in a letter to Edmond Malone where he sums up his response by noting that the former Mrs. Thrale "seems to have had no *affection* for our great friend, but merely the attachment of vanity."[72] The "dark, uncharita-ble cast" of Hawkins's *Life* again revealed the absence of genuine affec-tion. Boswell's aim was to get right for his contemporaries and for posterity what they had gotten wrong. His biography is meant to show us that Johnson was fully worthy of affection and love and indeed was esteemed and loved, not only by himself but by numerous others.[73] That is again why Boswell's Johnson is not and could not be simply Boswell's Johnson.

Objective truth, in the scientific sense of a guarantee of uniform and entirely predictable results, something that is always the same under the same circumstances, something that will always yield the same response, is no part of the flux of human relationships and can never be one of the fruits of biography. But to acknowledge this is not to acknowledge that any biographical work can be reduced to mere subjectivity, that its real truth can only be found in the biographer's particular angle of vision and not in whom he writes about. Objectivity and subjectivity are clearly contrary poles in human knowledge, but in most instances there is an inextricable mixture of the two. Boswell's portrait of Johnson in the *Life* as an act of human knowledge is no exception to that rule. He does not maintain that everybody thought and felt the same way about Johnson; he cannot guarantee that everyone will respond the same way to his portrait in the *Life*. What he does show us is that enough people saw and heard what he saw and heard, enough people felt what he felt to guarantee that we are responding to significant objective truths about Johnson the man. Boswell's *Life of Samuel Johnson* deserves its pride of place because of that objectivity, because it includes more, much more from others than any other biography by a contemporary of Johnson and because it captures so vividly what was evanescent and volatile about Johnson, especially the emotional qualities of his human relationships. That is something no modern biographer can ever hope to duplicate.

Notes

An award from the University of Alabama's Research Grants Committee provided the time for a final revision of this essay.

1. Bertram H. Davis has argued the case for Hawkins's Johnson most fully. See *Johnson before Boswell: A Study of Sir John Hawkins' "Life of Samuel Johnson"* (New Haven: Yale University Press, 1960). For an earlier insight into the case that can be made for Hawkins, see Harold Nicholson, *The Development of English Biography* (New York: Harcourt, Brace, 1928), 95–97. Robert E. Kelley

and O M Brack, Jr., have provided important tools for assessing the minor biographies by other contemporaries of Johnson that, in turn, establish a context for the major biographies by Mrs. Piozzi, Sir John Hawkins, and Boswell. The texts can be found in *The Early Biographies of Samuel Johnson* (Iowa City: University of Iowa Press, 1974); Kelley's and Brack's own assessment of those texts can be found in *Samuel Johnson's Early Biographers* (Iowa City: University of Iowa Press, 1971). See also Paul Korshin, "Robert Anderson's *Life of Johnson*," *Huntington Library Quarterly* 36 (1973): 239–253. It is worth noting that Bishop Percy had a hand in Anderson's biography.

2. This is a crucial point in Richard B. Schwartz's argument for restricting Boswell's *Life of Johnson* to a minimal role in Johnson studies. See *Boswell's Johnson: A Preface to the "Life"* (Madison: University of Wisconsin Press, 1978), 87–88. Donald Greene has also argued this point. See " 'Tis a Pretty Book, Mr. Boswell, But—," *Georgia Review* 32 (1978): 22–23, reprinted in this volume. For yet another version of this argument, see Paul Fussell, *Samuel Johnson and the Life of Writing* (New York: Harcourt Brace Jovanovich, 1971), 39–40.

3. Doubters about Boswell's traditional pride of place, if there be any, may consult one of the standard histories of biography. Examples can be found in Harold Nicholson, *The Development of English Biography*, 107; Mark Longaker, *English Biography in the Eighteenth Century* (Philadelphia: University of Pennsylvania Press, 1931), 407; and Donald A. Stauffer, *The Art of Biography in Eighteenth Century England* (Princeton, N.J.: Princeton University Press, 1941), 432. John A. Garraty offers a crisp statement of the traditional view of Boswell's pride of place in the field of biography: "Since his day biographers have refined and expanded his methods, sharpened and polished his tools. They have not really pushed much beyond him. Biography, after 1791, had reached maturity" (*The Nature of Biography* [New York: Knopf, 1957], 57).

4. My position here is close to that of William R. Siebenschuh, particularly the one he argues in his most recent book, *Fictional Techniques and Factual Works* (Athens: University of Georgia Press, 1983): "I argue, ultimately, that although Boswell's portrait of Johnson is limited and incomplete in many senses, Boswell's achievement represents a nearly perfect compromise between the power of his literary art and the generic demands of the biographical form in which he writes" (p. 63). I have found Siebenschuh's contributions to current discussion of Boswell's *Life* among the most valuable we have had, but I have my differences with him. Though not great, they are important. First, he is too willing to appease Boswell's detractors. Boswell's portrait of Johnson is limited and incomplete, I will concede, but only in a "few" senses, maybe "some," but certainly not "many." Second, I am unhappy with Siebenschuh's choice of the word "image" and all that it implies. For example, "Boswell makes us believe we are seeing Johnson 'warts and all' when, in fact, what we are seeing is a carefully controlled image" (p. 64). I prefer the word

"idea" over the word "image" because I believe it more accurately captures the task Boswell had set for himself in the *Life*. He was, I believe, trying to be true to his idea of Johnson while writing. To conceive of an idea guiding his craft is to see something far more flexible and protean than what is implied by "image," which typically connotes something static and fixed. The current popularity of "image" is apparently due to the enormous influence of Ralph Rader's essay, "Literary Form in Factual Narrative: The Example of Boswell's *Johnson*," in *Essays in Eighteenth-Century Biography*, ed. Philip B. Daghlian (Bloomington: Indiana University Press, 1968), 3–42, reprinted in this volume. Certainly it is picked up by Richard Schwartz in *Preface to the "Life*," p. xii and passim, though Schwartz can hardly be accused of intending to praise Boswell. Siebenschuh is, perhaps self-consciously, writing within this tradition. But he comes closer to my sense of Boswell when he acknowledges that "In the *Life* Boswell is more concerned with truth than he is with facts per se" (p. 73). Yes, the truth of his idea of Johnson. The question was how to convey it. Third, I am uneasy with what he calls, for lack of a better term, "fictionalization," something he finds characteristic of the greatest literary achievements in factual narrative. But this "fictionalization," it seems to me, is characteristic in one way or another of all biography, indeed of all writing. The issue is really the kind and quality of the fictionalization, not that it is present. That belief probably marks me as one who sees merit in the work of Jacques Derrida, though I would hardly qualify as a true disciple. See *Of Grammatology*, trans. Gayatri Chakravorty Spivak (Baltimore: Johns Hopkins University Press, 1976) and *Writing and Difference*, trans. Alan Bass (Chicago: University of Chicago Press, 1978).

5. *Boswell's Life of Johnson, Together with Boswell's Journal of a Tour to the Hebrides and Johnson's Diary of a Journey into North Wales*, ed. George Birkbeck Hill, rev. L. F. Powell, 6 vols. (Oxford: Clarendon, 1934–1964), I, 25. All future citations from Boswell's *Life of Johnson* will be from the Hill-Powell edition; they will for the most part be included in the text.

6. Marshall Waingrow, ed., *The Correspondence and Other Papers of James Boswell, Relating to the Making of the "Life of Johnson"* (New York: McGraw-Hill, 1969), 267. All future references to these materials will be to Waingrow's edition, with the title abbreviated as *Correspondence-Life*.

7. Davis, *Johnson before Boswell*, 29.

8. For a fuller discussion of the importance of these principles in Johnson's theory and practice of biography, see my essay, "Excellence in Biography: *Rambler* No. 60 and Johnson's Early Biographies," *South Atlantic Bulletin* 44, no. 2 (1979): 21–23.

9. Sir John Hawkins, Knt., *The Life of Samuel Johnson, LL.D.*, ed. Bertram H. Davis (New York: Macmillan, 1961), 81.

10. Frederick A. Pottle, "The *Life of Johnson*: Art and Authenticity," in *Twentieth-Century Interpretations of Boswell's "Life of Johnson*," ed. James L. Clifford (Englewood Cliffs, N.J.: Prentice-Hall, 1970), 72–73.

11. For an authoritative account of Boswell's record of Mrs. Thrale's unflattering opinion of Elizabeth Montagu's *Essay on Shakespeare* (1769) and how it would lead to the infamous Postscript to her *Anecdotes*, see Mary Hyde, *The Impossible Friendship: Boswell and Mrs. Thrale* (Cambridge, Mass.: Harvard University Press, 1972), 100–110. See also Waingrow, *Correspondence-Life*, 418–420, 435–436.

12. Bertrand Bronson has analyzed some of the differences between the Boswell of the journals and the Boswell of the *Life*. See "Boswell's Boswell," *Johnson Agonistes and Other Essays* (1944; reprint, Berkeley and Los Angeles: University of California Press, 1965), 44. It might be worth mentioning that here Bronson prefers the Boswell of the journals. Paul K. Alkon focuses on Boswell in his role as narrator as distinct from Boswell the character in "Boswell's Control of Aesthetic Distance," *University of Toronto Quarterly* 38 (1969): 174–191. See also Frank Brady, "Boswell's Self-Presentation and His Critics," *Studies in English Literature* 12 (1972): 545–555. David L. Passler makes some interesting points about Boswell's use of autobiography even for events before 1763—something Passler sees as part of Boswell's complex use of time in the *Life*. See *Time, Form, and Style in Boswell's "Life of Johnson"* (New Haven: Yale University Press, 1971), 24–25.

13. The following passage near the end of the *Life* seems to confirm my point that Boswell's use of autobiography in the *Life* is indeed purposeful: "I now relieve the readers of this work from any farther personal notice of its authour, who if he should be thought to have obtruded himself too much upon their attention, requests them to consider the peculiar plan of his biographical undertaking" (IV, 380).

14. Waingrow, *Correspondence-Life*, 319.

15. Ibid., 598. See also Boswell's *Life of Johnson*, III, 312. Charles N. Fifer provides a fine summary of how the rift between Boswell and Percy developed in "Boswell and the Decorous Bishop," *JEGP* 61 (1962): 48–56.

16. Waingrow, *Correspondence-Life*, 597.

17. William R. Siebenschuh has a helpful discussion of how Boswell handles the more unpleasant aspects of Johnson's personality in the *Life*. See *Form and Purpose in Boswell's Biographical Works* (Berkeley and Los Angeles: University of California Press, 1972), 63–75.

18. Jean H. Hagstrum, "Johnson and the *Concordia Discors* of Human Relationships," in *The Unknown Samuel Johnson*, ed. John J. Burke, Jr., and Donald Kay (Madison: University of Wisconsin Press, 1983), 42–44.

19. The most important work done on Johnson's politics is Donald Greene, *The Politics of Samuel Johnson* (New Haven: Yale University Press, 1960), along with his edition of Johnson's *Political Writings*, vol. 10 (1977) of *The Yale Edition of the Works of Samuel Johnson* (New Haven: Yale University Press, 1958–). Kelley and Brack identify Joseph Towers, Whig and dissenting minister, as the early biographer most responsible for the myth of Tory Johnson. See *The Early Biographers of Samuel Johnson*, 68. For treatments of Johnson's religious

views, consult Maurice J. Quinlan, *Samuel Johnson: A Layman's Religion* (Madison: University of Wisconsin Press, 1964); Chester F. Chapin, *The Religious Thought of Samuel Johnson* (Ann Arbor: University of Michigan Press, 1968); and Charles E. Pierce, *The Religious Life of Samuel Johnson* (Hamden, Conn.: Archon, 1983).

20. *The Letters of Samuel Johnson with Mrs. Thrale's Genuine Letters to Him*, ed. R. W. Chapman, 3 vols. (Oxford: Clarendon, 1952), no. 505, II, 156 and no. 578, II, 251. All future references to Johnson's letters will be to Chapman's edition, with the title abbreviated to *Letters*.

21. E. L. McAdam, Jr., *Dr. Johnson and the English Law* (Syracuse, N.Y.: Syracuse University Press, 1951). Thomas M. Curley discusses Johnson's role in the Vinerian law lectures delivered by Sir Robert Chambers in "Johnson's Secret Collaboration," in *The Unknown Samuel Johnson*, ed. Burke and Kay, 91–112. Curley's edition of Chambers's Vinerian law lectures will be published soon by the University of Wisconsin Press.

22. See Sven Eric Molin, "Boswell's Account of the Johnson-Wilkes Meeting," *Studies in English Literature* 3 (1963): 307–322. Ralph W. Rader includes a perceptive discussion of this episode as part of his overall argument in "Literary Form in Factual Narrative," 22–27.

23. John Butt, for one, has also drawn attention to this point. See *Biography in the Hands of Walton, Johnson, and Boswell* (Los Angeles: University of California Press, 1966), 38–39.

24. Ralph Rader also sees significance in this point. See "Literary Form in Factual Narrative," 16–17. Rader's emphasis is on universality; mine on objectivity.

25. See P. A. W. Collins, "Boswell's Contact with Johnson," *Notes and Queries* 201 (1956): 163–166. Interestingly, this now famous calculation was done to correct Croker's much lower estimate, that Boswell had only spent 276 days in Johnson's company.

26. See James L. Clifford, "The Authenticity of Anna Seward's Published Correspondence," *Modern Philology* 39 (1941): 113–122; and James D. Woolley, "Johnson as Despot: Anna Seward's Rejected Contribution to Boswell's *Life*," *Modern Philology* 70 (1972): 140–145.

27. Waingrow, *Correspondence-Life*, 111.

28. As Marshall Waingrow has shrewdly observed, "there is more of Sir Joshua Reynolds in the *Life* than meets the eye." See Waingrow, *Correspondence-Life*, 119, n. 1. According to Frederick Pottle, Reynolds was "a loyal and affectionate friend, the closest of all Boswell's London friends after Johnson and Edmond Malone" (*James Boswell: The Earlier Years, 1740–1769* [New York: McGraw-Hill, 1966], 431).

29. Even a rough count gets into three figures. See the index to the Hill-Powell edition (1964), VI, 333–337.

30. For a confirmation of this point, see ibid., I, 523.

31. For a fuller description of Johnson's relationship with Thomas Warton, see John A. Vance, *Joseph and Thomas Warton* (Boston: Twayne, 1983), 8–11, and "Samuel Johnson and Thomas Warton," *Biography* (forthcoming).

32. Charles N. Fifer provides a useful summary of Langton's biography in *The Correspondence of James Boswell with Certain Members of The Club*, ed. Charles N. Fifer (New York: McGraw-Hill, 1976), lii–lxxv. Future references to these materials will be to Fifer's edition, with the title abbreviated as *Correspondence-Club*. An earlier, considerably less informative account of Langton can be found in George Birkbeck Hill, *Dr. Johnson: His Friends and His Critics* (London: Smith, Elder, 1878), 248–279.

33. This is the estimate of James L. Clifford, an extraordinarily careful scholar. See *Dictionary Johnson: Samuel Johnson's Middle Years* (New York: McGraw-Hill, 1979), 127. Levet's role in the meeting is confirmed in a letter from Johnson to Langton, dated 2 March 1782, informing him of Levet's death: "My dear old friend Mr. Levet to whom, as he used to tell me, I owe your acquaintance, died a few weeks ago suddenly in his bed" (*Letters*, no. 770, II, 470). For the possibility of unreported preparations for that first meeting in which Joseph Spence may have played a key role, see Charles N. Fifer, "Dr. Johnson and Bennet Langton," *JEGP* 54 (1955): 504–506.

34. *Letters*, no. 70, I, 71.

35. Ibid., no. 732, II, 429.

36. According to the complaints of his friends, Langton spent too much time in London. In fact, the expense of maintaining a second household in London was part of the reason he had difficulty making ends meet, despite an income in the range of 4,000 pounds a year, in contrast to Boswell's income of 1,800 pounds a year as laird of Auchinleck and Johnson's government pension of 300 pounds a year.

37. A persuasive piece of evidence for the closeness between Johnson and Langton appears in Boswell's notes of his interview with the Reverend William Adams in June 1784. It is all the more persuasive because the point of the story is to show the closeness between Adams and Johnson, not that between Langton and Johnson. "In the year 1766 he was dreadfully afflicted with low spirits. Dr. Adams called at his house. Mrs. Williams said nobody had been admitted to him for some days but Mr. Langton. But he would see Dr. Adams. He found Mr. Langton with him" (Waingrow, *Correspondence-Life*, 24).

38. It is clear from his journals that Boswell first heard about this incident from Johnson himself. It is just as clear that he confirmed the details of the incident with Langton before writing up the account that appears in the *Life*. There he supplies a list of the scriptural texts whose "drift" so unsettled Johnson. See *Boswell: The Applause of the Jury, 1782–1785*, ed. Irma S. Lustig and Frederick A. Pottle (New York: McGraw-Hill, 1981), 216.

39. *Boswell in Search of a Wife, 1766–1769*, ed. Frank Brady and F. A. Pottle (New York: McGraw-Hill, 1956), 175.

40. *Thraliana: The Diary of Mrs. Hester Lynch Thrale (Later Mrs. Piozzi) 1776–1809*, ed. Katharine C. Balderston, 2 vols. (Oxford: Clarendon, 1942), 1:106.

41. *Boswell for the Defence, 1769–1774*, ed. William K. Wimsatt, Jr., and Frederick A. Pottle (New York: McGraw-Hill, 1959), 139.

42. See *Correspondence-Club* and *Correspondence-Life*.

43. Irma Lustig notes the complex way Boswell also handled the contributions from the Reverend William Adams. See "Fact into Art: James Boswell's Notes, Journals, and the *Life of Johnson*," in *Biography in the 18th Century*, ed. J. D. Browning (New York: Garland, 1980), 138.

44. Thomas M. Curley has provided the most complete account of the importance of travel to Johnson. See *Samuel Johnson and the Age of Travel* (Athens: University of Georgia Press, 1976).

45. Charles Fifer's summary of the problems in Langton's writing is certainly to the point: "His letters . . . are disorganized and undirected; they reflect a mind which diffused itself too widely to be effective. His sentences are too long and too involved; where one word would have sufficed he uses three" (*Correspondence-Club*, lxxv).

46. See "The Chronology of the Making of the *Life*," in Waingrow, *Correspondence-Life*, li–lxxviii.

47. Donald Greene disputes Boswell's reputation for accuracy by challenging the authenticity of the famous Billingsgate anecdote in the *Life* (IV, 26), noting that long ago E. L. McAdam found that the story had been printed material before Boswell was even born. See Greene, "'Tis a Pretty Book," 25. It might be worth pointing out that this incident was reported by Langton (IV, 26), not Boswell. If the story is indeed fabricated, either in its substance or in its ornaments, Boswell can be blamed only for reporting what he had reason to believe was authentic, not for inventing it. Moreover, if the same words that Langton said Johnson used, or words very close to them, can be found in earlier printed material, that does not necessarily mean that he did not use them, especially if we consider Johnson's extraordinary verbal memory.

48. It would be hard to improve on Charles Fifer's assessment of Langton's willingness to let the truth be told: "Extraordinarily tolerant, he allowed Boswell to print all Johnson's wounding remarks about himself without any remonstrance, though Boswell's occasional suppressions of his name furnished him no real protection. It would seem that, like Boswell, he could tolerate anything Johnson said as soon as he had become convinced that Johnson's love for him was unalterable. Unlike Percy, unlike even Reynolds, Langton was unreservedly cooperative. By such magnanimity, if for nothing else, he deserved his epithet of "worthy." (*Correspondence-Club*, lxx). Hester Thrale Piozzi, however, was not quite as understanding when she learned from reading the *Life* that Johnson could be a "back Friend" (see *Thraliana*, 2:810–811).

49. That Johnson was aware that such gossiping might be blameworthy is made clear in an incident reported by Boswell. The two had just attended

church and listened to a sermon on evil-speaking. When they came outside, Johnson said to Boswell, perhaps archly, that what they had just heard "was very applicable to *us*" (III, 379).

50. For the text of *Idler* 67, see *The Idler and The Adventurer*, ed. W. J. Bate, John M. Bullitt, and L. F. Powell, vol. 2 (1963) of *The Yale Edition of the Works of Samuel Johnson* (New Haven: Yale University Press, 1958–), 207–211. After reviewing Langton's correspondence, it would be difficult to disagree with Charles Fifer's conjecture that "Johnson revised that essay before it was printed" (*Correspondence-Club*, lvi).

51. John Wain considers Langton's essay in his recent biography of Johnson. See *Samuel Johnson* (New York: Viking, 1975), 225–227. Much as I appreciate Wain's discussion of the essay's themes, I cannot understand why he would believe that Johnson did not catch Langton's "drift" on this topic.

52. *William Shaw: Memoirs of the Life and Writings of the Late Dr. Samuel Johnson and Hester Lynch Piozzi: Anecdotes of the Late Samuel Johnson, LL.D. during the Last Twenty Years of His Life*, ed. Arthur Sherbo (New York: Oxford University Press, 1974), 86.

53. For a discussion of her inaccuracies, see Irma S. Lustig, "Boswell at Work: The 'Animadversions' on Mrs. Piozzi," *Modern Language Review* 67 (1972): 11–30; and Hyde, *The Impossible Friendship*, passim.

54. Hawkins, *Life*, 327. Davis's edition of Hawkins's *Life* is an abridgment, but only because Davis eliminated more than three hundred pages of Sir John's digressions, digressions that tell us much about life in the eighteenth century but little about Johnson (see xxix, xviii–xx).

55. *Correspondence-Club*, lii. Bertram Davis claims that all the members of the Club, including Langton, "sided" with Boswell and turned over all their memorabilia to him (*Johnson before Boswell*, 34), but he offers no details. Elsewhere, however, Davis portrays Hawkins's relationship with Langton very favorably, noting that Langton was even awarded a mourning ring for Sir John, according to the terms of his will. See *A Proof of Eminence: The Life of Sir John Hawkins* (Bloomington: Indiana University Press, 1974), 371, 374. Moreover, it seems clear that Langton did cooperate with Hawkins, that, at the very least, he was the source for the stories about the gift of the *Dictionnaire* and about his own contribution to the *Idler* series. He also contributed another famous story, that of Johnson composing one of his *Idlers* in a white-heat at Langton's room in Oxford. Hawkins did use this story but, perhaps characteristically, felt it deserved only a footnote. See Hawkins, *Life*, 300, n. 23.

56. Greene, " 'Tis a Pretty Book," 37.

57. Waingrow, *Correspondence-Life*, 250.

58. John Butt notes that Boswell's legal training is what probably helped him most when it came to determining the authenticity of what he had learned about Johnson from others. See *Biography in the Hands of Boswell*, 45.

59. Waingrow, *Correspondence-Life*, 241, n. 4.

60. Ibid., 88.

61. See James L. Clifford, *Young Sam Johnson* (New York: McGraw-Hill, 1955), 312–315.

62. Elizabeth Desmoulins remains, and will probably always remain, an obscure figure about whom little is known. But what we do know of her can hardly increase our confidence in the exactness of her testimony. Donald and Mary Hyde speak of her "ill temper" and a "lack of intellectual interest" that was "incapable of development"—not the characteristics, one would think, of an entirely reliable informant. See "Dr. Johnson's Second Wife," in *New Light on Dr. Johnson*, ed. Frederick W. Hilles (New Haven: Yale University Press, 1959), 148.

63. The two most successful efforts at bridging this gap are, to my mind, Walter Jackson Bate, *The Achievement of Samuel Johnson* (1955; reprint, Chicago: University of Chicago Press, 1978) and Donald Greene, *Samuel Johnson* (New York: Twayne, 1970). Though more restricted in its focus, Jean H. Hagstrum's *Samuel Johnson's Literary Criticism* (1952; reprint, Chicago: University of Chicago Press, 1967) also deserves mention.

64. For one opinion on how few uses we should have for the *Life*, see Schwartz, *Preface to the "Life,"* 90–105. Donald Greene would allow the *Life* to be used for examples of Johnson's table talk. See "'Tis a Pretty Book," 29.

65. William Siebenschuh also believes that noting the role of the imagination is the key to any satisfactory interpretation of the *Life*. See "Who Is Boswell's Johnson?" in *Studies in Eighteenth-Century Culture*, ed. Harry C. Payne, vol. 10 (Madison: University of Wisconsin Press, 1980), 353, 355. George Mallory believed the effect of the *Life* was to make us "feel better" and "want especially to love other men." See *Boswell the Biographer* (London: Smith Elder, 1912), 145.

66. For the argument that the real point of Boswell's *Life* is to make Johnson looks ridiculous, see Donald Greene, "Reflections on a Literary Anniversary," *Queen's Quarterly* 70 (1963): 198–208. This essay can be found in slightly abridged form in Clifford, *Twentieth Century Interpretations*, 97–103.

67. "Of all his intimates and Friends, I think I never could find any who much loved him Boswell & Burney excepted—Mr Murphy too loved him as he loves People—when he sees them—All the others would rather not have seen him than seen him as far as I have been able to observe; & as to Burney had they been more together, they would have liked each other less" (*Thraliana*, 1:182). If Boswell was quite as hurt as we have been told (Lustig, "'Animadversions' on Mrs. Piozzi," 27) when he learned from the publication of Johnson's letters to Mrs. Thrale that he apparently loved her more than him, he might have been consoled by what he could have read in her diaries if he ever could have had the chance to read them. There she says unequivocally: "He loved Mr Boswell sincerely" (*Thraliana*, 1:166). Frank Brady, Boswell's most recent biographer, also feels that the affection between the two was en-

tirely genuine. See *James Boswell: The Later Years, 1769–1795* (New York: McGraw-Hill, 1984), 161–162.

68. James L. Clifford, *Hester Lynch Piozzi (Mrs. Thrale)*, 2d ed. (Oxford: Clarendon, 1968), 207. For an otherwise dense and satisfying biography, Clifford places surprisingly little emphasis on Hester Thrale's feelings for Johnson. Perhaps he felt these feelings were too obvious for discussion; perhaps, too, he avoided a direct treatment of the subject because the relationship between the two had been the cause of so much snickering in the past, not excluding Boswell's sophomoric ode on their supposed nuptials.

69. Not much is known about Catherine Chambers. Aleyn Lyell Reade reports on what little is known. See *Johnsonian Gleanings*, 11 vols. (1922; reprint, New York Octagon, 1968), 3:77 and 10:51, 89.

70. Davis, *Johnson before Boswell*, 178.

71. Frank Brady believes that Boswell's desire to delay the publication of his *Life* until he had had a chance to see Hawkins's was merely an excuse for his own tardiness. *The Later Years*, 351. I think the delay was crucial. As Maximillian E. Novak writes, the earlier biographical pieces by Mrs. Piozzi, Sir John Hawkins, and Fanny Burney "provide a means of judging Boswell's picture of Johnson, and they confirm the greatness of Boswell's *Life*" (*Eighteenth-Century English Literature*, Macmillan History of Literature [London: Macmillan, 1983], 181).

72. Waingrow, *Correspondence-Life*, 143.

73. William C. Dowling notes the importance of affection in the *Life* and draws attention to how Boswell increasingly surrounds Johnson with friends such as Reynolds, Langton, and Burke near the end. Unfortunately, affection for Dowling is merely the retreat of Johnson (and Boswell) from a world too hard to understand. See "Biographer, Hero, and Audience in Boswell's *Life of Johnson*," *Studies in English Literature* 20 (1980): 490–491. He repeats this point in *Language and Logos in Boswell's "Life of Johnson"* (Princeton, N.J.: Princeton University Press, 1981), 158–161. Fredric V. Bogel sees the achievement of the *Life* in Boswell's ability to convey Johnson's sense of presence to himself and to others, thereby redefining our sense of the heroic as an authentic sense of self. See *Literature and Insubstantiality in Later Eighteenth-Century England* (Princeton, N.J.: Princeton University Press, 1984), 173–194. Approaches to the *Life* through the heroic will almost always have an unfortunate but predictable result, an emphasis on awe at the expense of affection. Dowling is an exception only in that his conception of the heroic leads to condescension, not awe.

The Laughing Johnson
and the Shaping
of Boswell's *Life*

hether we accept or reject the conclusions of Donald Greene and Richard Schwartz,[1] their work has made us at least question the authenticity of the Johnson who appears throughout the pages of Boswell's *Life*. We have learned or have been assured—and are thus obligated, I would argue, to tell our students— that a fairly complete knowledge of Johnson the man *cannot* be gleaned merely from a reading of the *Life*. Just how much of the *real* Johnson may be discovered in Boswell's book, how much Boswell cre- ated the Johnson of popular legend, or how much evidence from the *Life* one should use with confidence are matters on which few totally agree; even so, they are significant questions that no modern reader can afford to ignore. But the disturbing finality of Schwartz's title, "Boswell's Johnson,"[2] has a special command of our attention, and as a result we scrutinize with both fascination and skepticism the figure who looms, delights, debates, grumbles, shouts, and bullies his way through the world's favorite literary "biography." Our desire to know the real Johnson is a major reason why we are so uncomfortable with the possibility that the Johnson in the *Life* may be largely or even in a small degree a creation of Boswell's art. The more some of us come to accept Greene's and Schwartz's theses, the more we wish to hurl bricks at the temple, the more we distrust the portrait of Johnson, and the more we reject the value of the *Life* as a biographical source.

Although I find convincing many of Greene's and Schwartz's conclusions about the false impression of Johnson one draws from the *Life,* I wish to take issue with the belief that *on the whole* we are engaged with Boswell's Johnson.[3] I qualify my assertion because I will not deny that in sections of the *Life* Boswell deliberately contrasts, creates, selects, emphasizes, or recalls those aspects and moments of the Johnson he remembered or wished his readers to know. My argument is that throughout the *Life* we see, to continue the critical vernacular, *Johnson's* Johnson; that is, a persona *he* deliberately advanced to surprise, shock, aggravate, and confuse his friends, acquaintances, and even his enthusiastic future biographer. The *Life* reveals to us upon careful examination a man who, rather than being the object of Boswell's manipulation, enjoyed controlling events himself and eliciting predictable responses from those in his company. We can therefore exonerate Boswell from several counts of the charge that he shaped Johnson into semifiction if we become more aware of Johnson's unique sense of humor as it manifests itself in the pages of the *Life.*

Even though readers have taken much pleasure in the frequent illustrations of Johnson's wit, they have not realized adequately enough how much the various demonstrations of his humor have helped to shape our, as well as Boswell's, impressions of him. Readers have for too long emphasized the tragic, philosophical, and combative Johnson depicted in the *Life;* too little space has been devoted to his marvelous though deceptive sense of humor. We may discover that in general the *Life* does give us the essence of Johnson, and not a reshaped creation of Boswell, but that to arrive at that essence we must occasionally see through the fictional persona Johnson himself established. We may moreover find that we have frequently wasted our time attempting to justify or understand a memorable Johnsonian utterance when the remark was never meant to reflect his true assessment.

Walter Jackson Bate has taken great pains to remind us that the Johnson who walked into Tom Davies's bookshop on that mid-May afternoon in 1763 had been moving precariously close to a breakdown, "and only by the most heroic effort, exerted day after day, could he pull himself together."[4] Bate's depiction explains why Johnson found so much stability and comfort in the hours spent socially with friends. And as the increasingly popular theory goes, Johnson found a much needed release from his mental anguish in laughter, that temporary palliative and dilutant of depression. Bate considers at some length Johnson's humor and wit, arguing quite rightly that it was not a "special or minor aspect of his personality but something interwoven with it at almost every point." Evidence of Johnson's delight in laughter is easy to find—Hester Thrale, Arthur Murphy, John Hawkins, and Boswell, among his closest associates, attest to the broad conception Johnson had of humor, from, as Bate again writes, "the playful to the aggressive, from the naive to the intellectually complicated, and from his unexpected talent for buffoonery and mimicry to almost every kind of wit."[5] And few can forget the vision of Johnson, stricken by the thought of Chambers making Langton's will, sending forth thunderous peals of laughter that vibrated the night air from "Temple-bar to Fleet-ditch."[6] But with a few other exceptions this is *not* the Johnson one recalls from the *Life*.[7] This is not the Johnson that looks at us from the famous portraits of Reynolds, James Barry, and John Opie; nor from the many nineteenth-century characterizations of events from the *Life*;[8] nor from the covers of modern texts.[9] Those moments of Johnson's indulging his humor seem to rise pleasantly in the *Life*, but they are quickly suppressed and supplanted by the gruff, aggressive, rational, yet prejudiced personality we have come to know.[10]

Boswell, it should be stressed at the outset, did not consciously conceal Johnson's humorous side. At times he signaled the nature of his friend's comments by including in parentheses indicators such as "smiling," "laughing," "laughing heartily," "chuckling and laughing," "laughing immoderately," or "with a complacent smile," "with a pleasant smile," "with a hearty laugh," "with a good humoured pleasantry," and "with a hearty loud laugh of approbation." And Boswell reminded the reader in other ways of Johnson's sense of humor: "I have known him at times exceedingly diverted at what seemed to others a very small sport. . . . [Johnson] could not help laughing. . . . [He said] To laugh is good. . . . You may laugh in as many ways as you talk. . . . I never knew a man laugh more heartily." But in this last remark Boswell sours the image of the laughing Johnson by adding, "We may suppose, that the high relish of a state so different from his habitual gloom, produced more than ordinary exertions of that distinguishing faculty of man, which has puzzled philosophers so much to explain."[11] And Boswell repeated this observation at the end of the *Life:* "Though usually grave, and even awful, in his deportment, he possessed uncommon and peculiar powers of wit and humour" (IV, 428).

The laughing Johnson is evident in the *Life,* but again one senses a reluctance by Boswell and the reader to emphasize the image to any large extent—as if it would damage the time-honored impression of the sober moralist, vigorous debater, and at times pompous commentator on literature, society, and politics.[12] Assuredly, many of Boswell's comments make difficult our seeing Johnson any other way: Boswell "beheld him with a reverential awe," had a "high veneration" for him, and considered him the "Colossus of Literature" and a man of "weight and dignity." "[I]f you should advise me to go to Japan," he told Johnson, "I believe I should do it."[13] And the reader has not needed these observations to draw the same conclusions, especially since Johnson apparently displays in his conversation those venerable characteristics of the famous image.

But Johnson's character was at times under the spell of an impish spirit, and it was often part of his design to make his remarks ambiguous and deceptive. Frequently the victim of Johnson's humor, Boswell was not always aware or sure of the context of his friend's conversation and therefore could not inform the reader with certainty if Johnson actually meant what he said. This is not to claim that Johnson was never consciously curt, angry, and insensitive, but we must consider the possibility that on many occasions what appeared somber and serious may well have been an extension of Johnson's sense of humor and his desire to deceive and control events. As Johnson told Arthur Murphy, "I sometimes say more than I mean, in jest, and people are apt to think me serious."[14]

Boswell once said to Johnson regarding the conversation of the night before, "you tossed and gored several persons" (II, 66). Readers have long concentrated on the goring without appreciating well enough the tossing, for it was in the latter that Johnson took his most delight; that is, in keeping his friends, acquaintances, and enemies off balance and defensive. Readers of the *Life* should be cognizant of the many times Johnson teased his friends for the purpose of annoying and embarrassing them and entertaining himself and others in his company—the kinds of occasions on which one's assertions must not be taken literally. Regarding Johnson's supposed bias against Scotland, throughout the *Life* he lambastes the country, its government and church, and its citizens, including its luminaries—men like the historian William Robertson, whom Johnson truly respected yet would not allow to escape censure when Boswell brought up his name. The famous response to Boswell's admission at their initial meeting—"I do indeed come from Scotland, but I cannot help it": "That, Sir, I find, is what a very great many of your countrymen cannot help" (I, 392)—was obviously meant to tease and shock the starstruck and thus vulnerable young man; it was not simply the response of a cantankerous though witty middle-aged English celebrity. And like many of us whose affection for another is triggered by a teasing remark or affectionate insult (and what *was* Johnson's demeanor when he spoke these words—scowling and apparently serious or more likely bemused with tongue in cheek?), Johnson would continue to make the joke as a reminder to him and Boswell of the initial stimulation of their relationship. But he also knew such references were bound to stir Boswell's patriotism and vanity and elicit the inevitable defense of his native country.

Boswell may have believed he was directing Johnson's responses when mentioning Scotland, but in reality it was Johnson who conducted this symphony of wit and humor. Drawing from these moments in the *Life* an image of Johnson as John Bull, readers have usually taken quite literally and out of its proper context Boswell's remark in 1768: "His prejudice against Scotland appeared remarkably strong at this time." And in support of his nation Boswell responded to Johnson's back-handed dismissal of Scotland's literary lions: "But, Sir, we have Lord Kames," to which Johnson replied, "You *have* Lord Kames. Keep him; ha, ha, ha! We don't envy you him" (II, 53).[15] Here we should picture Johnson with a devilish smile inching upward, staring incredulously at Boswell's defensive posture, and then applying the *coup de grâce* with a *playfully* derisive laugh. And during the famous dinner with Wilkes, Johnson thoroughly enjoyed tormenting Boswell, patronizing and embarrassing him in a good-natured way in front of company the Scot wished to impress: "[Y]ou know he lives among savages in Scotland, and among rakes in London. . . . And we ashamed of him" (III, 77).[16]

On one occasion when Boswell questioned Johnson's assertion that Garrick's death "eclipsed the gaiety of nations," Johnson cut off the questioning with the following remark, spoken, I would argue, with a wry smile on his lips and a twinkle in his eye—perhaps even winking at Beauclerk, Reynolds, and others as he said it: "Why, Sir, some exaggeration must be allowed. Besides, nations may be said—if we allow the Scotch to be a nation, and to have gaiety,—which they have not. *You* are an exception, though. Come, gentlemen, let us candidly admit that there is one Scotchman who is cheerful" (III, 387–388). Here is an excellent illustration of Johnson's using Boswell and his nationality to amuse an audience. Johnson is in control here, fully aware of what the response to his anti-Scots pose would be—from Boswell and from others in their company. And yet many readers still cherish the notion that Boswell held the leash, tossing out mention of Scotland as a bone that Johnson would retrieve and then chew.

Boswell probably did not know when he met the older man that Johnson was used to company that teased, challenged, and jockeyed for dominance. Because Garrick, perhaps above all others, so enjoyed needling Johnson, it is no wonder that Johnson frequently paid back in kind—especially with his sweeping denunciation of players. We surely should not believe that Johnson was always serious when he made derogatory remarks at the expense of the stage. As for Goldsmith, Johnson found early the chink in the Irishman's armor, which he could easily pierce with teasing and at times with bold humor. Johnson took delight in infuriating Goldsmith by calling him "Goldy," and how he must have grinned when a German (perhaps Swiss) acquaintance of theirs interrupted Goldsmith and said, "Stay, stay— Toctor Shonson is going to say something" (II, 257). Like many with roguish spirits, Johnson could not resist jabbing a helpless opponent, even though his teasing occasionally went too far, with the result that he was forced to apologize if feelings were bruised too deeply. But Goldsmith, ironically since he was often the butt of Johnson's humor, noted perceptively that Johnson *"has nothing of the bear but his skin"* (II, 66)—an observation applicable not just to his argumentative side but to his teasing nature as well.

Few of his friends escaped Johnson's baiting: to Hester Thrale, proud of her culinary talents, Johnson said "with a smile," "Mrs. Abington's jelly, my dear Lady, was better than yours" (II, 349). In the 1750s Garrick made the mistake of telling Johnson that some readers had objected to his quoting in the *Dictionary* "authorities which were beneath the dignity of such a work, and mentioned Richardson." Probably overjoyed that Garrick had walked so unknowingly into his trap, Johnson replied, "I have done worse than that: I have cited *thee*, David" (IV, 4). And even in his grave Garrick was not safe: Johnson seemingly took delight in recalling a story of Samuel Foote, who "had a small bust of Garrick placed on his bureau. 'You may be surprized (said he) that I allow him to be so near my gold;—but you will observe he has no hands'" (May 1783; IV, 224).

Appropriately, Garrick made what is perhaps the most vivid and discerning comment regarding Johnson's habitual teasing nature: "Rabelais and all other wits are nothing compared with him. You may be diverted by them; but Johnson gives you a forcible hug, and shakes laughter out of you, whether you will or no" (II, 231). This was Johnson's way; through his vigorous and brash method of needling he "shook" laughter or at least a begrudging smile from his many friends. He could not abide in social situations a dour countenance or an air of pomposity or solemnity. Johnson saw the corrective and purgative benefits to be derived from exposing oneself to the kind of teasing he endured from others and indulged in with alacrity and pleasure: "A man should pass a part of his time with *the laughers*, by which means any thing ridiculous or particular about him might be presented to his view, and corrected" (IV, 183). And an appreciation of this aspect of his character again helps to counter the popular view that he was usually "set up" and his wit and argumentative talents exercised by Boswell. Johnson was more often in command, drawing forth expected responses not only from Boswell but from many in his company. He may not have always known when to cease, but he certainly enjoyed keeping his friends off-stride and defensive in the jocular environment in which he frequently lived.

Another manifestation of Johnson's humor and a reflection of how he delighted in confounding and annoying others and keeping his true thoughts concealed, distorted, or ambiguous was his penchant for making outlandish statements for their shocking effect. Part of the Johnson myth has come from misunderstanding this characteristic of his. Johnson is without question guilty of perpetuating the myth (and therefore of shaping the *Life* itself), for *he* decided what to say and how, thus leaving himself open to the charge of bigotry, insensitivity, and intolerance. But, again, readers must be careful in assigning to Johnson any qualities "reflected" in some of the more memorable passages in the *Life*.

Boswell recalled the time when Johnson spoke warmly of Jacobitism to old Mr. Langton's niece, Miss Roberts: "My dear, I hope you are a Jacobite" (I, 430). We can only guess at how often in the past two hundred years this passage has been trotted out as strong evidence of Johnson's political prejudices. But the remark was more likely meant to raise the eyebrows of Langton, who while a Tory in sympathy had an affection for the Hanoverians. Although Johnson's frequent broadsides against Whiggism have been placed in their proper political contexts by Donald Greene and more recent commentators, we should not forget that Johnson would have known how such assessments would startle, aggravate, and provoke those in his company, whether friends, acquaintances, or enemies—none were excluded by Johnson. He was one of those rare individuals who enjoys stirring things up—like the wit of today who drops an anti-administration slur into a room full of staunch Republicans, knowing full well the reactions forthcoming. Johnson must have relished the opportunity to shock and anger Gibbon, Boswell, and others in his midst when he noted that little *authentic* history was being written: "all the colouring," he said, "all the philosophy, of history is conjecture" (III, 365–366). Even though Johnson could argue this point intellectually (after all, it makes perfect sense considering the legacy of historical skepticism in the eighteenth century), part of Johnson's intent was likely to shock and annoy Boswell and Gibbon—or anyone else who would assume the remark to be a slight against history. That Gibbon did not, as Boswell put it, "step forth in defence of that species of writing" because he "probably did not like to *trust* himself" with his famous contemporary, may well have disappointed Johnson, who would have expected a lively exchange. Almost certainly aware at that time (April 1775) of Gibbon's ongoing historical work on the Roman Empire, Johnson was willing to suppress or distort his own appreciation of history in order to confound and antagonize.

This desire to shock and upset, which is as much an extension of his sense of humor as it is a reflection of his combative side, may help to explain many of his most disturbing utterances in the *Life:* for example, his challenge to the "great republican" Catharine Macaulay that she allow her footman to dine with them (Johnson said he "*put on* a very grave countenance"); Johnson's almost incomprehensible defense of the Spanish Inquisition, to the "utter astonishment of all the passengers" in the coach; his refuting Berkeley's complex and sophisticated arguments by "striking his foot with mighty force against a large stone"; his seeming endorsement of male adultery: "Sir, a wife ought not greatly to resent this. . . . wise married women don't trouble themselves about infidelity in their husbands"; his apparent disregard for the fate of his friends: "Sir, that sympathetick feeling goes a very little way in depressing the mind"; his boast that he would "not have left [Samuel Foote] a leg to cut off" had the comic mimicked him in public; his impatience toward the teaching of children: "I should *not* have a pleasure in teaching [them]"; his characterization of Fielding as a "blockhead" to an "astonished" Boswell; his curt statement to James Elphinston, "No, Sir; do *you* read books *through?*"; his seemingly uncritical characterization of Gray as a "dull fellow": "He was dull in a new way, and that made many people think him GREAT"; and his callous pronouncement to Hester Thrale that in order to "maintain the subordination of civilized society" he would ostracize financially and familially any daughter of rank who made a "mean marriage." We might add to the list his characterization of actors as no better than "dancing dogs"; his dismissal of sculpting as best measured by its difficulty rather than by its artistic merit: "You would not value the finest head cut upon a carrot"; his brash statement that no one but a "blockhead" ever wrote "except for money"; his refusal to admit that men can be ruined by inordinate wagering; his memorable toast at Cambridge "to the next insurrection of the negroes in the West Indies";

and his apparent unwillingness while composing the *Lives of the Poets* to visit Lord Marchmont to learn of some particulars of Alexander Pope: "I don't care to know about Pope."[17]

All of these unforgettable responses, many having been explained in the context of Johnson's literary, social, and political beliefs, have helped enormously to shape the Johnson recalled from a reading of the *Life*. Accordingly, we should not be surprised when our colleagues and students characterize Johnson as cantankerous, at times callous and unfeeling, bullying, impatient, often critically unsound, unappreciative of artistic achievement, insensitive and patronizing to women and children, and unwilling to stretch his mind beyond the narrow confines of his own prejudices. Anyone who has studied Johnson carefully, however, knows that all of the negative impressions left by these famous comments and reactions are contradicted by accounts in other biographical sources, by Johnson's own writings, and by other sections of the *Life* itself. Although in several instances Boswell attempted to explain that Johnson was only "talking for victory" (for instance, when he cast aspersions at the historical work of William Robertson: "Sir, I love Robertson, and I won't talk of his book"), Johnson's shocking pronouncements obfuscated the more truthful addenda offered by Boswell and thus almost precluded the reader's setting Johnson's remarks in their proper contexts. Johnson, then, was most responsible on many occasions for shaping his own image. His retorts were too good, too shocking, and too memorable to be diluted by Boswell's caveat to the reader.[18]

Readers of the *Life* can more easily understand, enjoy, and appreciate some of Johnson's famous responses when they assess them as an extension of his desire to shock those in his company and to elicit from them predictable reactions. Although he was perceptive in comprehending his friend's true estimation of Robertson, Boswell could not understand Johnson's "violent declamation against the Corsicans," especially since he knew of Boswell's high regard for the islanders and his recently published *Account* of them (II, 80). But the reader should see that accordingly Boswell was vulnerable to this incorrigible aspect of Johnson's humor—and that, being naturally defensive about his pet project, he was too easy of a mark. Those of us who have been treated similarly by more devilish colleagues, those who make disparaging remarks about our special subject of interest, can easily sympathize with Boswell's position.

Aware of Sir Adam Fergusson's interest in a stable political system, Johnson could be confident of drawing forth a spirited reaction when he stated matter-of-factly, "I would not give half a guinea to live under one form of government rather than another. It is of no moment to the happiness of an individual" (II, 170). Johnson could not have meant this literally; nor could he have been serious when he observed to Boswell and Hester Thrale that men in general "do not care much about" their children: "I myself should not have had much fondness for a child of my own." Rather than an outburst of self-pity or a reflection of his occasional melancholy, this remark must have been uttered for its shock value. After all, how could Johnson expect Hester Thrale to respond any differently than she did: "Nay, Sir, how can you talk so?" (III, 29). How indeed, considering Johnson's fondness for the Thrale children and their affection for him. Even though he at times offers an explanation for Johnson's observations, here and elsewhere in the *Life* Boswell allows the comment to stand, without qualification, therefore giving it the weight of a legal pronouncement. But more than a matter of leaving out important details, Boswell was not always able to gauge Johnson's mood as he made these incomprehensible and often disturbing statements. Did Johnson have a slight smile on his lips? His tongue in his cheek? His eyes rolling slightly upward perhaps? That readers of the *Life* have been shocked and angered by and defensive about these memorable passages would be, ironically, what Johnson would have expected, since he was hoping to elicit the very same responses from those who heard the words originally.

At one point, Boswell depicts Johnson's apparent shift from a serious and aggravated mood to one of near-boyish delight when a gentleman, who decided to incur the wrath of Johnson by discussing metaphysical matters, said in earnest, "But really, Sir, when we see a very sensible dog, we don't know what to think of him." Johnson, "rolling with joy at the thought which beamed in his eye, turned quickly round, and replied, 'True, Sir: and when we see a very foolish *fellow,* we don't know what to think of *him.*'" Johnson then "rose up, strided to the fire, and stood for some time laughing and exulting" (II, 54). This is one in-

stance in which we can visualize with ease the effect of Johnson's humor
on his retorts, but in many other memorable sections of the *Life* we are
not given such unmistakable clues to his frame of mind. There are
scenes in which Johnson's demeanor, observations, and arguments cannot be characterized as mere teasing or as attempts to shock his friends
and acquaintances; they are rather reflections of his love of misstatement with the intention of confusing and keeping offstride many who
might wish to predict his response.

Because his performance was usually superb, Johnson, like most
good actors who are proficient at what they do, frequently had his
stage role represent his true personality. His ability to intimidate
Boswell on their initial meeting must have amused him considerably,
although Tom Davies could see through Johnson's persona: "Don't be
uneasy," he told Boswell, "I can see he likes you very well" (I, 395).
Again, Boswell was not always able to detect when Johnson was deliberately deceptive in his demeanor and conversation, even though
Johnson had told him from the beginning, "Poh, poh! . . . never mind
these things"; that is, his apparent brusqueness at their meeting (I,
399). Boswell mentioned several times that, given Johnson's reputation for "bigotry," he was "surprized" to hear from him many "liberal"
sentiments (I, 405). Obviously, Johnson had been in the habit of misleading others before he met Boswell.

"Mr. Ogilvie was unlucky enough," Boswell recalled in the *Life*, "to
choose for the topick of his conversation the praises of his native
country. . . . he observed, that Scotland had a great many noble wild
prospects." Johnson responded, "I believe, Sir, you have a great
many. . . . But, Sir, let me tell you, the noblest prospect which a
Scotchman ever sees, is the high road that leads him to England!" (I,
425). Boswell does not give us enough information to ascertain
whether Johnson said this red-faced with anger, grinning or suppressing a laugh, or with a serious air. I would guess that he made this
memorable retort with a straight face, for to do so would make the jest
even more effective; there is, as we know, something awkward in a
marvelous witticism coming from the mouth of an angry man, and it
is somewhat diluted when emanating from the lips of a laughing man.
Johnson would have thoroughly enjoyed uttering a remark with an
inscrutable look on his face, his victim looking stunned and then per-

plexed, trying to determine just in what spirit the comment was delivered. Readers have laughed at the brilliance of the reply but have wrongly tended to place it in the context of Johnson's "uncontrollable" anti-Scots bias.

A few other examples will serve to illustrate the deceptive quality of Johnson's humor in the *Life*. On the way to Harwich in August 1763, Boswell "ostentatiously gave a shilling to the coachman, when the custom was for each passenger to give only six-pence." Quite rightly, Boswell admitted in retrospect, Johnson "scolded" him about making the coachman "dissatisfied" with the amount the others had given (I, 465–466). Boswell's defense of Johnson's parsimonious nature aside, might it be that Johnson's "scolding" was an extension of that inscrutable side of his humor that encouraged him to say with apparent seriousness what he did not really mean? Our knowledge of Johnson's humanitarianism and generosity to the downtrodden and common citizen is inconsistent with the portrait emerging from this scene in the *Life;* that is, Johnson as class conscious and cheap.

We might also consider these possibilities: were Johnson's criticisms of Swift, Gray, and Fielding exaggerated because he wished to be deceptive and at odds with popular opinion? Was Johnson suppressing a smile, rather than displaying aggravation, when he answered Boswell's point about the benefits of drinking? "You know," Boswell said, "drinking drives away care, and makes us forget whatever is disagreeable. Would not you allow a man to drink for that reason?" Johnson responded, "Yes, Sir, if he sat next *you*" (II, 193). Was Johnson deliberately trying to confuse Boswell by asserting that marriages would be "as happy, and often more so, if they were all made by the Lord Chancellor" (II, 461)? Considering again Johnson's humanitarianism and keen understanding of human weaknesses, would he actually preside, as he said, over harsher laws punishing pre- and extramarital sex— especially when recalling Boswell's inclinations in those directions (III, 17–18)? And could he really have dismissed the morals and principles of tradespeople and farmers as he appears to have done in May 1778 (III, 353)? Each of these scenes has been used, to Johnson's discredit, as evidence of his true personality—as if his words were to be taken literally, without any regard to context. Similarly, Boswell's occasional cataloging of Johnsonian utterances (e.g., II, 471–473) does not consider their contexts; nor does he scan Johnson's face for any indication of his mood or penchant for humor and deception.

We must remember that in certain situations, when Scotland, the Whigs, or the Americans were mentioned, Johnson would in a sense entertain his listeners by voicing opinions (some clearly outrageous) they would expect to hear. But we must be careful to note a significant difference between this form of entertainment and the longstanding view that Johnson was amusing to others as a passionate and argumentative man, *controlled* by his own prejudices and stimulated by Boswell's clever designs, who made others laugh (and readers of the *Life* as well) *despite* himself, despite the seriousness of his views. I would argue instead that he enjoyed entertaining those who looked forward to his brash, controversial, and at times incomprehensible statements on familiar topics, but that he did so *with the intention* of amusing some and shocking others in his company. He was *not* controlled by his own prejudices or manipulated by Boswell or anyone else. Johnson's notorious assessment of actors is a case in point. He at times delighted in allowing his humor to take his remarks into the realm of absurdity, much as many of us take an odd pleasure in distorting and exaggerating the deficiencies of our students or administrators. Boswell: "We respect a great player, as a man who can conceive lofty sentiments, and can express them gracefully." Johnson: "What, Sir, a fellow who claps a hump on his back, and a lump on his leg, and cries '*I am Richard the Third*'?" (III,184). Boswell reminds us that he had "the best side of the argument" and that Johnson's was "most fallacious reasoning," but he seems not to have considered the possibility that Johnson *knew* and *wanted* his opinions to be outrageous, unfair, and provocative. The reader, however, tends to nod in Boswell's direction and wonders how the Great Cham of literature could be so shortsighted regarding the merits of actors like Garrick.

Assuredly, Johnson's deceptive demeanor could border on the insult, but for the sake of a humorous or shocking retort he would risk—or occasionally encourage—the displeasure of his company. When a solicitous gentleman praised the merits of his brother ("When we have sat together some time, you'll find my brother grow very entertaining"), Johnson responded, most likely with a straight face, "I can wait" (IV, 21). On another occasion, a gentleman no doubt bored

Johnson with his defense of Berkeley's philosophy that "nothing exists but as perceived by some mind." Johnson bid farewell to the departing man with "Pray, Sir, don't leave us; for we may perhaps forget to think of you, and then you will cease to exist" (IV, 27). And, not surprisingly, Johnson shone in environments where the insult was greatly appreciated. After being peppered by "some coarse raillery" while sailing on the Thames, Johnson quickly loaded and fired in retaliation, "Sir, your wife, *under pretence of keeping a bawdy-house,* is a receiver of stolen goods" (IV, 26).[19]

Johnson little feared risking the displeasure of others, because he had the ability—and he knew he did—to amuse himself and his friends with a joke at another's expense and then to soothe the feelings of the injured party, who usually could not perceive that Johnson's remarks were diversionary and not as serious and literal as they sounded. He once attempted to upset the Quaker Mrs. Knowles by refusing to give credence to her judicious assessment of the inequality between the sexes. He therefore offered a seemingly enthusiastic and prejudicial view he certainly would not actually endorse: "[W]omen have all the liberty they should wish to have. We have all the labour and the danger, and the women all the advantage."[20] (And how many modern students have come to dislike Johnson because of this response, not comprehending his real designs?) Later in their conversation, however, he flattered Mrs. Knowles by agreeing with one of her observations on Christianity: "Very well, indeed, Madam. You have said very well" (III, 289–290). He furthermore believed he could torment Goldsmith with impunity because he could easily restore himself to the Irishman's good graces. On one occasion, Goldsmith was brooding over a Johnsonian "reprimand." Johnson then said to some of his friends, probably with a wink of his eye, "I'll make Goldsmith forgive me"—which he did—"and they were on as easy terms as ever, and Goldsmith rattled away as usual" (II, 256).

As I have noted, although Boswell is perceptive and kind enough at times to qualify Johnson's remarks as "talking for victory," he was, like Johnson's other friends, the victim of Johnson's inscrutable ways. Other than his understandably perplexed reaction to the initial meeting at Davies's bookshop, we might recall Boswell's sense of rejection and betrayal stemming from Johnson's "rude attack" at Reynolds's home on 2 May 1778. When he next saw Johnson, he opened his heart to his older friend, complaining that no one had "a greater respect and affection" for Johnson and that he should therefore have been treated with more courtesy. Apparently taking the rebuke to heart, Johnson said, "I am sorry for it. I'll make it up to you twenty different ways, as you please." The possible teasing and patronizing air of this response should be considered, but one should especially note Johnson's reaction to Boswell's attempt at expressing metaphorically his feelings about being attacked by a close friend in the company of strangers: "I don't care how often, or how high he tosses me," Boswell had told Reynolds, "when only friends are present, for then I fall upon soft ground: but I do not like falling on stones, which is the case when enemies are present." "I think," he said to Johnson, "this is a pretty good image," to which Johnson replied, "Sir, it is one of the happiest I have ever heard" (III, 338). We should visualize Johnson responding with a patronizing look and a suppressed smile on his lips, as if patting Boswell on the head with his reply, mollifying his bruised ego with words of comfort. Here as elsewhere in the *Life* Johnson is in control of the events, manipulating his friends in a playful way, enjoying reactions such as Boswell's and unwilling to cease teasing even in the midst of an emotional moment for his victim.

A significant clue to Johnson's unusual sense of humor and his method of deceiving his company is evident in his assessment of one of Garrick's diversionary comments to Boswell. Had he to do it all over again, Garrick observed, he would not have played "those low characters," such as Abel Drugger, with whom he solidified his reputation. Noting Boswell's shock (which is another indication that the Scot was not always cognizant of subtleties or deliberate misstatement from those proficient at role playing), Johnson told him, "Garrick, Sir, was not in earnest in what he said." "Why, then," Boswell replied, "did he talk so?" Johnson: "Why, Sir, to make you answer as you did." Boswell: "I don't know, Sir; he seemed to dip deep into his mind for the reflection." Johnson: "He had not far to dip, Sir: he had said the same thing, probably, twenty times before" (III, 35). Who better to reveal Garrick's designs than a man who engaged frequently in the same kind of verbal deception?

The reader of the *Life* is certainly discouraged from contemplating the laughing and deceptive Johnson because of the desire or inclination to attribute every remark from Johnson as something *ex cathedra*. Throughout his work Boswell mentions Johnson's strict regard for the truth and his contempt for those who perpetrate falsehood. But advocating the truth in one's serious writing, whether of a moral, political, or historical nature, does not preclude violating the truth in one's conversation, especially in a lighthearted or humorous context. Johnson was a man with an enormous and often elusive sense of humor who believed life was all the more enjoyable for those moments of gaiety, playful deception, and outlandish statement. Why, we might ask, must Johnson be held so accountable for every word he uttered? There is, of course, a logical answer to this: like a highly publicized political figure of our time, Johnson has been perceived as someone who must always speak literally, because his importance might be diminished if we had to sort through a series of humorous and contradictory remarks in order to discover his true feelings about significant matters. Undoubtedly, several of his acquaintances thought less of him because he was elusive and prone to tease, shock, and confuse, but such a man he was.

Readers of the past two centuries have helped to encourage the monolithic view of Johnson by playing the parlor game, using the *Life* as support, of anticipating his behavior in any given situation. For example, one trusts there have been many occasions on which readers have thought, "I can imagine the fireworks if Johnson and Hume could ever have been at the same dinner table," or "Wouldn't it have been something if Johnson and Rousseau could have come to blows?" and so on.[21] We can dream such dreams because of our confidence in predicting the outcome, based on the immutable sense of Johnson's personality and his literary and political beliefs we have drawn from those memorable moments in the *Life*. But Boswell was likewise prone to prediction and was thus amazed at the way the Johnson-Wilkes meeting turned out. He no doubt thought he could foretell the result of such a confrontation, but both men turned the tables on him: "And we ashamed of him" (III, 77). Whereas many believe Johnson was initially determined to make the most out of a bad situation (that is, being trapped by Boswell into dinner with Wilkes and others of his ilk) but then found that a chemistry existed between him and the famous radical, I think it highly probable that Johnson made up his mind *not* to come to blows with Wilkes because to do so would have made his behavior predictable. Although genuine fondness appears to have grown between the men, we should not ignore the possibility that the success of the meeting was dictated for the most part by Johnson's desire to keep both Boswell and Wilkes offstride.

Boswell, of course, took credit for bringing the two warriors together and having them turn their swords into ploughshares. And frequently in the *Life* he gives evidence of his "power" to manipulate Johnson into interesting exchanges and responses: "Desirous of calling Johnson forth to talk, and exercise his wit" (II, 187). Many Johnsonians have been angered by what they perceive as Boswell's patronizing air in this remark and in his "ringmaster" mentality, which is also evident in "I diverted his attention to other topics" (III, 290).[22] Other than the occasion with Wilkes, Boswell enjoyed matching Johnson against his "natural" enemies, such as the radical freethinker Catharine Macaulay. Johnson's reaction to Boswell's intentions in this matter is important: "No, Sir: you would not see us quarrel, to make you sport. Don't you know that it is very uncivil to *pit* two people against one another?" (III, 185). Johnson disdained the idea that others wanted to control *him*, for he was too adept, in another context, at doing the same to them.

Boswell reminds us early in the *Life* that "the conversation of a celebrated man" will "best display his character" and then quotes from Johnson's *Rambler* 60 for corroborating evidence· the biographer, Johnson writes, must "display the minute details of daily life, where exteriour appendages are cast aside," for then will be laid "open to posterity the private and familiar character" of the man (I, 31–32). As the author of these words, Johnson would have known eventually what Boswell's designs on him were and he could have thus sent up occasional smokescreens to prevent his true nature from being revealed. Johnson told Hester Thrale how he so deceived Thomas Percy, who was interested in collecting Johnsoniana: "I have purposely suffered him to be misled, and he has accordingly gleaned up many Things that are not true."[23] What Boswell did not comprehend when he quoted from the *Rambler* essay was that all of these keys to an understanding of a man's character are of little use if the biographical subject, aware that he is being scrutinized, decides to change the locks. Thomas Tyers said Johnson was like a "ghost" because he never spoke until spoken to (III, 307); but the characterization is even more accurate than Johnson would have admitted, for it suggests an illusive, ethereal specter leaving visual traces of its substance but no hard proof that it has actually come and gone.

When he came to realize that Boswell was taking down his conversations for posterity's sake, Johnson could not resist the opportunity to set up obstacles to the Scot's desire to know him intimately. We might expect that someone who senses his words may indeed become immortalized to pontificate, apologize, embellish, assuage, and explain—all with the purpose of creating an image he himself would want remembered. If Johnson did anything *consciously* to shape his image for posterity, it seems to me, he did so with the intention of misshaping it, leaving it shrouded in a haze of confusion, contradiction, and ambiguity. His famous reply to the excessively probing Boswell, "Sir, you have but two topicks, yourself and me. I am sick of both" (III, 57), indicates his displeasure not only at Boswell's interrogation but also at the very idea of laying himself open for accurate analysis.[24] To Johnson, such examination violated the privacy he so valued, and even though, as his correspondence and parts of the *Life* demonstrate, he at times opened his mind to his friends, these moments of self-revelation do not suggest that he enjoyed wearing his heart on his sleeve for a Boswell or anyone else to peck at. Unlike many famous literary figures, who would have their vanities titillated by the attention of a biographer, Johnson would have been emotionally on the rack knowing what a Walter Jackson Bate had done to his privacy.

The desire to be in control and protect his privacy is at the heart of much of his unique brand of humor. Other indications of his ability to disguise his true feelings and keep others off balance and unable to predict his behavior would be his habit of taking "the wrong side of a debate" and his unwillingness to provide the probing Boswell and Goldsmith with an answer as to why he has now (1766) ceased writing more frequently. Boswell: "But I wonder, Sir, you have not more pleasure in writing than in not writing." Johnson: "Sir, you *may* wonder." We might also recall his objection to the publication of a part of his correspondence and the work, *Johnsoniana; or a Collection of Bon Mots* (1776); his amusement at and evasive response to Boswell's and others' attempts to ascertain the correct "catalogue" of his works; and his angry and very revealing reply to Goldsmith's assumption that members of the Club had already "travelled over one another's minds": "you have not travelled over *my* mind, I promise you."[25] The conviction with which Johnson answered Goldsmith emphasizes his fervent wish to remain aloof from scrutiny. Being inscrutable, unpredictable, and elusive meant to Johnson being in control of events around him—and his sense of humor helped him achieve this state. Boswell has long been given both credit and censure for manipulating Johnson into confrontations, eliciting from him expected responses, and portraying him as a man *controlled* by other forces (his own physical infirmities and sudden explosions of vitriol, bigotry, and fear), but perhaps the most interesting irony of the *Life* is that Johnson was so often in control, not only of himself and his responses but also of those in his company.[26] Far from being a passive bear stimulated into action by a manipulative Boswell, Johnson led his friends (and unwittingly later readers of the *Life*) into a labyrinth of confusion, from which the victims struggled to extricate themselves with stereotypical judgments, wrong-headed assumptions, and patronizing airs: "Dr. Johnson and his dear idiosyncrasies." He would have been pleased, we can imagine, with the title of the latest collection of essays devoted to him, *The Unknown Samuel Johnson.*[27]

Clearly, not all of Johnson's controversial remarks recorded in Boswell's *Life* can be dismissed as expressions of his humor. Some will remain problematic and will require explanations infused with an understanding of Johnson's complex attitudes toward society, politics, and literature. I would argue, however, that many of the most memorable responses can be attributed to the impish spirit that often overcame him in social settings. Considering the evidence of Johnson's sense of humor and its various manifestations, the reader must weigh heavily the possibility that many of Johnson's unforgettable and disturbing statements and responses, those not corroborated by other biographical sources or by his own writings, were the effusions of the laughing, not the serious, Johnson.

Notes

1. Most notably in Donald Greene, "Reflections on a Literary Anniversary," *Queen's Quarterly* 70 (1963): 198–208, excerpts reprinted in James L. Clifford, ed., *Twentieth Century Interpretations of Boswell's "Life of Johnson"* (Englewood Cliffs: Prentice Hall, 1970), 97–103; Donald Greene, " 'Tis a Pretty Book, Mr. Boswell, But—," *Georgia Review* 32 (1978): 17–43; and Richard Schwartz, *Boswell's Johnson: A Preface to the "Life"* (Madison: University of Wisconsin Press, 1978).

2. Schwartz was not the first to examine "Boswell's Johnson," but his book (and the work of Donald Greene) gave the phrase a more pejorative connotation than it formerly had.

3. The range of opinion on the issue of "Boswell's Johnson" is broad. In addition to the remarks quoted in my introduction to this volume and John Burke's essay, "But Boswell's Johnson Is Not Boswell's Johnson," one might note the comments of James Clifford ("[Boswell was not] consciously distorting character or falsifying evidence. Like all great biographers, he was presenting the essential truth as he saw it"), Marshall Waingrow ("no matter how many new facts are brought to light, Samuel Johnson will always be somebody's hypothesis"), and Frederick Pottle ("Boswell's Johnson is always 'authentic.' . . .The conversations, though they appear to be pure Johnson, are in fact the quintessence of Boswell's view of Johnson"). See Clifford, *Twentieth Century Interpretations*, 15, 50, 71, 73.

4. Walter Jackson Bate, *Samuel Johnson* (New York: Harcourt Brace Jovanovich, 1977), 372.

5. Ibid., 480. Bate writes as well of the "connection" of Johnson's humor "with some of his most serious psychological problems" and the intimate relationship between his humor and "the secret of his genius generally and with what is, of course, a part of his genius, his style and powers of expression, especially in the conversations of his later years" (pp. 480–481).

6. All quotations from the *Life* will come from James Boswell, *The Life of Samuel Johnson, LL.D.*, ed. G. B. Hill, rev. L. F. Powell, 6 vols. (Oxford: Clarendon Press, 1934–1964). See II, 262.

7. Donald Greene believes that "in most readers' minds, after finishing the *Life*, there lingers around the image of Johnson an aura of unpleasant pomposity"; and Leopold Damrosch, Jr., argues that in the *Life* Johnson "appears

distressingly often as an irritable old man." Greene, "Reflections on a Literary Anniversary," in Clifford, *Twentieth Century Interpretations*, 102; Damrosch, "*The Life of Johnson:* An Anti-Theory," *Eighteenth-Century Studies* 6 (1973): 495.

8. The "Illustrated" *Boswell's* "*Life of Johnson*" (London: George Routledge and Sons) of the mid nineteenth century, for example, portrays such scenes as a bitter Johnson leaving the residence of his unsupportive patron Lord Chesterfield, Johnson in the company of Samuel Richardson and William Hogarth, Johnson buying fruit at Covent Garden with Beauclerk and Langton, Boswell's meeting of Johnson in 1763, Johnson and Boswell at the Mitre in the same year, Johnson reading Goldsmith's *Vicar of Wakefield*, Johnson's interview with George III, Johnson at St. Clement Dancs Church, Johnson bidding farewell to Madame De Boufflers, Johnson at Warley Camp, and Johnson and Wilkes in conversation. In each instance Johnson looks the same—old and dyspeptic. Even when the "artist" depicts Johnson in better humor, smiling as he plays with his cat Hodge or laughing heartily outside Temple Gate, laughter seems alien to the grotesque sourpuss that is the "illustrated" Johnson.

9. A refreshing exception would be the cover of the paperback ninth printing of *The Portable Johnson and Boswell*, ed. Louis Kronenberger (New York: Viking Press, 1966), on which Johnson is portrayed as an amiable middle-aged man. More representative would be the corpulent and fatigued figure that appears on the cover of the paperback Signet edition of Boswell's *Life* (New York: New American Library, 1968).

10. Several commentators have dealt with Johnson's explosive temperament—for example, William R. Siebenschuh: "[Boswell] develops incidents involving Johnson's sometimes violent temper in the context of greater and more impressive facts about his personality and character. Preserving all the vividness of Johnson's tumultuous spirit and its forcible expression in conversation and attack, he represents Johnson's outbursts and anger—even the most serious instances—in ways that always explain them to Johnson's credit and in some cases make them the occasion for powerful images of his greatness of heart." Siebenschuh, *Form and Purpose in Boswell's Biographical Works* (Berkeley: University of California Press, 1972), 65.

11. See *Life*, I, 449; II, 261, 262, 378. Jo Allen Bradham argues that in several scenes Boswell "positions Johnson as *alazon*, or the bragging over-speaker, against himself as the quiet, but eventually victorious *eiron*, the foxy fellow who holds his tongue and bides his time." "Because Boswell uses 'laughing' or 'smiling' hundreds of times to describe Johnson," Bradham concludes, "it follows naturally that as biographer he would treasure comic interludes. It is part of the decorum of the whole that the man of laughter (when he chose) and the man who could produce laughter in others (when he chose) would find his permanent portrait by one who could laugh at him, but lovingly." Bradham, "Comic Fragments in the *Life of Johnson*," *Biography* 3

(1980): 95, 103. Although Bradham's emphasis is on comedy in the *Life*, it characterizes the humorous Johnson, for the most part, as something shaped by Boswell's hand. Boswell added in the *Life* that Johnson's laugh "was a kind of good humoured growl. Tom Davies described it drolly enough: 'He laughs like a rhinoceros'" (*Life*, II, 378). In this case the laughing Johnson is portrayed as something bordering on the grotesque.

12. Two earlier commentators, G. B. Hill and A. S. F. Gow, remarked perceptively on this matter: "Johnson, as drawn by Boswell," Hill observed, "is too 'awful, melancholy, and venerable.'" Hill then quoted from Hawkins, Murphy, Hester Thrale, and Fanny Burney on Johnson's humor. Of these Burney's remark should be most often recalled: "Dr. Johnson has more fun, and comical humour, and love of nonsense about him, than almost anybody I ever saw" (*Life*, II, 262–263, n. 2). Gow wrote half a century ago that there was another side of Johnson "which Boswell knew, and has, indeed, touched upon, but to which he has, I think, deliberately done less than justice—I mean Johnson's capacity for boisterous, open-hearted, irrational laughter. . . . Boswell must stand arraigned for the fact that one of Johnson's most striking characteristics is all but absent from the *Life*." Gow, "The Unknown Johnson," in Clifford, *Twentieth Century Interpretations*, 83, 84.

13. *Life*, II, 149, 189; III, 65; IV, 14, 158. Irma Lustig believes that "Boswell's reverence for Johnson as moral and intellectual hero never failed. It is a fixed element of the friendship, and the motive and theme of the *Life*." Lustig, "The Friendship of Johnson and Boswell: Some Biographical Considerations," *Studies in Eighteenth Century Culture* 6 (1977): 200.

14. Murphy, *Essay on the Life and Genius of Samuel Johnson* (1792), rpt. in G. B. Hill, ed., *Johnsonian Miscellanies*, 2 vols. (1897; rpt. New York: Barnes and Noble, 1966), 1:357.

15. This essay assumes the validity of Frederick Pottle's position that "Johnson's conversation as Boswell reported it, is, for all its veridicality, an imaginative reconstruction, a recreation"; except for "particular sentences" or "some brief passages of an epigrammatic cast" Boswell did not record Johnson's conversation verbatim. Pottle, "The *Life of Johnson*: Art and Authenticity," in Clifford, *Twentieth Century Interpretations*, 71, 72. Many of the passages quoted in this essay would in all likelihood be among those sections Boswell quoted verbatim; regardless, Boswell no doubt captured the essence of Johnson's remarks—that is, in regard to *what* Johnson said, not necessarily *how* he said them or what he meant. A comparison of these passages in the *Life* with the original entries in the journals does not suggest that Boswell ignored, intentionally or innocently, significant information he had earlier recorded on the contexts of Johnson's conversation.

16. More recent commentators have begun to discuss Boswell's depiction of himself in the *Life*. See, for example, Frank Brady, "Boswell's Self-Presentation and His Critics," *SEL* 12 (1972): 545–555.

17. *Life*, I, 447, 465, 471; II, 56, 94, 95, 101, 173, 226, 327, 328, 404, 439; III, 19, 23, 200, 344.

18. One of Macaulay's famous assessments will illustrate the point: ignoring Boswell's several warnings that Johnson's true opinion of Robertson was distorted by his colorful outbursts, Macaulay wrote that Johnson "always spoke with contempt of Robertson." Macaulay's review of Croker's edition of Boswell's *Life of Johnson*, in James T. Boulton, ed., *Johnson: The Critical Heritage* (New York: Barnes and Noble, 1971), 428.

19. Regarding the authenticity of this anecdote, see John Burke's response to Donald Greene's observations (p. 200 [note 47] of this volume).

20. *Life*, III, 286–287. In this instance, Johnson failed to upset Mrs. Knowles, who appears to have seen through his facade: "The Doctor reasons very wittily, but not convincingly."

21. I am therefore surprised that such scenarios were not realized on Steve Allen's PBS show "Meeting of Minds."

22. A typical reflection of this attitude would be Ralph Isham's: Boswell "was always glad to take a rebuff if it drew the old boy out." See Clifford, *Twentieth Century Interpretations*, 92.

23. Katharine D. Balderston, ed., *Thraliana*, 2 vols. (Oxford: Clarendon Press, 1942), 1:173.

24. As Leopold Damrosch, Jr., notes, "we ought not to forget that the shape of Johnson's opinions must sometimes have been distorted by his irritation at being cross-examined" ("The *Life of Johnson*," 490).

25. *Life*, I, 441; II, 15, 60, 432; III, 321; IV, 183.

26. That this is not the way many see Johnson in the *Life* is also suggested in Hugo M. Reichard's "Boswell's Johnson, the Hero Made by a Committee," *PMLA* 95 (1980): 225–233. Reichard argues that the Johnson of the *Life* is "largely decided by others, by persons in his shadow." Most of Johnson's "celebrated remarks," Reichard adds, "are prepared for by others."

27. John J. Burke, Jr., and Donald Kay, eds., *The Unknown Samuel Johnson*, (Madison: University of Wisconsin Press, 1983).

Boswell's
Presentation of Goldsmith:
A Reconsideration

*B*oswell's *Life of Johnson* has been of great importance to our perception of Oliver Goldsmith, whom so devoted a Boswellian as Frederick A. Pottle has described as "in many ways the greatest literary figure of the era, certainly the most versatile genius, . . . [who did] work of high distinction in poetry, the essay, the novel, and the drama."[1] The authority of Boswell's presentation of Goldsmith remained in effect unchallenged until 1801, for no reliable biography existed, though collections of anecdotes about him appeared in early memoirs of Johnson, such as Mrs. Piozzi's *Anecdotes* and Sir John Hawkins's *Life*, both of which Boswell's biography successfully superseded.[2] For most of Goldsmith's contemporaries, David Garrick's witty phrase that he "wrote like an angel, and talk'd like poor Poll,"[3] summarized the prevailing view of him, and we find this conception of a Goldsmith of unreconciled opposites in the recollections of Mrs. Piozzi and Hawkins, Richard Cumberland's *Memoirs*, and Thomas Davies's *Life of Garrick*, as well as in Boswell's presentation of him in the *Life*. Most of Goldsmith's contemporaries appear to have regarded him as a foolish man who wrote extremely well, a view ironically rather like Macaulay's mid-nineteenth-century estimation of Boswell. However, from the three of Goldsmith's contemporaries who knew him best—Reynolds, Johnson, and Percy—we find the generally consistent view that he was a great writer *and* a great man.

I should like to consider the quality of Boswell's portrait of Gold-smith in the *Life of Johnson*, at times comparing it with extracts from his other papers, especially his journals, and comments on these by Goldsmith's most recent biographers; then to consider the views presented by Reynolds, Johnson, and Percy; and finally to offer an assessment of the relationship between Boswell and Goldsmith from their first meeting in 1762 until Goldsmith's death in 1774.[4]

Boswell met Goldsmith before he did Johnson, on Christmas Day, 1762, at the house of Thomas Davies, who would introduce him to Johnson five months later on 16 May 1763. At this first meeting he described Goldsmith as "a curious, odd, pedantic fellow with some genius," noting that "It was quite a literary dinner."[5] Goldsmith next appears in Boswell's journal when he was attending the theatre on 3 February 1763: "I was amused to find myself transported . . . to the gay, gilded theatre. . . . Luckily, Dr. Goldsmith came into the seat behind me. I renewed my acquaintance with him, and he agreed to keep the same place for the night. His conversation revived in my mind the true ideas of London authors, which are to me something curious, and, as it were, mystical."[6] Then Boswell did meet Johnson at Davies's house on 16 May. Among Johnson's miscellaneous comments that made their way into Boswell's journal from their conversation at the Mitre on 25 June is the following: "Dr. Goldsmith is one of the first men we have as an author at present, and a very worthy man too. He has been loose in his principles, but he is coming right."[7]

When Boswell came to write up this section of his journal for the *Life* in the late 1780s, he broke his narrative and inserted his character sketch of Goldsmith:

> As Dr. Oliver Goldsmith will frequently appear in this narrative, I shall endeavour to make my readers in some degree acquainted with his singular character. . . . He had sagacity enough to cultivate assiduously the acquaintance of Johnson, and his faculties were gradually enlarged by the contemplation of such a model. To me and many others it appeared that he studiously copied the manner of Johnson, though, indeed, upon a smaller scale. . . . No man had the art of displaying with more advantage as a writer, whatever literary acquisitions he made. *"Nihil quod tetegit non ornavit."* . . . It has been generally circulated and believed that he was a mere fool in conversation; but, in truth, this has been greatly exaggerated. (I, 411–412)

Boswell believed Goldsmith showed a typically Irish trait in that his words outran his thoughts, resulting in comically jumbled expression. He further describes him as "what the French call *un étourdi*," arguing that his vanity and desire for attention led him to careless and thoughtless talk, and repeats old gossip that Goldsmith was angry when the Horneck sisters got more attention than he did during their trip to France in 1770. Boswell continues,

> He, I am afraid, had no settled system of any sort, so that his conduct must not be strictly scrutinised; but his affections were social and gener- ous, and when he had money he gave it away very liberally. His desire of imaginary consequence predominated over his attention to truth. When he began to rise into notice, he said he had a brother who was Dean of Durham, a fiction so easily detected, that it is wonderful how he should have been so inconsiderate as to hazard it. (I, 414–415)

Boswell concludes his sketch by mentioning Goldsmith's exaggeration of the prices his writings could command—four hundred pounds for his novel—and adds Johnson's correction that *The Vicar of Wakefield* brought Goldsmith only sixty pounds.[8]

Boswell recognized that his view of Goldsmith was different from Reynolds's, for he included in the *Life* a note commenting on the pop- ular perception of the Irishman as "a mere fool in conversation":

> Sir Joshua Reynolds mentioned to me that he frequently heard Gold- smith talk warmly of the pleasure of being liked, and observed how hard it would be if literary excellence should preclude a man from that satis- faction, which he perceived it often did, from the envy which attended it; and therefore Sir Joshua was convinced that he was intentionally more absurd, in order to lessen himself in social intercourse, trusting that his character would be sufficiently supported by his works. If indeed it was his intention to appear absurd in company, he was often very successful. But with due deference to Sir Joshua's ingenuity, I think the conjecture too refined. (I, 412, n. 6).

Ironically, James Beattie, whom Goldsmith resented and despised for what he believed was shoddy, trivial work (Beattie's *Essay on Truth*), wrote to Sir William Forbes on 10 July 1788: "Goldsmith's common conversation was a strange mixture of absurdity and silliness; of sil- liness so great, as to make me sometimes think that he affected it."[9] We know that Reynolds's observation, and Beattie's too, was soundly based from Goldsmith's 1759 letter to his older brother Henry, first printed in Percy's "Life": "It is a good remark of Montaign's that the wisest men often have friends with whom they do not care how much they play the fool."[10]

Reynolds apparently composed his sketch of Goldsmith's personality in 1776, perhaps at the request of Percy, who was then collecting materials for Goldsmith's biography.[11] And Reynolds's sketch remains the most detailed, nearly contemporary account that we have of Goldsmith by someone who knew him very well, although it remained unknown for nearly two hundred years. Reynolds begins by arguing that Goldsmith's genius was generally acknowledged and that he was neither a fool nor a weak man, even though many of his contemporaries believed that he was one or the other or both.

> A great part of Dr. Goldsmith's folly and absurdity proceeded from principle, and partly from a want of early acquaintance with that life to which his reputation afterwards introduced him. . . . He was of a very sociable disposition. He had a very strong desire, which I believe nobody will think peculiar or culpable, to be liked, to have his company sought after by his friends. To this end, for it was a system, he abandoned his respectable character as a writer or a man of observation to that of a character which nobody was afraid of being humiliated in his presence. This was his general principle. (Pp. 46–47)

While Reynolds noted Goldsmith's desire for attention at virtually any cost, he believed that at times he did try to behave with more decorum but found that behavior hard to maintain, and so dropped back into his old habits. As a result, he got the attention he wanted by singing or dancing or even standing on his head. Reynolds offers further explanation of Goldsmith's unique behavior:

> The Doctor came late into the great world. He lived a great part of his life with mean people. All his old habits were against him. It was too late to learn new ones, or at least for the new ones to sit easy on him. . . . This disadvantage, joined to an anxious desire and impatience to distinguish himself, brought him often into ridiculous situations. As he thought, and not without reason, that he had distinguished himself by his writings, he imagined therefore he ought at all times and in all places to be equally distinguished from the rest of the company, which, if neglected, he thought it incumbent on him to do that little service for himself. (Pp. 47–48)[12]

Admitting Goldsmith's extreme envy, Reynolds argues that when Goldsmith was part of a group he made things happen, enlivened the conversation, and, if people made fun of him, was still eagerly sought out the next day.

> Goldsmith had no wit in conversation, but to do him justice, he did not much attempt it. When in company with ladies he was always endeavouring after humour, and as continually failed; but his ill success was equally diverting to the company as if he had succeeded. If they laughed, he was happy and did not seem to care whether it was with him or at him. But when he was in company with the philosophers, he was grave, wise, and very inclinable to dispute established opinions. This immediately produced a general cry. Every man had arguments of confutation ready, and he himself was at once placed in the situation he so much loved, of being the object of attention of the whole company. (Pp. 53–54)

Thus, Reynolds portrays Goldsmith far more sympathetically than Boswell, but the portrait was lost for almost two hundred years.

The only direct comments by Johnson on Goldsmith or his works I have been able to discover appear in his unsigned, highly complimentary review of *The Traveller* in the *Critical Review* for December 1774 and in the epitaph he composed for Goldsmith's memorial tablet in Westminster Abbey. The review of *The Traveller* ends, "Such is the poem, on which we now congratulate the public, as on a production to which, since the death of Pope, it will not be easy to find anything equal."[13] All other remarks he made about Goldsmith's personality or writing have been filtered through some other mind, but Boswell's descriptions are undoubtedly the most important, if only because they are the most extensive. A well-known anecdote from the *Life* illustrates Boswell's typical handling of Johnson's comments about Goldsmith. The anecdote appears in the *Life* for 9 April 1778, four years after Goldsmith's death. Johnson is recalling Goldsmith's being questioned at some unspecified time in the past about *The Traveller:* "[Anthony] Chamier once asked him, what he meant by *slow*, the last word in the first line of 'The Traveller.' . . . Did he mean tardiness of locomotion? Goldsmith, who would say something without consideration, answered, 'Yes.' I was sitting by, and said, 'No, Sir; you do not mean tardiness of locomotion; you mean, that sluggishness of mind which comes upon a man in solitude'" (III, 252–253). Obviously,

Johnson is here being the Great Cham, interrupting in a rude, brusque way, and Goldsmith never gets a chance to say anything about his intended meaning. But a note on this passage in the Hill-Powell *Life* quotes John Forster's *Life and Times of Oliver Goldsmith*, pointing out that the word *slow* easily carries both meanings, that the physical movement and the mental action correlate with each other.

When Percy, who certainly knew Goldsmith far better than Boswell did, came to write the summary that concludes his 1801 "Life," he drew on firsthand knowledge of Goldsmith dating back to 1759, when the Reverend James Grainger introduced the two men.[14] Percy's summary of Goldsmith's character touches on many of the same points that Boswell and especially Reynolds had, but with very different emphases from Boswell's. When Boswell writes of Goldsmith's giving away money "very liberally," he suggests Goldsmith was an imprudent spendthrift. Percy's treatment of this trait in Goldsmith's character stresses not Goldsmith's irresponsibility with money but, as one might expect from a bishop, Goldsmith's compassion and charity:

> He was generous in the extreme, and so strongly affected by compassion, that he has been known at midnight to abandon his rest, in order to procure an asylum for a poor dying object who was left destitute in the streets. Nor was there ever a mind whose general feelings were more benevolent and friendly. He is however supposed to have been often soured by jealousy or envy; and many little instances are mentioned of this tendency in his character: but whatever appeared of this kind was a mere momentary sensation, which he knew not how like other men to conceal. It was never the result of principle, or the suggestion of reflection; it never imbittered his heart, nor influenced his conduct.[15]

In judging Goldsmith's literary achievements, Percy offers no insights of his own but rather paraphrases and quotes Johnson as reported by Boswell, though without the undercutting qualifications we find in the *Life*. Percy's interpretation of Goldsmith is far less incisive than that of Reynolds, for he fails to mention the possibility that Goldsmith sometimes assumed a mask in social settings.

Despite the relatively wide circulation of Percy's "Life,"[16] Boswell's less sympathetic sketch, with its many more readers, seems to have provoked the notion prevailing among Goldsmith's nineteenth-century biographers that the Scot misrepresented Goldsmith. Sir James

Prior, Goldsmith's first full-scale biographer, clearly expresses this view, and Prior's major followers—Washington Irving, John Forster, Austin Dobson, and William Black—all echo it.[17] And two of Goldsmith's most recent biographers, both, like Morgan and Hart, writing after the publication of Reynolds's sketch, take slightly different views. Ralph Wardle argued in 1957 that "the careful reader of the *Life* [*of Johnson*] will discover, as he proceeds, that Boswell's attitude becomes less disapproving."[18] Arthur Lytton Sells's 1974 biography generally skirts the problem, but Sells does notice a shift in Boswell's attitude toward Goldsmith after the success of *She Stoops to Conquer.*[19]

Boswell's letter to Goldsmith of 29 March 1773 mentions that his daughter Veronica was born the same day that Goldsmith's play opened, and he continues warmly: "I intend being in London this spring and promise myself great satisfaction in sharing your social hours. In the mean time, I beg the favour of hearing from you. I am sure you have not a warmer friend or a steadier admirer. While you are in the full glow of theatrical splendour, while all the great and gay in the British Metropolis are literally hanging upon *your smiles,* let me see that you can *stoop to write* to me," and his postscript on the wrapper adds, "Pray write directly. Write as if in repartee."[20] When Boswell wrote this letter and ten others to announce his daughter Veronica's birth, he had already made specific plans to leave for London the following day. As Wimsatt and Pottle observe, Boswell's letter to Goldsmith was designed to secure an autograph reply from Goldsmith to add to his collection of letters from famous men. They describe his behavior as "innocently unscrupulous" and his letter to Goldsmith as "one of the most successfully artificial that he ever wrote."[21] Although Boswell arrived in London on 2 April 1773, he did not call on Goldsmith until five days later.

Replying in a very friendly fashion, Goldsmith reported to Boswell the troubles he had had with the play:

> It has kept me in hot water these three months. . . . I promise you, my Dear Sir, that the stage earning is the dirtiest money that ever a poor poet put in his pocket, and if my mind does not very much alter, I have done with the stage. . . . When I see you in town, and I shall take care to let Johnson, Garrick, and Reynolds know of the expected happiness, I will then tell you long stories about my struggles and escapes, for as all of

you are safely retired from the shock of criticism to enjoy much better comforts in a domestic life, I am still left the only *poet militant* here, and in truth I am very likely to be *militant* till I die, nor have I even the prospect of an hospital to retire to.[22]

John Ginger, Goldsmith's most recent biographer, reverts to the prevailing nineteenth-century view: "There were few grounds for compatibility—least of all the streak of egotism which could be observed in both men. . . . Boswell resented Goldsmith's nearness to Johnson and was young and humourless enough to be at a loss as to what Johnson could see in him. All these factors contributed to the predominantly hostile portrait which is inserted in *The Life of Johnson* at Goldsmith's first eruption into the story."[23] Ginger also argues that "There is enough praise in the opening section of the portrait to give an appearance of fairness, and when he presents 'greatly exaggerated' reports of his subject's 'foolish' conversation in order to sweep them away Boswell even poses as counsel for the defense. Having disarmed the reader, he introduces the major criticisms, that Goldsmith was vain, naive, foolish, and dishonest—introducing at least one anecdote which reveals his inability to understand a certain straight-faced vein of humour in the expatriate Irishman,"[24] a reference to the anecdote concerning Goldsmith's behavior with the Horneck sisters during their 1770 visit to France. Ginger's comments do not agree very well with the journal accounts that we have of Boswell's early meeting with Goldsmith, and certainly not with the anecdotes involving Goldsmith from 1772 until his death in 1774. Ginger apparently believes Boswell's early dislike of Goldsmith caused him to present a virtual attack on his personality when he came to write the *Life of Johnson* in the late 1780s. The journal accounts do not support this view.

Both Morgan and Hart concentrate on Boswell's reports of Goldsmith's conversation, his personal idiosyncrasies, and Johnson's remarks on the merits of his writing. Hart especially points out that despite the unflattering portrait of Goldsmith drawn for 1762 in the *Life*, Boswell's accounts of Goldsmith for 1772 and 1773 show most of the incisive criticisms of Johnson for which Goldsmith is best remembered, that *"He has nothing of the* [roughness of] *the bear but his skin"* (Boswell's emphasis), that Johnson would have the little fishes in the fable talk like whales, as well as some of Johnson's most cutting remarks about Goldsmith's ignorance: "It is amazing how little Goldsmith knows. He seldom comes where he is not more ignorant than any one else" (II, 66, 231, 235).

But one instance demands more comment. On Good Friday, 9 April 1773, Boswell reported to Johnson Goldsmith's remark (to Boswell, the date of remark not given), "As I take my shoes from the shoemaker, and my coat from the taylor, so I take my religion from the priest." Boswell somewhat self-righteously regrets this loose way of talking, and Johnson takes the bait: "Sir, he knows nothing; he has made up his mind about nothing" (II, 214–215). Since Boswell gives no context for the remark, we cannot possibly know the exact tone of Goldsmith's voice. It may very well have been exasperation with Boswell, who certainly had no hesitation about asking anyone anything and could and did badger Johnson, especially on religious matters, to the point where Johnson would shut him up very brusquely (see, for example, II, 107–108). Goldsmith's remark to Boswell tells us nothing significant about Goldsmith's religious thought or practice, though it certainly provides a splendid piece of bait for Boswell to use, and Johnson rises to take it in a way that very likely distorts our notions of Johnson's opinion about Goldsmith.

Boswell's mainly favorable anecdotes about Goldsmith nearly all appear in passages dating from the last two years of Goldsmith's life (1772–1774), following the general recognition of Goldsmith's talent in the wake of *The Traveller* (1764), *The Vicar of Wakefield* (1766), *The Good Natur'd Man* (1768), *The Deserted Village* (1770), and the recent triumph of *She Stoops to Conquer*. Boswell's attitude toward Goldsmith at this time strongly resembles his early 1763 assertion that "the true ideas of London authors . . . to me are something curious, and as it were, mystical." After dining at General Oglethorpe's on 10 April 1772, he wrote in his journal, but did not include in the *Life*, a very revealing passage: "I felt a completion of happiness. I just sat and hugged myself in my own mind. Here I am in London, at the house of General Oglethorpe, who introduced himself to me just because I had distinguished myself; and here is Mr. Johnson, whose character is so vast; here is Dr. Goldsmith, so distinguished in literature. Words cannot describe our feelings. The finer parts are lost, as the down on a plum; the radiance of light cannot be painted."[25]

We may notice, then, as Fifer has pointed out, that the portrait in the *Life* differs considerably from the impressions of Goldsmith that Boswell recorded in his journal at the time he was actually experiencing Goldsmith as a person. In the journal, Boswell's interest in Goldsmith begins as a kind of generalized admiration, and this feeling persists as late as 1772. The first signs of Boswell's shifting attitude appear in those anecdotes, already noted, in which Goldsmith gets the better of Johnson in conversation. In March 1773 we find him flattering Goldsmith very directly and virtually ordering up the kind of letter he wants from him, not so much just for news of him, but a letter that will make a suitable addition to his collection of letters from the great and famous. Both Goldsmith's letter and his greeting to Boswell when Boswell finally did get around to calling on him in early April of 1773 show Goldsmith's genuinely warm response. Fifer describes Boswell's attitude as "not only friendly, but genuinely cordial," but a close examination suggests that Wimsatt and Pottle's description of it as "innocently unscrupulous" is more accurate for the solicitation of the letter. Certainly, Boswell acted from mixed motives, as we all do, desiring physical evidence in the letter that his relationship with the literary lion of the moment was close and intimate, and surely there is nothing wicked in such a desire, though Boswell's failure to call on Goldsmith may be somewhat more culpable.

Boswell's portrait in the *Life*, written at least ten years after Goldsmith's death, is something else again. His character sketch inserted after his *Life* entry for 25 June 1763 (I, 411–415) shows markedly lukewarm enthusiasm, with nearly all the praise highly qualified. Thus, Morgan is right when he calls Boswell's *Life* sketch remarkably similar to the other descriptions of Goldsmith drawn by most of his contemporaries, but the *Life* sketch is noticeably different from the estimates made of him by those who knew him best, i.e., Johnson, Percy, and Reynolds. To Johnson, acute critic that he was, Goldsmith's talent was already evident before Boswell met Johnson in 1763, though Johnson, as one of the literary insiders, undoubtedly knew much more of what Goldsmith had written than Boswell, the visitor newly arrived from Scotland, could possibly know. Johnson's perception of this talent presumably led to Goldsmith's being a charter member of the Club before he had published anything with his name signed to it and before he was well known to the general public.[26]

To Boswell, as to most of their contemporaries, Goldsmith remained a puzzle, a fool in public, though at the same time the finest practicing writer of the period 1762 to 1774, perhaps "a greater literary figure than Johnson for the whole post-Pope Georgian period," as Frederick Pottle has said.[27] Even though Boswell faithfully records Johnson's high praise of Goldsmith as both writer and man, he does not appear to have understood why Johnson thought as he did. Boswell knew Reynolds's interpretation of Goldsmith's personality and specifically rejected it as "too subtle," though Reynolds's interpretation finds confirmation in Goldsmith's early letter to his brother. In a sense, the common thread that runs through both Morgan's and Hart's studies is true: Boswell's presentation of Goldsmith is balanced, but, as Fifer points out, even when Boswell shows the Irishman's often keen insight into Johnson's personality, Boswell has usually made him Johnson's conversational foil, even when, as sometimes happens, Goldsmith gets the better of Johnson. Boswell's purpose, of course, was to reveal Johnson's character and personality as fully as possible and in as much detail as possible, so that quite obviously his presentation of Goldsmith was incidental to his central aim.

At the same time that Boswell seems not to have understood Goldsmith's personality, he nevertheless could show considerable personal concern for Goldsmith's difficulties as a *"poet militant,"* as Goldsmith describes himself in his letter to Boswell. In the journal entry for 13 April 1773, written during the period I have drawn on so heavily already, Boswell records that Johnson and Goldsmith called at his lodgings to take him to Oglethorpe's for dinner, where the other guests were a Miss Lockwood, "a very well-behaved woman, and a fine girl, [and] a Miss Scott, a natural daughter of the late Duke of Buccleuch."[28] Wimsatt and Pottle gloss this passage: "Miss Lockwood was present, along with Goldsmith, at Oglethorpe's again on Thursday 29 April. Apparently some kind of benevolent plot was on foot to bring the two together."[29] Three letters in the Yale Boswell Papers tell a fuller story.[30]

On 14 August 1773 Boswell wrote Oglethorpe from Edinburgh: "How does Miss Lockwood do? I hope you have carried our friend Goldsmith to visit her. I wrote to him, some time ago, to give attention to a plan which might perhaps be successfull; and if so would place him in a comfortable situation for life; and I am not afraid that the Lady would have reason to repent of her choice." Oglethorpe replied on 16 September: "As for the unfortunate Knight of Parnassus, Goldsmith, Alas! Amongst the other nymphs, she whom you mention'd in yours, enlightend our shades; names are not for the post. But Goldsmith was by cruel fates deny'd. What prevented his complying with my frequent invitations, and the History of the Ghost in Flanders, which you desire, & wonderful adventures must by me—reserv'd as a deposit to gratify your curiosity, and reward your appearance, pursuant to your written promise." Boswell's last comment on the scheme appears in his reply to Oglethorpe of 3 December: "So, our friend Goldsmith did not come to any amorous rendezvous in your groves with the Lady whose favour and gold I was desirous he should obtain. Your hints were encouraging enough to him. But I fancy he will never resolve to engage himself for life in any state whatever."

Do these letters add to our understanding of Boswell's portrait of Goldsmith in the *Life*? Unfortunately, we cannot tell how Miss Lockwood and Goldsmith took to each other, since Boswell's journal entry for 13 April 1773 consists almost entirely of a discussion between Johnson and Goldsmith of luxury, with Johnson presenting a Mandevillean defense to Goldsmith's attack on it. Boswell then notes, "We drank tea with the ladies [presumably after dinner when the gentlemen had rejoined the ladies], and Goldsmith sung Tony Lumpkin's song and a very pretty one to the tune of *Balamagairy* which he had designed for Miss Hardcastle; but as Mrs. Bulkeley, who played the part, could not sing, it was left out," and adds later in the entry, "I have forgotten much of this day's conversations."[31] The significant difference between the journal and the entry for this day in the *Life* (II, 217–219) is that the ladies' names are suppressed. Thus Boswell concentrates our attention on the exchange between Johnson and

Goldsmith. Had he kept Miss Lockwood and Miss Scott in the account, many readers might wish to know more about them, information the journal itself does not supply. Only the letters make clear the reason for Miss Lockwood's being there.

During the last two years of Goldsmith's life, 1772–1774, Boswell's interest in him probably reached its highest point, a point high enough that he would solicit a letter of, he hoped, some length and intimacy from Goldsmith about his new successful play, knowing full well that he would be in London before a reply from Goldsmith could reach him. He refrained from calling on Goldsmith for five days after his arrival—hardly the actions of a close or devoted friend. Such behavior undoubtedly shows the complex mixture of Boswell's motives: after his return to Edinburgh, he could also be scheming with Oglethorpe to set up a financially advantageous marriage for Goldsmith, one that would allow him to stop doing compilations for the booksellers—though of course *Animated Nature,* contracted for in 1769, would have had to be finished. Boswell's concern for what he believed was a reasonable solution to Goldsmith's problems appears to have been disinterested and to have claimed a certain amount of his time during nine months, although, almost certainly, had the marriage taken place Boswell would have let his friends and the public at large know of his part in arranging it. However mixed his motives may have been, in 1773 he was interested enough in Goldsmith's well-being to try to arrange this marriage for him or at least to lay the groundwork for what might turn into a marriage. The letters show us far more about the complexity of Boswell's motives and behavior than they do of Goldsmith's. They may cause us to think better of Boswell than we might otherwise, were we to rely upon the evidence of the *Life* alone.

Boswell, like most of Goldsmith's contemporaries who wrote of him (Mrs. Piozzi, Sir John Hawkins, Thomas Davies), gives little sense of having understood his personality. Garrick may well have crystallized most contemporary opinion about Goldsmith with his witty couplet as surely as did Horace Walpole's purported description of him as an "inspired ideot" (*Life,* III, 412, n. 6). With Goldsmith's close friends, it is another matter. As far as we know, Goldsmith revealed to Percy more detailed personal information than he ever did to any other person, although Percy's grasp of his complex character is the least acute left by Goldsmith's closest friends. Johnson's view of Goldsmith we see mainly in Boswell, so that it has become almost inextricably mingled with Boswell's presentation of Goldsmith. Reynolds's analysis of his personality provides us with the best contemporary insight into Goldsmith's behavior, insight that helps us reconcile Goldsmith's social conduct—his desire to amuse, to be the center of attention, to be liked, not to be neglected in society—with his literary achievements. Reynolds's belief that Goldsmith often behaved in a deliberately outlandish fashion in society rests firmly on many years' experience of intimate friendship. Goldsmith's own letter to his brother Henry, written long before he met Reynolds about 1761, confirms Reynolds's interpretation and further shows that Goldsmith believed social gatherings were times for relaxing, even for playing the fool with his friends—a far different view of conversation from Johnson's. Goldsmith obviously could and did play the fool on various occasions Boswell has recorded, but Boswell usually offers little or no interpretation, since his concentration centers on Johnson. Thus, to Boswell, Goldsmith's antics often strike a discordant note, and what was almost certainly intended as jest was taken in earnest and gave rise to the genius-fool paradox that most of his contemporaries saw and that the *Life of Johnson* has perpetuated. However, knowing Goldsmith's literary gifts in comedy gives us some tentative insights into judging his social behavior. Such knowledge surely also gives us a Goldsmith whose literary talents and social personality merge into a coherent, comprehensible whole.

Notes

1. "Introduction," *Boswell's London Journal, 1762–1763*, ed. Frederick A. Pottle (New York: McGraw-Hill Book Company, 1950), 30.

2. No authorized biography of Goldsmith appeared until 1801, when what is commonly called the "Percy Memoir" was prefixed to the first "authorized" edition of Goldsmith's works. Percy did not see the "Memoir" through the press and was deeply disturbed at the inclusion of additional material without his consent. The most readily available form of the "Percy Memoir"—more properly "The Life of Oliver Goldsmith"—is Richard Harp's edition of 1976

(Salzburg Studies in English Literature, Romantic Reassessment 52 [Salzburg: Institut für Englische Sprache und Literatur, 1976]). See also Katharine C. Balderston, *The History and Sources of Percy's Memoir of Goldsmith* (Cambridge: University Press, 1926).

3. Quoted in James Boswell, *The Life of Samuel Johnson, LL.D.*, ed. George Birkbeck Hill, rev. and enlarged by L. F. Powell (Oxford: Clarendon Press, 1934–1964), I, 412, n. 6. All references are to this edition and future citations will appear parenthetically by volume and page number.

4. We have three studies concentrating on Boswell's treatment of Goldsmith in the *Life:* Lee Morgan, "Boswell's Portrait of Goldsmith," in *Studies in Honor of John C. Hodges and Alvin M. Thaler*, ed. Richard Beale Davis and John Livesay (Knoxville: University of Tennessee Press, 1961), 67–76; Paxton Hart, "The Presentation of Oliver Goldsmith in Boswell's *Life of Johnson*," in *Re: Arts and Letters* 3 (1970): 4–15; and Charles N. Fifer's sketch in Boswell's *Correspondence with Certain Members of the Club* (New York: McGraw-Hill Book Company, 1976), l–li. Morgan sets out to show "that the portrait of Goldsmith in Boswell's works is substantially the same as the portrait painted by Goldsmith's other contemporaries and biographers, and at the same time to disprove the prevalent notion that Boswell despised Goldsmith" (p. 67). He also argues that Boswell's presentation of Goldsmith "involves one of the main tests of Boswell's achievement—the accuracy of his portraits of lesser characters in the *Life of Johnson*" (p. 67), an argument I find unconvincing, since it is quite possible, if not likely, that Boswell's insight into all of the people who appear within the *Life* is not equally keen. Morgan also believes that Reynolds's long-lost portrait sketch of Goldsmith "agrees almost completely with Boswell's" (p. 69), a judgment, as we shall soon see, I cannot endorse. Hart argues along similar lines but really disagrees with Morgan: "In *The Life of Johnson* Boswell actually presented a remarkably balanced appraisal which is corroborated in Boswell's private papers, and which comes much closer than is generally realized to the full truth of the poet's character as revealed by his best friend Sir Joshua Reynolds" (p. 4). Thus, for Hart, Reynolds's analysis of Goldsmith's personality is "the full truth," which Boswell's presentation approaches but does not reach. Fifer finds a "pervasive chilliness" in the *Life* portrait of Goldsmith, although Boswell's journal "gives a different impression." Boswell's "strategy" in the *Life* is "to characterize Goldsmith mainly through Johnson's utterances," which "in fact consist mainly of vivid and unsparing disparagement of Goldsmith's oddities and foibles." Fifer adds that Boswell's presentation of Goldsmith puzzled both Reynolds and Malone and is difficult to explain (pp. l–li).

5. *London Journal*, 105. Pottle's note on this passage adds, "It is hard to tell from the tone of the entry whether Boswell knew any of his writings."

6. Ibid., 176.

7. Ibid., 285.

8. Two of these illustrative examples are questionable, at least, and Boswell was working from a hearsay anecdote. Boswell recognized that the story about Goldsmith's purported claim that his brother was dean of Durham was dubious at best, since in his second edition he added the following note to that passage: "I am willing to hope that there may have been some mistake as to this anecdote, though I had it from a Dignitary of the Church. Dr. Isaac Goldsmith, his near relation, was Dean of Cloyne, in 1747" (I, 414, n. 6). The one involving the "two beautiful young ladies with their mother" alludes to an incident that occurred during Goldsmith's visit to France with Mrs. Kane Horneck and her two daughters, Catherine and Mary, in July of 1770. Goldsmith appears to have been deliberately playing the fool. Mary Horneck Gwynn told Sir James Prior many years later, "I am sure . . . that on many occasions from the peculiar manner and assumed frown of countenance, that what was often uttered in jest was mistaken by those that did not know him for earnest." This reminiscence is quoted in Ralph Wardle, *Oliver Goldsmith* (Lawrence: University of Kansas Press, 1957), 3, from James Prior, *Life of Oliver Goldsmith* (London: John Murray, 1837), 2:290–291. John Forster, *The Life and Times of Oliver Goldsmith,* 5th ed. (London: Chapman and Hall, 1871), 2:217, gives substantially the same information, which is quoted in *Life,* I, 414, n. 2, but without Forster's note on the passage: "[James] Northcote, with less excuse, has repeated it (*Life of* [*Sir Joshua*] *Reynolds* [London, Colburn, 1818]); but in later years he apologised for having too hastily done so, having since been better informed by Mrs. Gwynn [Mary Horneck's married name]. . . . On the other hand, Mr. Croker, who had received from Mrs. Gwynn some notes for his Boswell, is careful to remind us that 'the good-natured construction which the kind old lady was willing, after a lapse of above sixty years, to put on Goldsmith's behavior, she did not express in her previous communication with me, though it had afforded so obvious an opportunity of correcting the alleged injustice; and after all, it can be only a matter of opinion whether the vexation so seriously exhibited by Goldsmith was real or assumed.'"

9. *Life,* III, 518, Powell's Appendix F, glossing the discussion of Goldsmith's personality in *Life,* 9 April 1778, III, 252. Powell quotes only this one point from Beattie's 10 July 1788 letter to Forbes, but earlier in the letter Beattie describes his introduction to the Thrales by Johnson and then shifts to a discussion of Goldsmith's envy: "He envied even the dead; he could not bear that Shakespeare should be so much admired as he is." He obtusely adds, "But surely Goldsmith had no occasion to envy me; which, however, he certainly did, for he owned it (though when we met he was always very civil); and I received undoubted information, that he seldom missed an opportunity of speaking ill of me behind my back." Sir William Forbes, *An Account of the Life and Writings of James Beattie, LL.D.* (Edinburgh: A. Constable and W. Creech; London: Longman et al., 1806), 2:233–234. The sentence Powell quotes follows immediately afterward.

10. Percy, "Life," 59; also available in *Collected Letters of Oliver Goldsmith,* ed. Katharine C. Balderston (Cambridge: University Press, 1928), 65. Balderston, 65, n. 1, dates the letter about 13 January 1759, from the postmark "13IA."

11. Reynolds, *Portraits,* ed. Frederick W. Hilles (New York: McGraw-Hill Book Company, 1952). See Introduction, p. 34. Page numbers of quotations from Reynolds's portrait will appear parenthetically within the text.

12. Reynolds's view that Goldsmith's association with "mean people" had affected his manners for the worse may be true, but it is also true that much of Goldsmith's behavior reflects the norms acceptable in the Anglo-Irish society in which he grew up. Wardle, p. 4, quotes the Irish Lady Morgan as saying "some years later" that "in England, conversation is a game of chess, the result of judgment, memory, and deliberation—with us it is a game of battledore, and our ideas like our shuttlecocks are thrown lightly to the other, bounding and rebounding—played more for amusement than conquest and leaving the players equally animated by the game and careless of the results" (*Memoirs of Lady Morgan,* ed. W. H. Dixon (1862), quoted in Constantia Maxwell, *Dublin under the Georges* [London, 1936], 94–95). He also quotes (p. 19) from Catherine Hodson's narrative her account of one of her brother's "earliest [literary] productions," showing how middle-class morality was infecting Irish manners. In the anecdote the seven-year-old Goldsmith, as yet unbreeched, handles the hot kettle at teatime. Using the skirt of his "coat" as a potholder, he exposes his genitals to the ladies present, who giggle. The boy immediately recognizes the cause of laughter and tells his father, who promises him gingerbread as a reward for writing something about the incident. The last stanza of his short poem makes the point that "They [the ladies] laughed at that / Which sometimes else / Might give them greatest pleasure / How quickly they could see the thing / Which was their darling treasure" (*Collected Letters,* 163–164). Wardle believes it is "a curious story to emanate from a village rectory. Bishop Percy understandably omitted it from his Memoir of Goldsmith, but it tells a great deal. In the first place it reveals how uninhibited was the spirit which prevailed in the household at Lissoy. If Oliver Goldsmith later offended his staid friends in London, it was in part because he had been brought up among people who were anything but squeamish. Charles Goldsmith's suggestion was obviously indecorous, and so was his young son's poem. Neither Oliver nor his father stifled the impulse to violate the rules of decorum: both expected their friends to relish a joke without bothering whether it was in good taste. The taboos which prevailed in a more conventional society meant nothing to the Goldsmiths or their friends." In Goldsmith's own 1759 essay "A Description of the Manners and Customs of the Native Irish. In a letter from an English Gentleman," written for *The Weekly Magazine (Collected Works of Oliver Goldsmith,* ed. Arthur Friedman [Oxford: Clarendon Press, 1966], III, 28), his persona writes, "the Irish protestants are on the contrary [to the English] affable, foolishly prodigal, hospitable, and

often not to be depended upon. This difference from their ancestors they have acquired from their long conversation with the original natives, who carry all these faults to a vicious extreme." W. E. H. Lecky's first volume of his *History of Ireland in the Eighteenth Century* describes behavior among the Anglo-Irish county and clerical families as far closer to that which the Reverend Charles Goldsmith's family followed than Wardle seems to have known. Rather than being indecorous and taboo-ridden and showing dubious taste, their social peers seem to have been behaving very much like the Goldsmiths. English social behavior was undoubtedly undergoing great changes throughout the eighteenth century, largely because of the influence of the *Spectator* and the similar attitudes shown by Beau Nash at Bath, as Goldsmith's own *Life of Richard Nash* suggests. Goldsmith there treats both Nash and his microcosmic "realm" comically. Acceptable social behavior during the second quarter of the eighteenth century in Anglo-Irish society was certainly not the same as that of English society of the same date. The freer spirit of the seventeenth century lived on in Ireland well past the time when its racy gusto had fallen victim to Addison's withering genteelism and proto-Victorianism.

13. [Samuel Johnson], Review of *The Traveller, Critical Review* 18 (1764): 462. The review has been reprinted in *Goldsmith: The Critical Heritage*, ed. G. S. Rousseau (London: Routledge and Kegan Paul, 1974), 29–33.

14. Shortly afterward, Percy visited Goldsmith at his slum lodging in Green Arbour Court. In the 1801 "Life," 60, Percy very carefully describes his visit as that of "a friend," rather than using first person, perhaps because he thought it inconsistent with his dignity as a bishop. Wardle, *Oliver Goldsmith*, 93, notes that Grainger, whom Goldsmith had known while both reviewed for Griffiths's *Monthly Review*, introduced the two men the evening of 21 February 1759, and Percy's visit to Goldsmith's lodgings occurred on 3 March 1759. They continued to see a great deal of each other throughout the rest of Goldsmith's life. Wardle also notes (pp. 251–252) that Percy had agreed to act as Goldsmith's biographer on 21 April 1773, and on 28 November Goldsmith dictated a long memorandum to him and gave him a bundle of manuscripts supplementing the information in the memorandum. Balderston reprints the memorandum in *History and Sources*, 12–17.

15. Percy, "Life," 117.

16. Balderston, *History and Sources*, thought that the 1801 edition was the only one, but Irving L. Churchill, "Editions of Percy's Memoir of Goldsmith," *MLN* 50 (1935): 464–465, discovered that the "Life" was reprinted at least six times from 1801 to 1816, three times in London and three times in New York, and believes there were probably other reprints, besides at least two other editions of Goldsmith's works containing biographical prefaces clearly based on Percy's "Life."

17. See Morgan, "Boswell's Portrait," 68–69, and Hart, "The Presentation," 4.

18. Wardle, *Oliver Goldsmith,* 289, quoted by Hart, "The Presentation," 12.

19. Arthur Lytton Sells, *Oliver Goldsmith: His Life and Works* (New York: Barnes and Noble, 1974), 168–169.

20. Boswell, *Correspondence,* 25, Boswell's italics; also printed in *Boswell for the Defence, 1769–1774,* ed. William K. Wimsatt, Jr., and Frederick A. Pottle (New York: McGraw-Hill, 1959), 152–153.

21. *Boswell for the Defence,* 151.

22. Boswell, *Correspondence,* 26; also printed in *Boswell for the Defence,* 153–154.

23. John Ginger, *The Notable Man: The Life and Times of Oliver Goldsmith* (London: Hamish Hamilton, 1977), 26.

24. Ibid., 28.

25. *Boswell for the Defence,* 104; Hart quotes part of the passage in "The Presentation," 12.

26. How well known Goldsmith was as an author is, of course, hard to determine, but William Rider's anonymous publication *An Historical and Critical Account of the Living Writers of Great-Britain wherein Their Respective Merits Are Discussed with the Utmost Candour and Impartiality* (London: printed for the author, 1762) praises him as the author of his *Essay on the Present State of Polite Learning in All Parts of the World, The Bee,* but especially for *The Citizen of the World:* "He is superior to most of them [his contemporaries] in Style, having found out the Secret to unite Elevation with Ease, a perfection in Language, which few Writers of our nation have attained to. Rider's whole account is reprinted in Rousseau, *Goldsmith: The Critical Heritage,* 157–158, and Rousseau's introductory note (p. 157) states, "His high appraisal of Goldsmith's prose style reflects an attitude popular in 1761–3. In December, 1761, for example, the *Court Magazine,* a miscellaneous work edited by Hugh Kelly, singled out Goldsmith, along with Johnson, Young, Gray, and a few others, from a list of fifty-six living authors and hailed him as a writer accomplished in 'taste and understanding.'" John Vance has pointed out to me that Kelly ranked Goldsmith sixteenth, Young first, Johnson second, Thomas Warton eleventh, and Smollett twenty-fourth. About the time the Club was being formed, Goldsmith was finishing *The Traveller,* for which Johnson wrote lines 424–434 and 437–438, the final couplet. Johnson's knowledge of Goldsmith's talent, then, went far beyond that of either Rider or the *Court Magazine.*

27. Letter to the author, 31 January 1983. Pottle clarifies his position in his "Introduction" to *Boswell's London Journal, 1762–1763,* quoted in note 1: "He [Goldsmith] is far from being as great a man as Johnson, and he never touched the heights of some lines in the *Vanity of Human Wishes,* but his *oeuvre* as a whole surpasses Johnson's as *writing.* If anything holds Goldsmith's reputation back, it is *facility:* he seems to compose so easily that with him good writing seems hardly a virtue" (Pottle's italics).

28. *Boswell for the Defence,* 180.

29. Ibid., 180, n. 6.

30. Reprinted through the kind permission of Yale University and the McGraw-Hill Book Company. In the Boswell Papers, Boswell's letter to Oglethorpe of 14 August 1773 is number 1995, Oglethorpe's reply of 16 September 1773 is number C2113, and Boswell's letter to Oglethorpe of 3 December 1773 is number 1996. I have not retained the letters' original paragraph divisions. I first published these letters in "Goldsmith and Miss Lockwood: Boswell and Oglethorpe's Matchmaking," *Yale University Library Gazette* 58 (1984): 150–151.

31. *Boswell for the Defence,* 181.

RICHARD B. SCHWARTZ

Epilogue: The Boswell Problem

*T*he Boswell problem, as I have termed it, is in fact a succession of problems, but all turn on a single issue. Biography is a combination of history and art and, as such, the demands placed upon it are different from the demands placed on history alone or art alone. Of course, in a certain sense all history is art and, for that matter, all science is art. If our human limitations keep us from achieving *essential* explanations and if our knowledge is, ultimately, at a distance from our subject so that our "learning" proceeds by analogy, then all of our "explanations" are stories, *likely stories* perhaps, as Plato termed them in the *Timaeus*, but stories nonetheless. In the case of biography, however, I think it is useful to take a common sense approach to the problem, for even though we might be persuaded that *all* human explanations are fictions (in the sense of coherent, convincing stories, not in the sense of lies), it is certainly true that biography is a different sort of "fiction" from the novel or the romance.

In the area of fact, for example, it is a matter of considerable importance that Johnson came to the London of 1737 rather than that of 1637 or 1837. It is important for us to know that he was married and that the marriage was without issue. It is important that he met Henry Thrale and it is interesting that he met Benjamin Franklin. We could list a multiplicity of facts concerning Johnson's seventy-five-year life. Some would be of greater and some of lesser importance, but when all of the known data were listed and all of the judgments registered concerning their comparative importance, one fact would be clear and that is that Boswell's *Life* is an inadequate record of the specific events of Johnson's life. That this should be the case should occasion neither surprise nor contempt for Boswell.

No reasonable person expects Boswell to have known everything or to have been in a position to reveal all that he did know in 1791. The criticism of the *Life* as history (and for the Johnsonians, the history side of the history/art pattern is likely to continue to be of primary importance) is not motivated by a desire to besmirch Boswell's reputation or impugn his abilities, but rather by the belief that the importance of Johnson is such that the very highest standards of precision and rigor must be applied. This point cannot be overstated. Johnson's life matters and it matters in profound ways.

I will not reiterate the praise that has been heaped upon Johnson nor belabor the fact that he is the second most frequently quoted English author after Shakespeare. I will, however, quote A. J. P. Taylor's recent comment that Johnson "carried English human nature to the highest point of which we have knowledge." Many would remove the adjective *English,* for they believe that Johnson is more than just the quintessential representative of English civilization. Indeed, his function has become more like that of a Christian saint, although the nature of his struggles and the availability of his pronouncements enable us to feel far closer to him than to more ethereal presences. Part of this feeling, of course, is based on biographical practice. We know that hagiographers have been far less concerned with vehicles than their tenors. The result is a distancing of their subjects, even a dehumanization of their subjects. Johnson—no less religious than most saints in either attitude or practice—strikes us as a more secular figure, though I believe that this is the result of failure on the part of hagiographers and not the result of his being insufficiently otherworldly.

Like Joshua Reynolds we go to Johnson to have our minds *qualified* and we welcome the continual retelling of his life as biography after biography issues from the press. Johnson is, purely and simply, a model, not a perfect one and not the only one, but one of the most important. Given that role (a role for which Boswell is, in considerable part, responsible), Boswell is held to the highest of standards and is sometimes found wanting. Biographers of lesser men are, in a sense, in a far more fortunate position. Certainly their works are subjected to less scrutiny, and the criticism of their works is neither as searching nor as insistent, for their subjects do not matter in the way that Johnson does.

With regard to the art side of the history/art pattern, Boswell has been more fortunate. He has had persuasive commentators who continue to point up his demonstrable skill in technique. Some are even prepared to collapse the history/art distinction and treat the *Life* as if it were no more than effective fictional narrative. While one could argue that history is art anyway, as I said earlier, one could also argue that the distinction simply does not matter. For example, Jonathan Culler has pointed to the work of speech act researchers who study human stories and find that their "truth" or "falsehood" is less important than their tellability. In other words, an individual can recount a story of absolute veracity and still receive the most dreaded of responses: "So what?" As we listen to stories we are engaged by their tellability far more than by their historical accuracy.

Historical accuracy (or the claim of it) is still a matter of importance, however. If history need never be distinguished from fiction, the eighteenth-century novelist would not use the leverage of historicity in writing art that pretends to be biography. Similarly, a Borges or a Pynchon would not write art that appeared to be history unless there was both thematic importance and reader interest in our struggle to disentangle fiction from fact and our occasional failure in the attempt. The fact that we make the attempt or make the assertion that, for important reasons, the two cannot be disentangled suggests the possibility that they could be and even should be.

In the case of a biography of a person such as Johnson the Culler point needs to be extended. The tellability of Johnson's life story is one of its initial attractions, but so is the tellability of Rochester's life story or Burns's. There are, it is clear, tellable life stories that do not need to be continually retold and that do not attract ongoing and intense scholarly attention the way that Johnson's does.

Johnson's life is retold for a number of reasons, and one of the most important of those reasons is the fact that Johnson serves as an intellectual and moral example. It is important that he opposed slavery both in word and deed. It is important that he refused opiates at the end of his final illness and it is important that he opposed the Seven

Years' War. It is important to know that he kissed and fondled another woman while his wife was still alive and that he devised a number of strategies to deal with the fluctuation in his moods and mental states. It is important that he resisted partisan politics and that he demonstrated his maturity, in good Eriksonian fashion, by helping younger writers to realize their potential and achieve their place.

Because he is looked to as a pattern of belief and behavior any alteration or potential alteration of that pattern based on new evidence is a matter of intense concern. Issues that would be considered trivial in other contexts here become important. Johnson kicks a stone and the incident is subjected to analysis in technical, philosophic terms. Johnson exchanges insults with a man traveling on the Thames and we attempt to determine whether or not Johnson's comment was original or derivative. The youthful Johnson steps on a duckling and commentators hasten to determine whether or not the doggerel verses describing the event are to be attributed to Johnson or to his father.

As with all such investigations, some are ingenious and fruitful, some trivial. The point is that no one hesitates to pursue such leads in the case of Johnson. It is assumed, *a priori,* that such investigations are always worth the effort. Thus, the body of information surrounding Johnson's life continues to grow. This process underlines the uneasiness of the history/art mix that constitutes biography. Art, we have always been told, is self-contained and immutable. We do not, like Bentley with Milton, try to "improve" it unless we wish to receive eternal ridicule. Art is perceived as a totality, a whole. History, on the other hand, is always subjected to question, challenge, and revision. It is always an open subject and the discussion of that subject is mutable and dynamic. It is never finished; it is never complete.

Thus, a defender of Boswell will use formalistic arguments and stress the artistic side of the *Life,* as if the biography of a historic person were directly comparable to a play, a poem, or a novel. Similarly, the student of Johnson will see our knowledge of Johnson's life as a continually unfolding story and Boswell's *Life* as an important but quite dated document.

I would approach this issue from a Johnsonian perspective. As a professional writer and not a professor of literature, Johnson knew that works of art could be altered and improved. He knew the conditions under which works of art are composed and the conditions under which they are printed and he had no qualms about enumerating the faults of a writer as great as Shakespeare or listing the ways in which Shakespeare's works could be improved, a practice that would today be viewed with great nervousness and suspicion.

Similarly, Johnson was, to say the least, aware of the fact that "history" has not been settled, that it is an endless and open subject. He knew and constantly stressed the fact that our imaginations can always outstrip present realities. The fact that a better biography of Johnson than Boswell's has not been *written* (assuming for the sake of argument that that might be true) would in no way keep us from employing Johnsonian principles and *imagining* a finer, more complete, and more faithful biography of Johnson. If the history/art pattern is one key facet of the Boswell problem, another is that imagined book—the collective biography of Johnson that exists in the minds of Johnson's students but not in print in the form of a continuous narrative.

For example, in the case of Boswell's portrait of Johnson, we are grateful for the marvelous *précis* of conversations in which Johnson participated and the reporting of direct, personal responses of those with whom Johnson came in contact. We do not, however, always find in Boswell the sensitivity to human psychology that we find in Bate's biography or the sensitivity to the life of a professional writer, especially one from a small town in Staffordshire, that we find in John Wain's. We do not receive a set of discriminations concerning the nuances of eighteenth-century English political ideology and practice and, hence, a true sense of Johnson's place therein. For that we turn to Greene. For all of his strengths, Boswell does not approach his subject with the common sense and broad humanity of Clifford. For that matter, though it is hardly to be seen as a fault, Boswell lacked the totality of commentary and information available to Clifford writing in the middle of the twentieth century. As we imagine a perfect biography we realize that we need far more information than Boswell gives us concerning his subject's youth, family life, and sexual experience. We do, however, have Irwin's discussions and speculations on the relationship between Johnson and his mother and Verbeek's suggestions on Johnson's autoeroticism. We do not know enough but we know enough to realize how limited Boswell's account is. We still lack a definitive account of Johnson's religious attitudes, but we have several volumes to which we may turn that go beyond Boswell. Our sense of Johnson's achievement as a thinker and critic is far clearer now than it was in the eighteenth century and we have recovered and seen texts that were overlooked in the past. The eighteenth century had the sale catalog of Johnson's library, but we are *using* it. Johnson's reaction to Renaissance and eighteenth-century currents in science and philosophy is now studied and we have come to see how important Johnson's relationship with the Thrales truly was.

Boswell could never be expected to recover single-handedly the material that is now available and he could never provide the multiple perspectives that that material demands if it is to be properly digested and understood. To the extent that biography is history and involves cumulative study and reflection, it is absurd to talk about Boswell's *Life* as a "perfect" biography. The very notion of perfection is, of course, absurd in this context. We might substitute the word *adequate* instead. Adequacy, however, is generally in inverse proportion to the complexity of the subject. The more simple the subject the more likely it will be that we can offer an adequate discussion or explanation of it. Again taking a common sense approach and without too much concern for philosophic nuance, we can say that certain biographies are, if not perfect or ideal, perfectly adequate. With Johnson, however, we confront Everest. No one, for example, has yet written the intellectual biography of the man who, in Adam Smith's famous comment, "knew more books than any man alive." That portion of Johnson's life alone brings the kind of response that Richard Bentley had when he received Isaac Newton's answer to his question concerning the work needed to prepare himself to read and understand the *Principia,* and yet that would only be a part of a truly adequate biography of Johnson. The material in Boswell, as valuable as it is, cannot hope to approach the material available to a student of Johnson in the latter part of the twentieth century, and yet that material is itself far from even beginning to approach adequacy. Boswell is surely to be praised for the comparatively large portion of the present whole that he himself provided, but the distance of that part from the "final" (i.e., adequate) whole is considerable.

What then are we to do with Boswell? The question itself may seem strange and even impertinent. I believe that the question is, in some ways, a pedagogical one. On the cover of an early edition of the Major Authors Edition of the Norton Anthology on my shelf Boswell sits between Johnson and Blake. The only other eighteenth-century figures enjoying this privileged position are Pope and Swift. In the third edition Boswell is dethroned (as are Mill and Shaw) to make room for Beckett and Auden. The Boswellians may be surprised to know that I would have sacrificed a number of individuals (Tennyson, Arnold, Hardy, Hopkins, Lawrence) to save Boswell but that is not really the point. The question is *how* we see Boswell and I do not believe that it is an idle question.

I believe, for example, that Boswell is one of the "major British authors," although I would approach his work as great autobiography rather than great biography. I have stated my reasons for this elsewhere and will not belabor them. If, however, we think of him, uncritically, as a "major author" with all of the fanfare attached to that position, it is extremely difficult to simultaneously think of his chief work as an important but in many ways misleading and inadequate secondary source for the study of Samuel Johnson.

Once enshrined in that hallowed position of greatness it is difficult to think of him in a position that appears to be a subordinate one, perhaps even an insulting one, and yet, in my judgment, that is what we must do. My assumption that it is not nearly so difficult to do that as others believe is built not only on a particular way of approaching Boswell and a particular view of the proper uses of Boswell's *Life of Johnson* but also on a far more heretical assumption, one that I am prepared to admit to though I lack the space to defend it in detail. To some extent I also question the usefulness of defending it, for some will find it so appalling as to refuse to consider it and others will agree with it readily.

The point is easily stated and involves a return to the notion with which I began; namely, the profound importance of Johnson. I believe that, to state it baldly, the eighteenth century has been mistaught. When I studied the seventeenth century in graduate school some twenty years ago, Arthur Barker instructed us to see everything in that period in relation to Milton. In a sense, all was minor but Milton.

More important, everything was clarified when compared to, contrasted with, or filtered through Milton. I believe that that same approach is the proper one for the eighteenth century and the figure against whom all is to be measured is Johnson. As rash as that statement might seem, it is not without precedent. C. S. Lewis's famous comments on Addison may ultimately be patronizing to Addison but I believe that his comments on the Tory satirists in that essay are entirely defensible. For all of their dazzling strengths, their ultimate narrowness is undeniable. Lewis writes: "I fully admit that when Pope and Swift are on the heights they have a strength and splendour which makes everything in Addison look pale; but what an abyss of hatred and bigotry and even silliness receives them when they slip from the heights!" Lewis assumes that breadth of interest, generosity of spirit, openness and curiosity, and what he terms a "'habit' of cheerfulness" are crucial norms. Measuring Pope and Swift against them points up Addison's strengths. As one reads the essay, however, the striking thing is how much stronger the case could have been made if Addison's name were systematically struck out and Johnson's substituted.

Another telling precedent for this point of view is, of course, Johnson's own view of early eighteenth-century literature and literary figures, a view so different from that which usually prevails. One thinks not only of his praise of Arbuthnot, his preference for Dryden over Pope, his views of Swift, and his comments on the type of mind that could seriously advance the arguments of the *Essay on Man*, but also of his comment on the correspondence of Swift and Pope:

> In the Letters both of Swift and Pope there appears such narrowness of mind, as makes them insensible of any excellence that has not some affinity with their own, and confines their esteem and approbation to so small a number, that whoever should form his opinion of the age from their representation, would suppose them to have lived amidst ignorance and barbarity, unable to find among their contemporaries either virtue or intelligence, and persecuted by those that could not understand them.

The problem with this view (if there is a problem) is that it is based on the attitude that writers should also be judged as thinkers and as men, that literary skill is a part of one's reputation but only a part. It is in that larger context, of course, that Johnson becomes the truly towering figure of his period. I say that with no wish to diminish his simultaneous importance as a great writer, but rather to stress the quality of the thought and character that suffuse his writings and result in a situation wherein we can read a small poem or seemingly minor essay and yet feel that connection with greatness that we may not sense in a "greater" work by another writer.

Seeing Johnson in that way, in my judgment, enables us to see Boswell in a subordinate role but one that need not and should not be thought of as a poor role. This, however, does not solve that part of the Boswell problem that is also a pedagogical one. What are we to do with the book itself—assign abridgments, use alternative biographies, or require students to read Boswell's *Life in toto*? Defenses of Boswell's art (by Paul Alkon, for example) point up the necessity of reading the entire book. Boswell's structural strategies cannot be appreciated if one reads abridgments. However, to assign some 1,400 pages or so of Boswell means (in this academic world) that much else will be excluded, including perhaps Boswell's *Tour* or a volume of his journal.

One of the key problems with the eighteenth century has always been the fact that many of its greatest accomplishments go untaught (and thus, to some extent at least, unstudied). We teach *Eloïsa to Abelard* rather than Pope's Homer. We teach Gibbon's memoirs rather than the *Decline and Fall*. Students do not often see the period's work in the editing of Shakespeare; they seldom see Johnson's dictionary; they read a smattering of periodical essays but have little sense of such activity beyond Addison, Steele, Johnson, Defoe, and sometimes Goldsmith. The constraints of academic calendars have served to misrepresent the period to generation after generation of students, at least in North America. Most students do not appreciate the period until they know it in depth and all of our academic structures in North America are there to ensure that they will not be able to explore the period and its long and complex materials in the way that they demand. Many eighteenth-century works are taught because they fit calendar requirements and though every period will make the following claim, I believe that the eighteenth century is misrepresented more than any other because of this situation. Not only are the period's major accomplishments often overlooked, but many minor dramatic and poetic works are taught simply because we do not have the time and latitude to prepare our students to encounter the eighteenth century as it should be encountered.

Moreover, the problem is not likely to be solved. Thus, the question of how one is to deal with Boswell is an important one. I believe that Boswell's *Life* must be taught *in toto*. The *Life* is a key secondary source for understanding Johnson, one that includes primary materials. In its own right it is a book that every educated person must read. There is no way to understand the biographical tradition or the manner in which we have arrived at the current state of Johnson and Boswell studies without reading it and, in my judgment, it is crucial for an understanding of Boswell himself, perhaps even more important than a reading of Boswell's journal volumes.

The twin dangers of the *Life*'s leading to a misinterpretation of Johnson and to the notion that Johnson and Boswell are Siamese twins must be kept in mind. The separation of Johnson and Boswell from one another within the course calendar can help ameliorate the problem. Another useful technique is to assign the *Life* at preregistration or, at the latest, during the registration period, so that the *Life* can be read before the course is really under way. This obviates the need to block out two weeks for reading time and presents the *Life* both as a prelude to something else as well as a book of sufficient importance to be singled out for separate consideration.

Two other pedagogical issues present themselves, the first practical, the second practical as well but also controversial. First, the teaching of Boswell and Johnson occurs at both graduate and undergraduate levels. As Richard Ohmann and many others have pointed out, the undergraduate major is structured (in general) like a thin Ph.D. program. The major fields, genres, themes, figures, and approaches are all covered. The doctoral student is expected to traverse a great deal of this ground; the undergraduate can perforce traverse very little. Thus, there is the constant temptation to give the young student more than he or she can handle, particularly in the eighteenth century, where the teacher assumes that his or her course is likely to be the sum total of the student's exposure to the subject. The problem is exacerbated with the teaching of Johnson and Boswell, for there is so much revisionist ground to cover and so many texts to examine. At the doctoral level this must be done; at the undergraduate level it simply cannot be done. We must resist these temptations, present both writers separately on their merits, and wait for time and later reading to fill in the gaps.

If Boswell is seen as he should be seen, this is not a great problem. My second pedagogical point is that the *Life should* function the way it *does* function. It is not a bible; it is a catechism. It serves some basic functions and sets out certain facts, judgments, and points of view. The mature student (like the mature theologian with a catechism) goes beyond it. It represents a body of truth, opinion, and interpretation against which we react. It is a preliminary to a later, larger discussion.

One of the major problems in contemporary education is that we have lost many of our "catechisms." Those texts that were once common property are no longer so and we have rebuilt Babel. This has been done, more often than not, on political grounds. When W. J. Bate lately decried this state of affairs so cogently (and, I might say, so moderately), he was immediately charged with seeking to protect *his* tradition or the tradition of white, male, western society. That, I believe, is rubbish. What needs to be protected is the possibility of communication. When Johnson talked of classical languages and literatures constituting a kind of *parole* for all men he was talking about a question of communication and the importance of a common "language" and common traditions. E. D. Hirsch has recently pointed to the manner in which we have helped perpetuate illiteracy by moving away from a shared set of readings in our schools. The political dimension of this process is a bogey, not a true problem. The Romans were imperialists and the Greeks pederasts but we could not understand ourselves, our history, and our civilization without understanding them. Boswell defended slavery and was skittish with intelligent women who threatened him but that is no reason to ban a book (or banish it) when it is a part of western intellectual life and the western literary and historical imagination.

Thus, while I would continue to offer revisionist approaches to the *Life,* I would also reassert the importance of our introducing students to it as an indispensable part of their education. When the book is challenged (as it should be), individuals are upset (as I have argued elsewhere) because literary associations are being shaken. The book is a part of our intellectual and spiritual lives and it is not a comfortable experience when we learn of its flaws, errors, or misrepresentations. On the other hand, it is a part of our lives for a number of good and important reasons. To allow our students to bypass or overlook it is to impoverish their lives and deny them the means to understand our present views of Johnson, of biography, and of the second half of eighteenth-century British culture.

In other words, we must see Boswell in different ways for different audiences and we must have the suppleness of mind to share an appreciation for Boswell's work with our students at the same time that we are continuing the revisionist process of subjecting the book to searching examination and correction. We must, in short, balance the art and history sides of the biographical form without excluding either. In the case of Boswell that is not an easy task, but it is certainly a most rewarding and important one.

Contributors

FREDRIC V. BOGEL is professor of English and director of the freshman seminar program at Cornell University. He is the author of *Acts of Knowledge: Pope's Later Poems* (1981), *Literature and Insubstantiality in the Later Eighteenth Century* (1984), and essays on eighteenth-century topics in *PMLA, Eighteenth-Century Studies,* and *Studies in English Literature*. His essay "Dulness Unbound: Rhetoric and Pope's *Dunciad*" won the 1984 James L. Clifford Prize, awarded by the American Society for Eighteenth-Century Studies.

JOHN J. BURKE, JR., is associate professor of English and director of the English honors program at the University of Alabama in Tuscaloosa. He has published articles on Defoe, Fielding, Hume, Johnson, and Scott and is coeditor of *The Unknown Samuel Johnson* (1983). He feels he has learned more about Johnson from Donald Greene than from any other scholar living or dead, with the possible exception of Boswell.

DONALD GREENE is Leo S. Bing Professor of English at the University of Southern California. Among his many publications are *The Politics of Samuel Johnson* (1960), *The Age of Exuberance* (1970), *Samuel Johnson* (1970), and (with James L. Clifford) *Samuel Johnson: A Survey and Bibliography of Critical Studies* (1970). He has also edited Johnson's *Political Writings* in the Yale Edition of Johnson's Works (1977) and an anthology of Johnson's writings (1984). He is currently writing a biography of the last twenty years of Johnson's life.

Contributors

Donald J. Newman teaches English and journalism at Mt. San Antonio College in Walnut, California. A former newspaper reporter, Newman is interested in the appearance of medicine and physicians in literature and is examining the materials relating to Johnson's medical problems and the medical portrait of Johnson in the *Life*.

Frederick A. Pottle is Sterling Professor Emeritus at Yale University. For over thirty years he has been the editor or coeditor of the "trade" editions of the Boswell papers. In addition to many essays, he is the author of *The Literary Career of James Boswell* (1929), *James Boswell: The Early Years, 1740–1769* (1966), and *Pride and Negligence: The History of the Boswell Papers* (1982).

Ralph W. Rader is professor of English at the University of California, Berkeley. His publications include various articles on the theory of form in the novel and other genres and a book, *Tennyson's "Maud": The Biographical Genesis* (1963).

Richard B. Schwartz is professor of English and dean of the Graduate School at Georgetown University. In addition to essays in *Modern Philology, Studies in English Literature,* and *Journal of English and Germanic Philology,* he has written *Samuel Johnson and the New Science* (1971), *Samuel Johnson and the Problem of Evil* (1975), *Boswell's Johnson: A Preface to the "Life"* (1978), and *Daily Life in Johnson's London* (1983). He has also edited *The Plays of Arthur Murphy,* 4 vols. (1979).

William R. Siebenschuh is associate professor of English and director of composition at Case Western Reserve University. He has published essays on Johnson, Boswell, biography, and autobiography, and two books, *Form and Purpose in Boswell's Biographical Works* (1972) and *Fictional Techniques and Factual Works* (1983).

John A. Vance is associate professor of English at the University of Georgia. He is the author of *Joseph and Thomas Warton* (1983), *Joseph and Thomas Warton: An Annotated Bibliography* (1983), *Samuel Johnson and the Sense of History* (1984), and essays on Milton, Dryden, Pepys, Cibber, Swift, Garrick, the Wartons, and Johnson. He is currently working on a critical study of Johnson's correspondence.

SAMUEL H. WOODS, JR., is professor of English at Oklahoma State University. He has published essays on Goldsmith in *Eighteenth-Century Studies, Studies in Burke and His Time,* and *Yale University Library Gazette.* He is also the author of *Oliver Goldsmith: A Reference Guide* (1982) and coauthor of *Introduction to Literature* (1968) and *Writing about Literature* (1971). He is presently writing a biography of Goldsmith.

Index